THE STATE OF COLLEGE ACCESS AND COMPLETION

Despite decades of substantial investments by the federal government, state governments, colleges and universities, and private foundations, students from low-income families as well as racial and ethnic minority groups continue to have substantially lower levels of postsecondary educational attainment than individuals from other groups. *The State of College Access and Completion* draws together leading researchers nationwide to summarize the state of college access and success and to provide recommendations for how institutional leaders and policymakers can effectively improve the entire spectrum of college access and completion.

Springboarding from a seminar series organized by the Advisory Committee on Student Financial Assistance, chapter authors explore what is known and not known from existing research about how to improve student success. This much-needed book calls explicit attention to the state of college access and success not only for traditional college-age students, but also for the substantial and growing number of "nontraditional" students. Describing trends in various outcomes along the pathway from college access to completion, this volume documents persisting gaps in outcomes based on students' demographic characteristics and offers recommendations for strategies to raise student attainment. Graduate students, scholars, and researchers in higher education will find *The State of College Access and Completion* to be an important and timely resource.

Laura W. Perna is Professor in the Graduate School of Education and Faculty Fellow at the Institute for Urban Research at the University of Pennsylvania, USA.

Anthony P. Jones is Director of Policy Research for the Advisory Committee on Student Financial Assistance in Washington, DC.

THE STATE OF COLLEGE ACCESS AND COMPLETION

Improving College Success for Students from Underrepresented Groups

Edited by
Laura W. Perna and
Anthony P. Jones

Routledge
Taylor & Francis Group

NEW YORK AND LONDON

First published 2013
by Routledge
711 Third Avenue, New York, NY 10017

Simultaneously published in the UK
by Routledge
2 Park Square, Milton Park, Abingdon, Oxon OX14 4RN

Routledge is an imprint of the Taylor & Francis Group, an informa business

Library of Congress Cataloging-in-Publication Data

CIP has been applied for

ISBN: 978-0-415-66045-7 (hbk)
ISBN: 978-0-415-66046-4 (pbk)
ISBN: 978-0-203-07409-1 (ebk)

Typeset in Bembo
by Apex CoVantage, LLC

Printed and bound in the United States of America by Publishers Graphics, LLC on sustainably sourced paper.

CONTENTS

FOREWORD

The current recession has permanently altered the landscape of the nation's higher education system, as institutions are challenged to operate in an environment marked by diminished state appropriations, rapidly escalating tuition, fluctuating commitments to financial aid, and the omnipresent need to secure essential resources while reducing operating costs. Traditional demands on colleges and universities to serve the multiple missions of teaching, research, and service have amplified as the nation turns to higher education as a driver of innovation and economic development. These pressures are further intensified by a growing emphasis on productivity, college completion, and heightened calls for public accountability.

As institutions struggle to adapt to these uncertainties and demands, there is a concomitant realization that, in the knowledge economy of the 21st century, our nation's intellectual edge and creative ingenuity can only be sustained by ensuring broad access to a postsecondary education. With few exceptions, it is critical for all Americans to attain some level of education beyond high school in order to compete in the global economy. As demonstrated through countless research studies, increased educational attainment results in higher personal income, a better-skilled and more adaptable workforce, fewer demands on social services, and higher levels of community involvement.

At a time when higher education is increasingly important, many Americans are, unfortunately, being left behind. While overall educational attainment levels have increased during the past two decades, considerable disparities exist and, in most states, these gaps are widening. Despite decades of substantial investments by federal and state governments, colleges and universities, private foundations, and other entities, students from low-income families and racial/ethnic minority groups continue to have substantially lower levels of educational attainment than individuals from other groups.

Compounding access problems for these underserved groups, the ability of the academy to respond to the demands and pressures placed upon it has been negatively impacted by reductions in state and federal operating support. The level of support for full-time students provided by state appropriations has declined significantly over the past two decades, while student fees continue to climb faster than inflation. The combination of increasing student fees and federal financial aid policy that accentuates loans constitutes a significant burden on college access and success for low- and middle-income families. At the same time that state support is declining, most states face increasing demand for higher education, a result of growing numbers of high school graduates coupled with displaced workers seeking job retraining and retooling.

As the administrations of several U.S. presidents and numerous national policy organizations have articulated, the United States has fallen behind other countries in terms of the educational attainment of its population. The importance of improving U.S. international competitiveness is emphasized by labor market projections that place a premium on skills and training beyond high school. As recently noted by the U.S. Bureau of Labor Statistics, analyses for the 2010–2020 decade consistently project an increase in occupations requiring some amount of postsecondary education. Concurrently, the importance of educational attainment to economic and social well-being is underscored by trends in benefits that accrue with higher levels of education. Since the early 1990s, for example, the wage premium associated with holding a bachelor's degree has grown significantly.

Scholars and policy leaders are examining questions about how states, institutions, and the federal government can respond to these changing circumstances and expectations. This volume is an extension of a seminar series organized in 2012 by the Advisory Committee on Student Financial Assistance, an independent source of advice and counsel to Congress and the Secretary of Education. The Advisory Committee is charged with reporting annually on the condition of college access and the adequacy of need-based grant aid for low- and moderate-income students. The Committee established the seminar series to inform its ongoing efforts, enhance awareness of the latest scholarly research on access and success, and ascertain researchers' recommendations for what is needed to better understand these issues.

The culmination of the Committee's efforts is represented by this volume. Here, leading researchers in higher education summarize the state of college access and success for students nationwide, providing recommendations on how federal and state policymakers, as well as institutional leaders, may effectively improve the entire spectrum of college access and success. Together, these chapters describe various trends in college outcomes, document persisting gaps in these outcomes based on student demographic characteristics, synthesize what is known and not known from existing research on access and persistence, and offer recommendations for strategies to ensure access and raise attainment for students. The volume also pays explicit attention to the state of college access and success not just for traditional college-age students, but for the substantial and growing number of nontraditional college students as well.

This collection will be important to scholars and researchers because it documents what is known and unknown about different dimensions of college access and success at various stages of the educational pipeline from college awareness and preparation to college completion. Furthermore, this volume serves as a guide for what federal and state policymakers and other stakeholders need to understand in order to make critical decisions to ensure that all of our citizens have the education and skills necessary to participate in the country's growth in economic strength and global competitiveness.

Brian E. Noland

ACKNOWLEDGMENTS

This book is the product of a yearlong seminar series organized by the Advisory Committee on Student Financial Assistance. At the request of the Committee, each of the lead authors in this volume convened a seminar (typically at the author's home institution) that was designed to disseminate information about the state of knowledge about a particular dimension of the pipeline to college completion. Attended by college administrators, faculty, and students, these seminars described the challenges that continue to restrict college access, persistence, and completion, particularly for students from groups that are underrepresented in higher education, and discussed potential solutions to these challenges. These seminars were the seeds for the chapters included in this volume.

This book would not have been possible without the engagement of these authors. It was a tremendous privilege to work with these individuals over the course of this project, as they are among the most respected researchers in the field of higher education administration. We are grateful for their important contributions to this project.

We are also thankful for the assistance of the Committee staff. Jeneva Stone provided thorough and invaluable editorial suggestions. Janet Chen and Elizabeth Kurban contributed thoughtful feedback as well as logistical assistance. William Goggin provided insightful advice on the project's scope and selection of seminar leaders/chapter authors. We are especially appreciative of the support and encouragement that he offered throughout the course of this project.

1

INTRODUCTION

Improving Postsecondary Access, Persistence, and Completion in the United States: Setting the Stage

Anthony P. Jones

Higher education in the United States has experienced tremendous growth in recent decades, due in large part to deliberate efforts of public policymakers to expand the nation's economy, meet workforce needs, improve the financial and social mobility of individuals and families, reduce discrimination and inequality, and develop a better-educated citizenry (Carnevale & Rose, 2012; Gilbert & Heller, 2010; Hutcheson, 2007). The chapters in this volume contend that significant progress has been made in broadening participation in postsecondary education, but several inequities still exist, especially for students most at risk for not entering or completing. These inequities prevent students and society from maximizing the benefits of higher education. This introduction sets the stage for the volume and provides broad context for the discussion and recommendations.

Expansion of higher education in the United States has occurred both in the number and types of institutions available as well as the number and characteristics of students enrolled. In terms of institutional increases, Table 1.1 shows that in the 2010–2011 academic year, there were 4,599 accredited institutions in the United States granting degrees at the associate's level or above, up from 4,182 in 2000–2001 and 3,231 in 1980–1981 (Snyder & Dillow, 2012; Snyder, Dillow, & Hoffman, 2008)—an increase of 10% within the last decade and 42% within the last three decades. The number of institutions in each of the major institutional sectors (i.e., 4-year and 2-year public, private nonprofit, and private for-profit) also has grown over these periods.[1] The most dramatic growth since the mid-1990s has occurred in the private for-profit sector (Snyder & Dillow, 2012; Snyder et al., 2008).

Mirroring these patterns, the number of students enrolling in postsecondary education has also increased dramatically, and the distribution of students among institutional types has shifted. Table 1.2 shows that, of the 18 million students

TABLE 1.1 Number of Accredited, Degree-Granting (2-year and 4-year) Institutions in the United States, by Sector

Academic Year	Total	Public	Private Nonprofit	Private For-Profit
2010–2011	4,599	1,656	1,630	1,313
2000–2001	4,182	1,698	1,695	789
1990–1991	3,559	1,567	1,649	343
1980–1981	3,231	1,497	1,569	165

Sources: Snyder and Dillow (2012); Snyder, Dillow, and Hoffman (2008).

TABLE 1.2 Total Undergraduate Enrollment at Accredited, Degree-Granting (2-year and 4-year) Institutions in the United States with Proportional Enrollment by Sector

Period of Enrollment	Total	Public	Private Nonprofit	Private For-Profit
Fall 2010★	18 million	76%	15%	10%
Fall 2000	13.2 million	80%	17%	3%
Fall 1990	12 million	81%	17%	2%
Fall 1980	10.5 million	81%	18%	1%

Source: Aud et al. (2012).
★Percentages add to more than 100 due to rounding.

enrolled in undergraduate education programs at degree-granting institutions[2] during fall 2010, 76% attended public institutions, 15% attended private nonprofit colleges and universities, and 10% were enrolled in private for-profit institutions (Aud et al., 2012). These data show a three-decade increase of 71% in overall undergraduate enrollment and a proportional shift from public and private nonprofit institutions to private for-profits. Growth in total enrollment in undergraduate degree-granting institutions is projected to increase further by 12%–17% over the 11-year period from 2007 to 2018 (Hussar & Bailey, 2009).

These trends suggest that college-going has become a more common experience. Clearly, the nation's higher education system has changed from a place once "reserved for a relatively small fraction of the population, something of a social and academic elite, to one frequented by a broad cross-section of students" (Kim & Rury, 2007, p. 305). Moreover, this expansion in enrollment has occurred for more than just the "traditional" student—that is, under age 25, White, and from middle- and upper-income households. Over the past two decades, several other groups have seen surges in college enrollment as well, including veterans, nontraditional-age students, racial and ethnic minorities, women, immigrants, and students from low-income families (Choy, 2002; Kim & Rury, 2007; Schuetze & Slowey, 2002; Snyder & Hoffman, 1991). Enrollment of students age 25 and older (one measure of "nontraditional") is projected to continue to grow in the coming years; between 2010 and 2020 the number of students age 25 and older is expected to increase by 20% while enrollment of students under age 25 is projected to rise by just 11% (Snyder & Dillow, 2012).

Nonetheless, as Laura Perna and Elizabeth Kurban as well as Don Heller note in their chapters in this volume, although the United States has enjoyed relatively high college access rates, challenges remain. One challenge is that educational attainment in the United States now lags behind that of many other developed nations (Organisation for Economic Co-operation and Development, 2011). Reflecting this trend, improving degree completion has become a centerpiece of national policy, as evidenced by President Obama's goal of returning the country to the top of world rankings in degree completion (Obama, 2009), and by the efforts of several foundations and organizations (e.g., see Bill & Melinda Gates Foundation, n.d.; Lumina Foundation, 2012; Southern Regional Education Board, 2010) to encourage national and state policy and institutional practice toward increasing degree completion.

Any attempt to reform or improve aspects of higher education to reach these degree completion goals must acknowledge several facts. First, both individuals *and* society benefit from an educational system that adequately prepares students to complete postsecondary coursework, enables entry to a postsecondary educational institution, and promotes students' successful progress to completion of their educational programs. Society benefits from increased participation in higher education in many ways, including higher rates of voting, adult literacy, charitable giving, and volunteerism, and lower rates of incarceration and utilization of public assistance (Baum, Ma, & Payea, 2010; Bowen, 1997). In turn, there are also numerous individual economic benefits to completing at least some postsecondary education; primary among these individual benefits are higher earnings and greater job satisfaction (Baum et al., 2010). In the 3-year period following the recession that began in 2007, and matching patterns that occur in better economic times, individuals with college degrees had the lowest unemployment rates and the best chances for getting hired (Carnevale, Smith, & Strohl, 2010). On average, lifetime wage earnings for an individual with a bachelor's degree are $1.1 million higher than for someone holding an associate's degree; even completing some college, but no degree or certificate, yields $473,000 in additional average lifetime earnings compared to an individual with only a high school diploma (Carnevale et al., 2010).

Second, public policies and programs have spurred tremendous expansion and improvement in college access and completion over time. Improvements in degree attainment rates for students from lower-income families and among most all racial, ethnic, and age groups (Berube, 2010) are attributable, at least in part, to public policies and legislation that removed barriers to and encouraged participation in postsecondary education (e.g., legislation to ban discriminatory admissions practices, creation of need-based student financial aid programs, the creation and expansion of 2-year public colleges and other sectors, etc.). Arguably one of the most significant of these is the Higher Education Act of 1965, as amended (HEA) for establishing several need-based student aid grant, work, and loan programs (including the Federal Pell Grant program). The HEA also has aided and strengthened minority-serving institutions, and advanced and expanded the TRIO programs (e.g., Upward Bound, Talent Search, Students Support Services), which are federally funded on-campus programs designed to promote college preparation and achievement for underserved student populations. Much of the expansion in individual opportunity and growth of the national economy are owed to such policies and programs.

Nonetheless, renewed attention by public policymakers and institutional leaders is required not only to raise further the nation's overall educational attainment rates, but also to remedy persisting gaps in college access and success across groups. As discussed in the chapters in this volume, although improvements have been made, substantial proportions of our population, especially students from low-income households and racial/ethnic minority groups, remain underprepared to take on and succeed in postsecondary coursework (see chapters by Conley; Long & Boatman), have unequal access to college enrollment (see chapters by Heller; Perna & Kurban), and struggle to persist to completion of their desired postsecondary credential (see chapters by Bragg; Melguizo, Kienzl, & Kosiewicz; Hossler, Dundar, & Shapiro). Further, there continues to be a need for new and different strategies for reaching out to, informing, and supporting students and families earlier in the educational process regarding benefits of and application processes for higher education (see chapters by Bragg; Conley; Long & Boatman; Heller; Melguizo, Kienzl, & Kosiewicz; Perna & Kurban).

Finally, raising educational attainment and reducing gaps in attainment across groups requires consideration by public policymakers and educational leaders across the entire spectrum of the college completion process, spanning awareness of college and financial aid, academic readiness and preparation, access and choice, persistence and transfer, and completion. Isolated attention to narrow or discrete parts of the process is insufficient. Focusing on enhancing one aspect of the spectrum at the expense of another only restricts opportunity and narrows the pipeline for students. For broad gains to be realized, each aspect must be considered in terms of its impact on the whole process.

Purpose of this Volume

This volume assesses the state of college access, persistence, and completion for students in the United States by identifying the problems that must be addressed, summarizing what is known and unknown from prior research about how to address these problems, and offering recommendations for federal and state public policymakers, campus leaders, and educational researchers who are interested in addressing these problems. Written by nationally recognized experts in higher education, the chapters in this volume address the following four questions:

1. What are the challenges that must be addressed in order to improve college attainment?
2. What is known from existing theory and research about how to improve college access and completion, particularly for groups of students that have been historically underrepresented in higher education?

3. What is not known from existing research and theory about how to improve college access and completion? What future research would improve the ability of policymakers and practitioners to take appropriate action?
4. What conclusions should federal and state policymakers and institutional leaders draw from this information? Given what we know, what actions should public policymakers and institutional practitioners be taking?

The chapters also include explicit attention to how to improve college access and completion among students from groups that are historically underrepresented in undergraduate higher education. For purposes of this volume, groups that are underrepresented in postsecondary education include students who are first-generation college students, from minority racial or ethnic groups, from families with low incomes, from nontraditional ages and backgrounds, or who have a combination of characteristics that signify underrepresentation (Kosoko-Lasaki, Sonnino, & Voytko, 2006; Ness & Tucker, 2008; St. John & Musoba, 2012).

The chapters in this volume examine the most important points of the pipeline toward college completion, with particular attention to the roles of academic preparation and affordability in college access, persistence, and completion. The volume also includes attention not only to the experiences of traditional-age students, but also to the experiences of nontraditional students. Collectively, the chapters also recognize the roles of multiple stakeholders in improving college access, persistence, and completion, including federal and state policymakers, as well as campus administrators and faculty. Moreover, while available research provides a number of critical insights into the challenges that must be addressed, the chapters also identify important areas for future inquiry.

In Chapter 2, Laura Perna and Elizabeth Kurban delve deeply into the college access and choice problem. Their chapter discusses the continued inequalities and stratification of college access and choice even as higher education opportunity and enrollment have grown. They offer a conceptual model for understanding the forces that influence students' enrollment and choice processes and outcomes. The chapter stresses the ways that the social, cultural, economic, and policy contexts in which students are embedded influence college access and choice, and discusses the primary predictors of these outcomes: financial resources, academic preparation and achievement, support from significant others, and information about college and financial aid.

In Chapter 3, Debra Bragg examines college access and completion among what has become the largest subgroup of students—nontraditional students. Bragg profiles the characteristics of the nontraditional student population and describes their pathways into and through postsecondary education. Drawing on available research, she describes how public policies and practices can influence these pathways, with particular attention to the role of financial aid for nontraditional students. Clearly more attention to the experiences of nontraditional students is required if the nation is to realize international competitiveness goals.

In Chapter 4, David Conley discusses proficiency approaches to ensuring that students are prepared to succeed in postsecondary coursework. Such approaches represent an emerging model for college and career readiness that goes beyond traditional measures of grades, courses taken, and standardized test scores by using demonstrated mastery and competency in key areas. Conley presents four areas of skills, knowledge, strategies, and techniques students must possess in order to be adequately prepared to succeed in postsecondary coursework. As the nation continues to work toward identifying appropriate measures of college readiness, Conley offers a model that applies to traditional classroom structures as well as online learning programs.

Also recognizing that too many students are inadequately academically prepared for college, Bridget Terry Long and Angela Boatman examine in Chapter 5 what is known and not known about the effects of remedial and developmental education programs on student outcomes. After describing the methodological challenges of identifying whether a particular program improves outcomes for participating students, the chapter discusses how the effects of these programs differ based on students' characteristics, particularly their level of prior academic preparation. The chapter also provides useful consideration of efforts to redesign approaches to offering remedial education as well as avoid the need for remedial education.

In Chapter 6, Don Heller updates the discussion on what has long been recognized as a critical factor to college access and success: the ability to pay college prices. Heller describes persisting gaps in college participation based on family income and presents trends in college tuition and financial aid. The chapter notes that research clearly and consistently demonstrates the importance of "net price" to enrollment, particularly for students from low-income families; the greater effects on enrollment for grants than for loans; and the greater negative effect of an increase in tuition than a decrease in aid. Heller offers a number of recommendations for the design of federal, state, and institutional financial aid policies and practices.

Tatiana Melguizo, Gregory Kienzl, and Holly Kosiewicz analyze in Chapter 7 the role that community colleges play in promoting transfer to and success in bachelor's degree programs. They present a conceptual framework of transfer behavior that identifies the student and institutional factors facilitating successful transfer to a 4-year institution. The framework stresses that, in order to transfer, community college students must meet the academic and social demands and possess the required information and financial resources. Their chapter argues that improving the alignment of educational and organizational policies will promote transfer; particularly important are governance and funding structures and transfer and articulation agreements.

In Chapter 8, Don Hossler, Afet Dundar, and Doug Shapiro offer an expansive discussion of the predictors of retention, persistence, and completion. The chapter provides attention to the theoretical perspectives for understanding both "retention" at one institution and "persistence" within the "system" of higher education and describes what is known from research about the effects of various policies and practices on these outcomes. The authors also discuss the methodological approaches and data necessary to further advance our understanding of these important outcomes.

In Chapter 9, Jim Hearn, Anthony Jones, and Elizabeth Kurban address college access, persistence, and completion issues from the state perspective. The authors focus on three areas of influence for state policy: affordability, accountability, and alignment. Affordability issues are front and center of many families' concerns about enrolling and continuing in college, accountability measures ostensibly affect educational program quality and promote better consumer information, and alignment initiatives enable postsecondary preparation and success. The chapter provides an assessment and understanding of these important aspects and provides recommendations for moving these efforts forward.

Recognizing the demand for research that establishes whether a particular policy or practice actually *causes* improvements in college access, persistence, and completion, Steve DesJardins and Allyson Flaster offer in Chapter 10 a useful review and critique of the contributions to knowledge of available research. Noting the methodological limitations of many existing studies, the chapter provides examples of the types of research designs and methods that will yield more rigorous statements about the effects and outcomes of programs and interventions that are designed to improve college access, persistence, and completion.

As conclusion, Laura Perna summarizes in Chapter 11 the lessons learned from the chapters presented in this volume. She notes the structural challenges that limit efforts to improve college access, persistence, and completion, including the lack of alignment between our nation's K–12 and higher education systems and the number, diversity, and autonomy of U.S. colleges and universities. While synthesizing the need for more research, she also identifies six steps that emerge from the chapters in this volume that policymakers and practitioners should take in order to further improve college access and completion, especially for students from low-income families and racial/ethnic minority groups.

Concluding Note

The chapters in this volume are designed to provide public policymakers, institutional leaders, and educational researchers with the necessary information and data to continue improvements in access, persistence, and completion for all students who are interested in pursuing postsecondary education. As decision makers are faced with competing priorities, rising costs of higher education, and persisting constraints on public resources, the goal must remain on policy decisions that decrease inequity, increase opportunity, continue economic growth, improve the nation's global competitiveness, and enhance the education of the citizenry. The chapters in this volume offer essential insights into how to achieve this goal.

Notes

1. There has also been a significant increase in postsecondary academic programs offered in electronic or online formats. While this change has had several impacts, many of them still emerging, the focus of this volume is on awareness, preparation, enrollment, persistence, and completion—not the method of delivery.
2. Additional data from the U.S. Department of Education (Snyder & Dillow, 2012) show that in the previous year, fall 2009, there were 539,000 students enrolled at accredited, nondegree-granting institutions in the United States. Such institutions do not award associate's or bachelor's degrees and, generally, only award career or technical training programs of less than two years in length.

References

Aud, S., Hussar, W., Johnson, F., Kena, G., Roth, E., Manning, E., . . . & Zhang, J. (2012). *The condition of education 2012* (NCES 2012–045). Washington, DC: U.S. Department of Education, National Center for Education Statistics.

Baum, S., Ma, J., & Payea, K. (2010). *Education pays 2010: The benefits of higher education for individuals and society*. New York, NY: College Board.

Berube, A. (2010). Educational attainment. In *State of metropolitan American: On the front lines of demographic transformation* (Chapter 4, pp. 104–117). Washington, DC: The Brookings Institution Metropolitan Policy Program.

Bill & Melinda Gates Foundation. (n.d.). *Why college completion?* Seattle, WA: Author. Retrieved from http://www.gatesfoundation.org/postsecondaryeducation/Pages/why-college-completion.aspx

Bowen, H.R. (1997). *Investment in learning: The individual and social value of American higher education*. Baltimore, MD: Johns Hopkins University Press.

Carnevale, A.P., & Rose, S.J. (2012). *The undereducated American*. Washington, DC: Georgetown University, Center on Education and the Workforce.

Carnevale, A.P., Smith, N., & Strohl, J. (2010). *Help wanted: Projections of jobs and education requirements through 2018*. Washington, DC: Georgetown University, Center on Education and the Workforce.

Choy, S. (2002). *Nontraditional undergraduates*. Washington, DC: U.S. Department of Education, National Center for Education Statistics.

Gilbert, C., & Heller, D. (2010). *The Truman commission and its impact on federal higher education policy from 1947 to 2010* (Working Paper No. 9). University Park: Pennsylvania State University, Center for the Study of Higher Education. Retrieved from http://www.ed.psu.edu/educ/cshe/working-papers/CSHE%20Working%20Paper%20%239

Hussar, W.J., & Bailey, T.M. (2009). *Projections of education statistics to 2018* (NCES 2009–062). Washington, DC: U.S. Department of Education, National Center for Education Statistics.

Hutcheson, P.A. (2007). Setting the nation's agenda for higher education: A review of selected national commission reports, 1947–2006. *History of Education Quarterly, 47*(3), 359–367.

Kim, D., & Rury, J.L. (2007). The changing profile of college access: The Truman commission and enrollment patterns in the postwar era. *History of Education Quarterly, 47*(3), 302–327.

Kosoko-Lasaki, O., Sonnino, R.E., & Voytko, M. (2006). Mentoring for women and underrepresented minority faculty and students: Experience at two institutions of higher education. *Journal of the National Medical Association, 98*(9), 1449–1459.

Lumina Foundation. (2012). *A stronger nation through higher education: How and why Americans must achieve a big goal for college attainment.* Indianapolis, IN: Author.

Ness, E.C., & Tucker, R. (2008). Eligibility effects on college access: Under-represented student perceptions of Tennessee's merit aid program. *Research in Higher Education, 49*(7), 569–588.

Obama, B. (2009). Remarks of President Barack Obama as prepared for delivery address to joint session of Congress. February 24, 2009. Retrieved from http://www.whitehouse.gov/the_press_office/Remarks-of-President-Barack-Obama-Address-to-Joint-Session-of-Congress/

Organisation for Economic Co-operation and Development (OECD). (2011). *Education at a glance 2011: OECD indicators.* Paris, France: OECD Publishing.

Schuetze, H.G., & Slowey, M. (2002). Participation and exclusion: A comparative analysis of non-traditional students and lifelong learners in higher education. *Higher Education, 44*(3), 309–327.

Snyder, T.D., & Dillow, S.A. (2012). *Digest of education statistics 2011* (NCES 2012–001). Washington, DC: U.S. Department of Education, National Center for Education Statistics.

Snyder, T.D., Dillow, S.A., & Hoffman, C.M. (2008). *Digest of education statistics 2007* (NCES 2008–022). Washington, DC: U.S. Department of Education, National Center for Education Statistics.

Snyder, T.D., & Hoffman, C.M. (1991). *Digest of education statistics 1990* (NCES 1991–660). Washington, DC: U.S. Department of Education, National Center for Education Statistics.

Southern Regional Education Board. (2010). *No time to waste: Policy recommendations for increasing college completion.* Atlanta, GA: Author.

St. John, E.P., & Musoba, G.D. (2012). *Pathways to academic success in higher education: Expanding opportunity for underrepresented students.* New York, NY: Routledge.

2

IMPROVING COLLEGE ACCESS AND CHOICE

Laura W. Perna and Elizabeth R. Kurban

What Is the College Access and Choice Problem?

Some argue that the United States does not have a college access problem (see, for example, Adelman [2007]). A review of overall trends in enrollment would seem to support this conclusion. Over the past three decades, the number of students enrolling in college has increased substantially. More than 21 million students were enrolled in degree-granting institutions at all levels in 2010, a 37% increase over the number enrolled in 2000, a 52% increase over the number enrolled in 1990, and a 74% increase over the number enrolled in 1980. The vast majority of enrollments are at the undergraduate level (86% in 2010; National Center for Education Statistics [NCES], 2012a).

Although impressive, these statistics mask continued college enrollment challenges. One is that college enrollment rates continue to vary based on race/ethnicity, family income, and other demographic characteristics (Baum, Ma, & Payea, 2010). Over the past two decades, college enrollment rates have been increasing among all race/ethnicity groups. Between 1990 and 2010, the share of high school graduates age 18 to 24 who were enrolled in degree-granting institutions increased from 32.7% to 46.3% among Blacks, 28.7% to 43.7% among Hispanics, and 40.4% to 48.5% among Whites (NCES, 2012a). Despite these increases, however, college enrollment rates are still lower for Blacks and Hispanics than for Whites. Following the same pattern, the percentage of high school graduates who enrolled in college within 12 months of graduating from high school has been increasing among Blacks, Hispanics, and Whites. But, the share of high school graduates who enrolled in college immediately in 2010 continues to be smaller among Blacks (62%) and Hispanics (60%) than among Whites (71%; NCES, 2012a).

Furthermore, as Don Heller describes in his chapter, college enrollment rates increase with family income, as has been true for many decades. Between 1998 and 2008, college enrollment rates rose only for three of the five quintiles—those in the lowest two quintiles (from 51% to 55% for those in the lowest quintile; from 51% to 57% for those in the second lowest quintile) and those in the highest quintile (from 79% to 80%; Baum et al., 2010). Yet even with these improvements, the share of recent high school graduates enrolled in college was still 25 percentage points lower for those in the lowest than the highest family income quintile in 2008 (55% versus 80%; Baum et al., 2010).

The types of colleges and universities in which students enroll also vary based on students' demographic characteristics (Advisory Committee on Student Financial Assistance [ACSFA], 2010; Baum et al., 2010). Among those who enroll, Blacks are relatively concentrated in for-profit colleges and universities. In terms of enrollment at the undergraduate and graduate levels in fall 2010, 19% of Black and 11% of Hispanic enrollments were at for-profit colleges and universities, compared with 10% of Whites and 5% of Asians (NCES, 2012a). Concurrently, Blacks and Hispanics are substantially underrepresented among undergraduates attending the nation's most selective colleges and universities. In 2010, Blacks represented 13% of all college-bound seniors, but no more than 8% of undergraduates at highly selective research universities such as the University of Chicago (5%), Harvard University (6%), the University of Pennsylvania (7%), and Princeton University (8%) (College Entrance Examination Board, 2011; U.S. Department of Education, 2011). Following a similar pattern, Hispanics represented 15% of college-bound seniors in 2010, but no more than 8% of undergraduates at these institutions.

College choice is also stratified by family income. Students from low-income families are relatively overrepresented among dependent students attending for-profit and public two-year institutions (Baum et al., 2010). In 2007–2008, dependent students with family incomes below $40,000 represented substantially higher shares of students attending private for-profit institutions (54%) and public two-year colleges (35%) than of students attending private not-for-profit doctoral-granting institutions (17%), private not-for-profit four-year nondoctoral granting institutions (23%), public doctoral-granting institutions (21%), and public four-year nondoctoral granting institutions (28%) (Baum et al., 2010).

Over the past decade, the stratification of institutional choice by income has increased. Between 1992 and 2004, college-qualified high school graduates (i.e., high school graduates who had taken at least Algebra II in high school) from low-income families shifted their college destinations away from four-year institutions to two-year institutions or even toward nonenrollment (ACSFA, 2010). About half (54%) of college-qualified students from low-income families enrolled in four-year colleges after graduating from high school in 1992, compared with only 40% of college-qualified students from low-income families who graduated from high school in 2004. At the same time, the share of low-income high school graduates attending two-year colleges increased from 21% in 1992 to 31% in 2004, and the share not enrolling in any postsecondary education increased from 20% to 23%. Although smaller in magnitude, a similar shift occurred for college-qualified high school graduates from moderate-income families (ACSFA, 2010). Clearly more needs to be done to promote college enrollment and choice, particularly with regard to reducing gaps across groups in these outcomes.

What Do We Know from Existing Theory and Research About How to Improve College Enrollment and Choice?

Drawing on a comprehensive review and synthesis of prior research, previous writing proposed a conceptual model for understanding students' college enrollment and choice processes and outcomes (Perna, 2006). The conceptual model is designed to bring order to the complexity of the college enrollment process and the many forces (operating at multiple levels) that influence college access and choice for different groups of students. The model reflects three assumptions: (1) fully understanding the college enrollment process requires attention to multiple theoretical perspectives, especially the economic theory of human capital as well as cultural and social capital theories; (2) college enrollment processes occur within, and are influenced by, multiple layers of "context;" and (3) college enrollment processes are not universal but vary across groups, and, as such, policy interventions will not effectively close gaps in enrollment and choice without recognizing the culture and circumstances of particular groups (Perna, 2006). For instance, as Tierney and Venegas (2009) argue, information needs and other aspects of the college enrollment process are likely different for students from undocumented immigrant families than for other students, and different for students raised by foster parents than for students raised by their biological parents.

Shown in Figure 2.1, the model identifies four nested contextual layers that influence students' college enrollment and choice. Starting inward and moving outward, the four layers are: (1) the individual's habitus (or student and family context); (2) the school and community context; (3) the higher education context; and (4) the broader social, economic, and policy context. Each layer influences an individual's college enrollment decisions directly and indirectly through other contextual layers.

At its core, the model assumes that students make college-related decisions as predicted by human capital theory; namely, students decide to enroll in college based on a comparison of the expected benefits with the expected costs. The expected benefits include both monetary and nonmonetary benefits, while the expected costs include the costs of attendance and foregone earnings. Also, as predicted by human capital investment models, calculations of the expected benefits and costs are influenced by an individual's academic preparation for college and availability of resources to pay the costs of attendance. Human capital theory does not assume that individuals have perfect and complete information about their

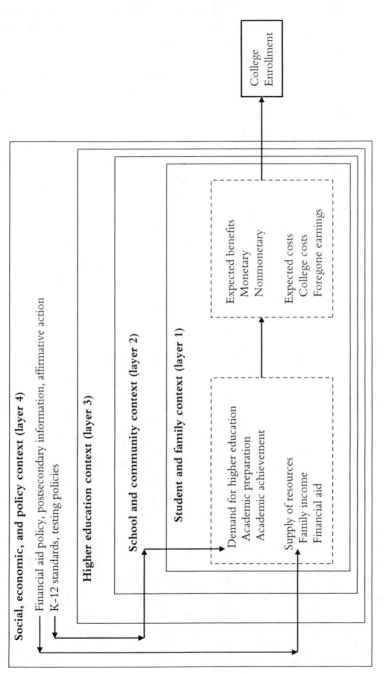

FIGURE 2.1 Conceptual Model of Student College Enrollment With Policy Linkages

Source: Perna, Rowan-Kenyon, Bell, Thomas, and Li (2008). The Ohio State University Press. Reproduced with permission.

academic readiness or other components of the model (e.g., financial resources, costs, and benefits), but that they decide to enroll in college based on available information. A decision is rational when based on available information regardless of the information's accuracy (DesJardins & Toutkoushian, 2005).

The conceptual model assumes that calculations of the expected costs and benefits are nested within several layers of context. With its attention to these layers, the conceptual model recognizes the differences in the resources that shape college enrollment and choice for different groups of students (McDonough, 1997).

The innermost layer, or the habitus, may be understood as the internalized system of thoughts, beliefs, and perceptions that is acquired from the immediate environment (McDonough, 1997). Rather than consider all possible postsecondary options, habitus defines and delimits the alternatives that are considered, how different alternatives are perceived and valued, and the choices that are made. These alternatives are determined by the social, organizational, and cultural contexts in which individuals are embedded, including class-based values and the organizational habitus of high school attended.

The school and community context (Figure 2.1, layer 2) reflects McDonough's (1997) notion of "organizational habitus," and recognizes the ways that social structures and resources facilitate or impede students' college enrollment processes. Research suggests that aspects of the school context may restrict college enrollment and choice for low-income students and racial/ethnic minorities. For instance, Stanton-Salazar (1997) argued that institutional agents, such as teachers, counselors, and middle-class peers, provide access to resources and opportunities, including information about college and help with college admissions requirements. Working-class minority students are especially dependent on nonfamilial institutional agents for essential college-related information, particularly if they are the first in their family or community to attend college. But because these mainstream institutional structures can operate on "subjective biases and interpersonal histories," they also can intrinsically alienate and exclude working-class minority students and limit the ability of these students to develop "trusting" relationships with institutional agents for support (Stanton-Salazar, 1997, p. 17).

The next layer (Figure 2.1, layer 3), the higher education context, recognizes the role that higher education institutions play in shaping students' college enrollment and choice. These institutions may be a source of information to students and their families about postsecondary enrollment options, conveying information passively through their location and geographic proximity to students' homes and, actively, through targeted marketing and recruiting efforts. The attributes and characteristics of higher education institutions may also influence student college choice, as students prefer to attend colleges and universities with particular characteristics, especially ones that are consistent with their personal and social identities. Higher education institutions also influence student college choice through their ability to select which applicants may enroll, as well as through the availability of enrollment slots.

The outermost layer (Figure 2.1, layer 4), the social, economic, and policy context, recognizes that college enrollment and choice are influenced, directly and indirectly, through other contextual layers, such as changes in social forces (e.g., demographic changes), economic conditions (e.g., unemployment rate), and public policies (e.g., state and federally sponsored student financial aid programs). Explicitly incorporating the social, economic, and policy context into the model recognizes the connections between policy and college choice outcomes identified by other researchers (e.g., Kirst & Bracco, 2004; Perna & Titus, 2004; St. John, 2003). For example, Kirst and Bracco (2004) argue that policy "signals," emanating from elementary and secondary education and/or postsecondary education about college admissions and placement requirements, play a critical role in students' knowledge about, and academic preparation for, college. Using multilevel analyses, Perna and Titus (2004) found that measures of four types of state public policies (direct appropriations to higher education institutions, tuition, financial aid to students, and elementary and secondary education) are related to the college enrollment patterns of 1992 high school graduates. St. John's (2003) framework posits that K–12 policies pertaining to schooling and school reform (e.g., standards and testing) shape K–12 attainment and achievement, while policy interventions (e.g., financial aid policies, postsecondary information, and affirmative action) influence postsecondary transitions and access, and college and university policies (e.g., financial and academic strategies) affect undergraduate and graduate student outcomes.

With the various contextual layers, this conceptual model highlights the complexity of college enrollment and choice processes and the many forces that contribute to outcomes. Attention to the contextual forces that influence college enrollment and choice provides a strong foundation for understanding how the primary predictors of college enrollment and choice influence outcomes.

What Are the Most Important Predictors of College Enrollment and Choice?

A review of prior research in light of this conceptual model reveals four categories of predictors that determine college enrollment and choice:

1. Financial resources
2. Academic preparation and achievement
3. Support from significant others
4. Knowledge and information about college and financial aid

Financial Resources

Available data and research clearly and consistently demonstrate that "money" matters to students' college enrollment and choice. As described earlier in this chapter, money—defined as family income—is related to both whether a student enrolls in college and the type of college the student attends (Baum et al., 2010). Research shows a positive relationship between family income and college enrollment even after controlling for other forces that influence college enrollment, including academic preparation and achievement and parental involvement (Kane, 1999; Perna, 2000).

An extensive body of research has examined the effects of student financial aid on college enrollment and choice. One recent synthesis (Perna, 2010a) identifies the following conclusions. First, the effects of student financial aid on college enrollment vary based on the type of aid. Nonetheless, research consistently shows that grant aid is positively related to the likelihood of college enrollment (Avery & Hoxby, 2004; Heller, 1997; Kane, 1999; Mundel, 2008). Moreover, while showing that both need- and merit-based aid are associated with increased college enrollment, some research shows that the magnitude of the positive effect is greater for need- than merit-based aid (Perna & Titus, 2004; St. John, Musoba, & Chung, 2004). In contrast, Heller (2008) concluded that prior research generally shows loans to have minimal effect on college enrollment and completion. But, Heller also speculated that loans may have a positive effect if more students received sufficient grant aid. Although some research has examined the effects of work-study on student persistence in college (e.g., Pascarella & Terenzini, 2005; St. John, 2003), little is known about the effects of work-study on students' college enrollment. In one of the few available studies, Avery and Hoxby (2004) found that, among high-ability high school seniors nationwide, the amount of work-study offered was positively related to the likelihood of enrolling after controlling for other student and institutional characteristics. The small number of available studies suggests that federal tax policies, including tax credits, deductions for higher education expenses and student loan interest, and tax-preferred savings programs, are unrelated to postsecondary access and choice (Long, 2004; Reschovsky, 2008).

A second conclusion that may be drawn from available research is that the effects of financial aid on college enrollment depend on a student's family income and race/ethnicity (Avery & Hoxby, 2004; Heller, 1997; Kane, 1999; Lillis, 2008; Mundel, 2008). As Don Heller describes in his chapter and as demonstrated in other research (Avery & Hoxby, 2004; Heller, 1997; Kane, 1999; Long, 2004), changes in tuition and financial aid have a larger effect on college enrollment for students from lower-income families than higher-income ones, and for African Americans and Hispanics than for Whites. Some evidence suggests that the effects of financial aid on students' choice of institution also vary by race. Kim (2004) found that, net of other variables, receiving grants was associated with a higher probability of attending the first-choice institution for Whites, and receiving loans was positively related to attendance for Asians, yet neither grants nor loans were related to the likelihood of attending the first-choice institution for Blacks or Hispanics.

A third conclusion from available research is that the effects of financial aid on enrollment and choice are mediated by various contextual forces (Perna, 2010a).

For instance, at the individual level, available research demonstrates variations in students' willingness to use loans to pay college-related expenses (Cunningham & Santiago, 2008; Perna, 2008); loans cannot have a positive effect on enrollment if students are unwilling to use them.

Characteristics of the high school context also mediate the effects of student financial aid. Students' perceptions and understanding of financial aid, including the availability of financial aid, criteria for receiving different types of aid, and the advantages and disadvantages of different types of aid, are determined in part by the information that they receive from high school counselors and other characteristics of the high school that they attend (Perna, 2008). But, data and research consistently document the absence of sufficient college-related counseling, especially at high schools attended by groups of students with low college-going rates (McDonough, 1997, 2005; Perna, Rowan-Kenyon, Thomas, et al., 2008). The average ratio of students to counselors at high schools nationwide in 2008–2009 was 261:1 (National Association for College Admission Counseling, 2010). Even when available, counselors are often unable to devote much attention to providing college counseling to students, as this type of counseling is typically only one of a counselor's many responsibilities (McDonough, 2005; Perna, Rowan-Kenyon, Thomas, et al., 2008).

The effects of financial aid on college enrollment and choice also depend on aspects of the higher education context, including the tuition and costs of attendance, as well as the other types and amounts of financial aid received (Perna, 2010a). The financial aid information that colleges and universities provide to students may influence students' and their families' perceptions and understandings of college costs. One challenge many students and their families face in understanding college costs is the lack of standardization of an institution's financial aid award letter. Particularly problematic are differences across colleges in definitions of the cost of attendance and the description of award components (e.g., subsidized versus unsubsidized loans; ACSFA, 2011).

The federal government has recently attempted to make information about the costs of attendance more transparent by requiring that, effective fall 2011, colleges and universities have an online "net price calculator" that estimates a student's net price of attendance. But, while the mandate (included as part of the Higher Education Opportunity Act of 2008) specifies that some information must be included, it does not require use of a common template for the net price calculator and requires only that the U.S. Department of Education develop a template for the financial aid award letter. Thus, even with this congressional attention, net price calculators and financial aid award letters continue to vary greatly in the content, formatting, and organization of information, making it difficult for students and their parents to make informed comparisons across colleges. The lack of standardization contributes to the complexities associated with understanding college costs and affordability (ACSFA, 2011).

The broader economic, social, and public policy context also informs the relationship between financial aid and college enrollment and choice. One relevant aspect of the public policy context is the availability of different types of aid. Nearly half of all aid awarded to undergraduates is in the form of loans (42% in 2010–2011, College Board, 2011), suggesting that, for many students, borrowing is required for college enrollment.

Academic Preparation and Achievement

Research consistently shows that measures of academic preparation and achievement are strong positive predictors of students' college-related outcomes (Perna, 2005a), including: high school graduation rates (Cabrera & LaNasa, 2000), college entrance examination scores (Horn & Kojaku, 2001), college enrollment rates (Perna, 2000; Perna & Titus, 2004), and attendance at more selective colleges and universities (Horn & Kojaku, 2001). The most common measure of academic preparation is now the highest level of mathematics taken; achievement is typically measured by test scores and high school grades (Perna, 2006).

As David Conley, Bridget Terry Long, and Angela Boatman describe in their chapters, the inadequacy of current levels of academic preparation is indicated by the high rates of participation in remedial or developmental education and the negative consequences of such participation for degree completion. About one-fifth of all first-year undergraduates took at least one remedial course in 2007–2008, with 10.9% of all first-year undergraduates taking at least two remedial courses that year (NCES, 2012a). Using data collected as part of the Achieving the Dream: Community Colleges Count initiative, Bailey, Jeong, and Cho (2010) found that 59% of the students attending the community colleges in the sample were referred to remedial math, and 33% were referred to remedial language arts. Those who are referred to remedial coursework often are challenged to complete a complex sequence of required courses. Bailey et al. also found that only a third of students referred to remedial math and 46% of students referred to remedial language arts completed the entire sequence of recommended developmental courses, which ranged from one to three courses, depending on the student's placement test score and the college's approach to developmental education.

Providing a partial explanation for observed differences in college enrollment and choice across groups, academic preparation and achievement are lower for groups that are underrepresented in higher education than for other students. For example, only 6% of Black and 8% of Hispanic high school graduates in 2009 took a rigorous academic curriculum (defined as at least four credits of English; at least four credits of math; biology, chemistry and physics; and at least three foreign language credits), compared with 14% of Whites and 29% of Asians (NCES, 2011). As one example of differences in commonly used measures of academic achievement, among those taking the Calculus AB Advanced Placement examination, only 5% of Blacks and 11% of Hispanics, but 23% of Whites and 25% of Asians scored a five (the highest score) in 2010 (College Entrance Examination Board, 2010). Similar patterns are present for examinations in other areas, including biology and calculus.

At the individual level, human capital theory assumes that students consider their academic readiness when weighing the costs and benefits of enrolling in college. But, academic readiness is influenced by the structures and contexts in which students are embedded.

Several aspects of the high school context influence students' academic preparation and achievement. Notably, high schools differ in terms of the availability of rigorous courses, as well as the procedures used to determine student participation in such courses. A descriptive examination of the availability of one rigorous curricular program (i.e., the International Baccalaureate [IB] diploma programme) reveals that, although IB is available in an increasingly diverse set of schools, the characteristics of participating students are somewhat less diverse (Perna et al., 2012). Moreover, the opportunity to participate in an available IB program varies across schools based on school-specific admissions practices.

Research also points to the importance of other characteristics of the high school context, including the extent to which college-related resources within a school are directed toward particular students. Some research suggests that, within schools, access to college counseling varies by academic achievement. More specifically, college counseling appears to be more common for students in Advanced Placement, honors, and college preparatory curricular tracks than for students in other curricular tracks (McDonough, 2005; Venezia & Kirst, 2005).

The higher education context also influences academic preparation for college. Particularly important is the alignment (or lack thereof) of curricula and assessments between K–12 and higher education (Kirst & Venezia, 2004). Developed and operated separately, K–12 and higher education systems are typically characterized by different curricular requirements, assessment systems, and accountability measures. In his chapter, David Conley describes some national (e.g., Achieve's American Diploma Project, Common Core State Standards) and state (e.g., Colorado, Texas, Wisconsin) initiatives designed to establish shared definitions of college readiness.

The broader public economic, social, and public policy context also plays a role in determining students' academic readiness for college. As one example, case study analyses of 15 high schools, 3 in each of 5 states, revealed that state-mandated high school exit examinations can have unintended consequences, particularly in schools with low performance on these tests (Perna & Thomas, 2009). In these schools, staff acted rationally, focusing available resources on efforts to improve the school's performance on the test, but leaving relatively few resources (e.g., counselor staff) for activities that more directly promote college enrollment for potentially college-qualified students.

The extent to which student financial aid programs that award financial aid based on academic achievement (i.e., merit-based aid) encourages improved academic readiness for college is unclear. Some have concluded that research does not establish whether merit-based aid programs improve students' academic readiness for college (Doyle, 2008; Dynarski, 2004). Another study that draws on data collected from the case study analyses of 15 high schools finds that students and their families are aware of the academic requirements to receive merit aid, but that at least some of these students take less rigorous courses in order to increase the likelihood of meeting the academic eligibility requirements for the aid (Perna & Steele, 2011).

Support from Significant Others

"Significant others" matter to college enrollment and choice in part because these relationships provide students with access to necessary college-related information (Perna & Titus, 2005). Most recent research focuses specifically on the role of parents. This research consistently shows that parental involvement in a student's education is associated with college-related outcomes, including the decision to enroll in a two-year or four-year college (Perna & Titus, 2005). The contributions of existing research are limited by a focus on the role of "parents" rather than other potential "significant others" and the tendency to define parental involvement using the norms of White, middle-class involvement, as well as the emphasis on traditional, nuclear family structures. Nonetheless, although parents typically have high educational aspirations for their children, many parents have limited involvement (using a traditional definition of involvement) because of economic, social, and psychological barriers as well as their limited direct prior experience with higher education (Rowan-Kenyon, Bell, & Perna, 2008).

Variations in the availability of college-related counseling in the high school attended (as described above) limit the extent to which the school can compensate for barriers that restrict parental involvement (McDonough, 1997). Some research shows variations in the availability of resources to promote college enrollment that may be accessed via parental involvement. Defining parental involvement as a form of social capital, Perna and Titus (2005) use multilevel analyses of data from a nationally representative longitudinal study to examine the effects on college enrollment of the extent to which a high school encourages parental involvement, the volume of different resources that may be accessed via social networks at the school, and the homogeneity of social networks at the school. The analyses show that, regardless of an individual student's social, economic, cultural, and human capital characteristics, the likelihood of enrolling in a two-year or four-year college after graduating from high school is positively related to the volume of resources that may be accessed through social networks at the school attended. The volume of resources is measured by the average levels of parental involvement, family income, parental education, and parental educational expectations at the school the student attends.

A smaller body of research suggests the importance of peers to students' college enrollment decisions. Perna and Titus (2005) found, even after controlling for a student's demographic and academic characteristics as well as other characteristics of the high school attended, that the likelihood of enrolling in a two-year or four-year college or university increases with the share of friends who plan to enroll. Moreover, high school students tend to attend the type of college (i.e., a two-year rather than a four-year institution) that their friends plan to attend. Other research shows that friends' college-going plans are even more important predictors of four-year college enrollment for low-income, urban, minority students than for other high school students (Sokatch, 2006).

In terms of the higher education and public policy context, research points to the role of precollege outreach programs in providing support for students and consequently promoting college enrollment. Although the findings may be out of date, some research suggests, however, that relatively few precollege outreach programs have a comprehensive and longitudinal approach to promoting college enrollment of historically underrepresented groups (Perna, 2002).

Knowledge and Information about College and Financial Aid

Existing reports and studies consistently document the absence of accurate knowledge of college prices and financial aid among high school students and their families (see Perna, 2005b, for one review). Levels of awareness and understanding of college prices and financial aid are particularly low among groups that are underrepresented in higher education (Perna, 2005b). Based on their review of prior research, Bowen, Kurzweil, and Tobin (2005) concluded that "there is solid evidence that a lack of information and a lack of understanding about the process of applying for college and for financial aid result in sub-optimal college-going decisions" (p. 318).

A variety of college-related outcomes (e.g., expectations, application, enrollment, and choice) are lower for students who have less knowledge and information about college prices and financial aid than for other students (Perna, 2005b). But, the direction of causality in these studies is ambiguous. In other words, research does not reveal the extent to which information is a cause or consequence of college-related outcomes (Perna, 2005b). One recent exception suggests that improved information may cause improved college-related outcomes. In the study, Bettinger, Long, Oreopoulos, and Sanbonmatsu (2009) use an experimental design with random assignment to show that simplifying the student financial aid process and providing assistance with completing the financial aid application form can improve college-going for individuals from low- to moderate-income families. Specifically, individuals from low- and moderate-income families who received assistance with completing and submitting the federal financial aid application form and personalized estimates of the net costs of attending a nearby public college or university were more likely to submit a financial aid application, enroll in college, and receive need-based financial aid than individuals who received only personalized estimates of the net costs or who received no information.

Context also influences the relationship between information and college enrollment. At the individual level, research demonstrates the importance of providing individually tailored information that recognizes a student's cultural background and other contextual forces (Perna, 2010a). For instance, using ethnographic methods, Valadez (2008) found that the selected students (12 high-achieving rural high school students who had immigrated from Mexico) made their college enrollment decisions by negotiating their own agency and preferences with the norms and expectations of their structural (e.g., high school) and cultural (e.g., family) contexts. The findings suggest the utility of approaches that consider the cultural perspectives and values, as well as the particular knowledge requirements, of immigrant students, in the provision of college-related information.

With regard to the high school context, qualitative research documents the challenges that counselors experience in their efforts to provide students with information related to college and financial aid (McDonough, 2005; Perna, Rowan-Kenyon, Thomas, et al., 2008). Especially in low-performing high schools, counselors often have numerous other noncollege-related responsibilities, including scheduling, testing, and providing personal and nonacademic counseling, and may not be trained in the nuances of college and financial aid application processes (McDonough, 2005; Perna, Rowan-Kenyon, Thomas, et al., 2008).

In terms of the higher education context, colleges and universities use varying approaches to communicate information to prospective students about college and financial aid. In one exploratory study, Perna, Lundy-Wagner, Yee, Brill, and Teran (2011) question the ways that many selective colleges and universities use their websites to communicate their "no loan" policies to prospective low-income students. Their analyses point to features of institutional communication strategies that may restrict the ability of low-income students to learn about the aid programs for which they may be eligible, including challenges locating the information, the use of future rather than present orientation in the presentation of the information, the absence of specific "how to" guidelines, and the lack of explicit recognition of the importance of need-based student aid.

In terms of the public policy context, some research suggests that knowledge of financial aid varies based on the characteristics of the aid. Although awarding financial aid based on academic criteria has been shown to have a smaller positive effect on college enrollment than awarding financial aid based on financial need (Perna & Titus, 2004), the eligibility and award criteria of merit-based aid are often relatively simple and transparent, and this approach appears to have some knowledge-related benefits (Perna & Steele, 2011). Using case study analyses of 15 schools, 3 in each of 5 states, Perna and Steele (2011) found that, although knowledge of financial aid was low at schools in all 5 states, students and parents attending the high schools in Florida and Georgia, 2 states with extensive state-sponsored merit-based aid programs, were aware of the availability of the aid and the criteria for receiving the aid. The analyses point to differences between the state need- and merit-based aid programs in the transparency and simplicity of available information as a potential reason for the differences in knowledge.

What Is Not Known from Existing Research About How to Improve College Enrollment and Choice?

Existing research provides a number of insights into the forces that contribute to college enrollment and choice, particularly for groups of students that have been historically underrepresented in higher education. Nonetheless, additional research is required in several areas in order to better inform federal policymaking.

Enrollment and Choice Decisions of Nontraditional Students

One area for future research is to better understand "nontraditional" college students and patterns of enrollment, where nontraditional is defined as anyone who does not enter college immediately from high school on a full-time basis. As Debra Bragg describes in her chapter, better understanding the college enrollment and choice processes and outcomes of nontraditional students is critical, given the changes that have occurred in the characteristics of college students. As the Advisory Committee on Student Financial Assistance (2012) points out in its report, *Pathways to Success: Integrating Learning With Life and Work to Increase National College Completion*, although still labeled "non-traditional," these students now represent "the largest subset of students in the nation," and include numerous subgroups with varying "circumstances, educational needs, and goals" (p. iii).

Clearly, research that focuses only on the college enrollment and choice decisions of 18-year-olds who transition into a not-for-profit college or university immediately after high school graduation misses a substantial share of the college-going population. In 2007–2008, only about half of all undergraduates were traditional age, defined as 19 to 23 years old. The share of students age 23 or below was substantially smaller at public two-year colleges (50.3%) and for-profit institutions (49.9% at less than two-year for-profit institutions; 33.6% at for-profit institutions of two years or more) than at public four-year nondoctoral granting (66.3%), public four-year doctoral granting (78%), private four-year nondoctoral granting (63.6%), and private four-year doctoral granting (67%) institutions (NCES, 2010).

Nontraditional College Enrollment Choices

Future research should also examine the decision of students to enroll in nontraditional ways, including the decision to attend part time, as well as the ways that working students can most productively balance the multiple and often competing responsibilities of employment and school (Perna, 2010b).

More attention is also needed to understand the enrollment and choice processes of the growing number of students attending for-profit institutions and online higher education programs. The share of students enrolled at degree-granting institutions who are attending for-profit institutions has increased substantially over the past decade, rising from just 3% in fall 1999 to 9% in fall 2009 (NCES, 2011).

Whether and How Particular Policies and Programs Improve College Enrollment

Additional research is also needed to better understand whether and how particular policies and programs improve college-related outcomes for different groups of students. Such research should identify the best approaches to addressing the following challenges:

How to use financial aid to improve academic preparation: Because most students and their families lack accurate and complete information about financial aid until they actually apply for aid, financial aid is likely not serving as a lever to encourage students to engage in other behaviors that promote college enrollment and success (Perna, 2010a). Particularly important is understanding ways that knowledge of financial aid may encourage students to become adequately academically prepared. How does information about different types of aid, provided at different points in a student's educational pipeline, shape a student's course taking and other academic preparatory behaviors?

How to provide meaningful access to rigorous academic preparation to all students: Rigorous academic preparation is required for students to gain access to and succeed in college (Perna, 2005a). But, how can the rigor of academic coursework be improved to ensure that all students are adequately academically prepared for college-level work without the need for remediation? Moreover, as other chapters in this volume (see Conley; Long & Boatman) ask, how can assessments be improved to ensure that students and their high schools know how well students are academically prepared for college?

How to encourage productive involvement of "parents" and other influential individuals among different groups of students: Although research consistently shows the positive effects on students' college-related outcomes of parental involvement, such research is limited by the reliance on definitions of involvement that reflect White, middle-class norms and the failure to consider nontraditional family structures. Future research should consider the contributions of a broader set of significant others and the ways to encourage productive assistance for college enrollment of these individuals.

How to provide accurate, usable information that promotes students' college-related outcomes: Much is unknown about the best ways to ensure that students and their families have accurate, usable information that promotes college-going and success. Among the unanswered questions are what types of information are required at what points along the educational pipeline and by what sources (e.g., counselor, website, and social media; Perna, 2010a)?

How to provide counseling about the "right" amounts of loans and work: Although some students are averse to using loans (Perna, 2008), other students are accumulating high amounts of debt. In 2007–2008, more than half (57%) of bachelor's degree recipients graduated with some amount of education debt; education debt exceeded $30,500 for 17% of 2007–2008 bachelor's degree recipients

(Baum & Steele, 2010). In addition, a notable fraction of students who borrow fail to complete their programs or degrees and still have a debt to repay (Gladieux & Perna, 2005). Research is required to understand the effects on college enrollment and choice of information about loan forgiveness programs and income-contingent repayment, particularly for loan-averse students.

Little is also known about how to counsel students about the trade-offs involved with using loans and employment to pay college costs. Some students choose not to borrow (or borrow limited amounts), but instead work substantial numbers of hours while enrolled to pay college costs (American Council on Education, Policy Center for Policy Analysis, 2006; Gladieux & Perna, 2005; Perna, 2010b). Employment is now the norm even among "traditional" undergraduates, as nearly half (40%) of undergraduates who were enrolled full time and under the age of 25 worked some number of hours in 2010 (NCES, 2012b). Between 2000 and 2010, the share of undergraduates under the age of 25 and enrolled full time working at least 35 hours per week varied between 6% and 9% (NCES, 2012b).

The available research on the effects of working while enrolled in college is quite consistent: students who work a modest number of hours per week (10–15 hours), on campus, are more likely than other students—even students who do not work at all—to persist and earn degrees (Perna, 2010b). Working a higher number of hours, especially when the employment is off campus, increases time to degree and reduces the likelihood of completing a degree (Titus, 2010). For some students, working while enrolled in college is necessary—without the earnings generated from employment, the student would have insufficient funds to pay the costs of attendance. In addition to providing students with necessary financial resources, employment may also have other benefits. Working may help a student explore career options. For adult students, working may be a fundamental part of their identity (Perna, 2010b). Some evidence suggests that students who work while enrolled earn higher salaries after college (Titus, 2010). Nonetheless, given that time is finite, working while enrolled in college necessarily reduces the time and energy available for academic engagement in college. Moreover, trying to meet the multiple and sometimes conflicting demands associated with simultaneously being a student, employee, parent, and so forth may create high levels of stress and anxiety, in addition to reducing the likelihood of completing a college degree (Perna, 2010b; Titus, 2010). From a societal perspective, working while enrolled may also reinforce social stratification and inequality, as students from lower-class backgrounds are more likely than students from upper-class ones to work high numbers of hours while enrolled (Perna, 2010b).

How are college enrollment and choice processes influenced by the contexts in which students are embedded: In addition, future research should consider the ways that particular dimensions of context influence college enrollment and choice processes. Clearly, college enrollment processes vary based on the cultural and other background characteristics of students, as well as the characteristics of the high schools that students attend; the local and national higher education context; and the broader social, economic, and public policy context. Future research should also identify the most relevant aspects of context that influence college enrollment of nontraditional students.

What Are the Implications of These Findings for Public Policy and Institutional Practice?

Despite the need for additional research, existing theory and research points to a number of conclusions and recommendations for policy and practice. Most generally, federal and state policymakers and college and university administrators should adopt policies and practices that recognize the changing characteristics of students (such as the growth in nontraditional students and nontraditional enrollment patterns) and postsecondary education institutions (particularly for-profit institutions).

Federal and state policymakers must also continue to support the collection and use of relevant data to more fully understand college enrollment and choice outcomes for students of different groups and the forces that contribute to these outcomes. With the encouragement of the federal Race to the Top initiative, a number of states are investing resources to improve their state education data systems and address current data limitations. Particularly important is improving the capacity of state educational data systems to longitudinally track students' educational experiences and progress across educational levels (e.g., between high school and college), across different educational sectors (from public colleges and universities to private colleges and universities), and into the workforce. Existing and new data collections, such as the federal government's Beginning Postsecondary Students Longitudinal Study, should also be expanded to track the postsecondary educational experiences of nontraditional undergraduates in addition to first-time, first-year undergraduates. Expanding data collection and analysis to include all students will more accurately represent the current landscape of U.S. higher education and provide the data needed to address many unanswered questions.

The review of data, research, and theory in this chapter also suggests the need for policies and practices that reduce the primary barriers to college enrollment and choice, particularly for students from underrepresented groups.

Financial Resources

Building on recommendations from the College Board's Rethinking Student Aid Study Group (2008), federal and state policymakers should maximize the availability of federal and state-supported need-based grants and target available funds to the lowest-income students. The federal government should also continue efforts to reduce the complexity of financial aid application processes and continue to identify mechanisms that increase the transparency of financial aid eligibility criteria and award amounts. State governments should encourage college affordability by providing sufficient and predictable appropriations to public colleges and universities and encouraging links between state appropriations, tuition, and student financial aid (Zumeta, Breneman, Callan, & Finney, 2012).

Along the same lines, college and university administrators should also work to ensure the affordability of college by minimizing increases in tuition, maximizing the availability of institutional grant aid, and targeting available institutional aid on students with the lowest family incomes. In addition, colleges and universities should review the information that they provide to students and their families about college costs and financial aid through net price calculators, financial aid award letters, and other mechanisms. In particular, colleges and universities should review communication strategies (e.g., institutional websites) to ensure available information is presented to effectively address the knowledge needs of low-income and first-generation college students (Perna et al., 2011).

Academic Preparation

Given the unambiguous importance of academic preparation to college enrollment and success and the low levels of academic readiness among many students, federal and state policymakers should encourage efforts that promote the availability of rigorous coursework, particularly in under-resourced high schools, and that promote achievement in these courses, especially among students from lower-income families and racial/ethnic minority groups.

Federal and state policymakers should also continue to support efforts to improve curricular alignment between K–12 and higher education so as to ensure college and career readiness. Two recent efforts are the PARCC (Partnership for Assessment of Readiness for College and Careers) Consortium and the Smarter Balanced Assessment Consortium. PARCC has 24 member states (including the District of Columbia), whereas Smarter Balanced has 27 member states; 5 states are members of both (i.e., Alabama, Colorado, North Dakota, Pennsylvania, and South Carolina). Both PARCC and Smarter Balanced are state-led consortia designed to develop assessments in English language arts/literacy and mathematics that are aligned with the Common Core State Standards (CCSS). Released in 2010 by the National Governors Association and Council of Chief State School Officers, the CCSS have been adopted by 45 states (Center for K–12 Assessment & Performance Management, 2012). The U.S. Department of Education awarded grants to PARCC and Smarter Balanced to develop assessments aligned with the CCSS. Member states have agreed to implement the new assessments starting with the 2014–2015 academic year; although states may also adopt state-specific standards, CCSS must represent at least 85% of a state's total standards (Center for K–12 Assessment & Performance Management, 2012). Each state may determine its own approach to implementing the standards and must pay the associated costs. It remains to be seen whether these initiatives will effectively promote students' academic preparation for college. Regardless, as David Conley concludes in his chapter, ensuring college readiness among high school graduates is an area where all states require greater progress.

State policymakers should also encourage high schools to offer courses and curricula that ensure college readiness. They should also ensure that state assessments not only provide valid and reliable assessments of college readiness, but also provide information to high schools and students about how students might become adequately academically prepared to enter and succeed in college without remediation. When students are not sufficiently prepared, schools should provide students with the opportunity to correct deficiencies (Conley, this volume; Long & Boatman, this volume; Roderick, Nagaoka, & Coca, 2009; Tierney, Bailey, Constantine, Finkelstein, & Hurd, 2009).

Support from Significant Others

Policymakers and practitioners should also encourage programming that facilitates college-related support from significant others and provides students and their families with college-related information. One mechanism for providing support, encouragement, and information to improve the college enrollment process is precollege outreach programs (Perna, 2002).

Sponsored by the federal government, state governments, colleges and universities, philanthropic organizations, and private businesses, precollege outreach programs focus on improving college readiness, particularly among students from historically underrepresented groups (Perna, 2002). The federal government has been involved in supporting such programs since the establishment of the Upward Bound program in 1964. Now one of the Federal TRIO programs, Upward Bound, is specifically targeted toward improving high school graduation, college enrollment, and college completion among students from groups underrepresented in higher education. All student participants in Upward Bound "must be either from low-income families or potential first-generation college students," and at least two-thirds of students must be both; "the remaining one-third must be either low-income, first-generation college students, or students who have a high risk for academic failure" (U.S. Department of Education, 2012).

Based on their review, Tierney et al. (2009) concluded that, although many existing studies have critical limitations, available rigorous research points to the benefits of precollege outreach programs such as Philadelphia's Sponsor-a-Scholar Program and the federal Talent Search program. Their review also points to the benefits of having a network of adults and peers who support a student's college-going aspirations. This type of support program may also be an important source of college-related information.

Information

Federal and state policymakers, as well as college administrators, must recognize the many forces that limit the availability of college-related counseling in the high schools that students attend (McDonough, 2005; Perna, Rowan-Kenyon, Thomas, et al., 2008). Federal and state policymakers should not only support programming that promotes college-related information, particularly among disadvantaged groups of students, but also build on efforts like the net cost calculator to encourage and promote early awareness and understanding of financial aid.

College administrators should also develop efforts to promote student and family understanding of college costs, the availability of financial aid, and financial aid application processes (Tierney et al., 2009). In addition to considering the presentation of financial information (described above), colleges and universities should review the methods used to provide counseling to prospective and current students about types of financial aid available, and the trade-offs between grants and loans. Colleges and universities should also help students make more informed decisions about private loans, reducing use of this financing mechanism by providing counseling, excluding these loans from financial aid offers, and systematically tracking the impact of students' decisions to use them (Reed, 2011).

Ideally, programs to improve college-related information would focus on improving student and family knowledge of higher education benefits, college expenses, mechanisms for paying for college, and financial aid application processes and procedures (ACSFA, 2008). Programs should adopt the 10 guidelines the Advisory Committee on Student Financial Assistance (2008) developed from a review of available research: intervene beginning in the sixth grade and through high school completion; involve parents and their families; mentor each student; complete the federal financial aid application form; modify program services to recognize the school context; recognize language and cultural needs; coordinate programming with other community organizations; promote peer integration; evaluate program performance; and promote financial literacy as well as knowledge of financial aid.

Conclusion

Clearly, more progress is needed to ensure that all students, regardless of family income and race/ethnicity, have the opportunity to enroll in the college or university of their choice. Although more research is needed, particularly with regard to the college enrollment processes of nontraditional students and nontraditional enrollment choices, available theory and research provides federal and state policymakers and campus leaders with a framework for understanding fruitful policies and practices. The time to act is now.

References

Adelman, C. (2007). Do we have an access problem? *Change*. Retrieved from http://www. carnegiefoundation.org/change/sub.asp?key=98&subkey=2385

Advisory Committee on Student Financial Assistance (ACSFA). (2008). *Early and often: Designing a comprehensive system of financial aid information*. Washington, DC: Author.

Advisory Committee on Student Financial Assistance (ACSFA). (2010). *The rising price of inequality: How inadequate grant aid limits college access and persistence.* Washington, DC: Author.

Advisory Committee on Student Financial Assistance (ACSFA). (2011). *The bottom line: Ensuring that students and parents understand the net price of college.* Washington, DC: Author.

Advisory Committee on Student Financial Assistance (ACSFA). (2012). *Pathways to success: Integrating learning with life and work to increase national college completion.* Washington, DC: Author.

American Council on Education, Center for Policy Analysis. (2006). *Working their way through college: Student employment and its impact on the college experience.* Washington, DC: Author.

Avery, C., & Hoxby, C.M. (2004). Do and should financial aid packages affect students' college choices? In C. Hoxby (Ed.), *College choices: The economics of where to go, when to go, and how to pay for it* (pp. 239–302). Chicago, IL: University of Chicago Press.

Bailey, T., Jeong, D.W., & Cho, S.-W. (2010). Referral, enrollment, and completion in developmental education sequences in community colleges. *Economics of Education Review, 29*(2), 255–270.

Baum, S., Ma, J., & Payea, K. (2010). *Education pays 2010.* Washington, DC: College Board. Retrieved from http://trends.collegeboard.org/downloads/Education_Pays_2010.pdf

Baum, S., & Steele, P. (2010). *Who borrows most: Bachelor's degree recipients with high levels of student debt.* Washington, DC: College Board.

Bettinger, E.P., Long, B.T., Oreopoulos, P., & Sanbonmatsu, L. (2009). *The role of simplification and information in college decisions: Results from the H&R Block FAFSA experiment* (Working Paper No. 15361). Cambridge, MA: National Bureau of Economic Research.

Bowen, W.G., Kurzweil, M.A., & Tobin, E.M. (2005). *Equity and excellence in American higher education.* Charlottesville: University of Virginia Press.

Cabrera, A.F., & LaNasa, S.M. (2000). Understanding the college choice of disadvantaged students. *New Directions for Institutional Research.* San Francisco, CA: Jossey-Bass.

Center for K–12 Assessment & Performance Management. (2012). *Coming together to raise achievement: New assessments for the common core state standards.* Princeton, NJ: Educational Testing Service. Retrieved from http://www.k12center.org/rsc/pdf/Coming_Together_April_2012_Final.PDF

College Board. (2011). *Trends in student aid 2011.* Washington, DC: Author.

College Entrance Examination Board. (2010). *Advanced placement exam summary reports.* New York, NY: Author.

College Entrance Examination Board. (2011). *SAT trends: Background on SAT takers in class of 2010.* New York, NY: Author.

Cunningham, A.F., & Santiago, D.A. (2008). *Student aversion to borrowing: Who borrows and who doesn't.* Washington, DC: Institute for Higher Education Policy.

DesJardins, S.L., & Toutkoushian, R.K. (2005). Are students really rational? The development of rational thought and its application to student choice. In J.C. Smart (Ed.), *Higher education: Handbook of theory and research: Vol. 20* (pp. 191–240). Dordrecht, The Netherlands: Kluwer Academic Publishers.

Doyle, W.R. (2008). Access, choice, and excellence: The competing goals of state student financial aid programs. In S. Baum, M. McPherson, & P. Steele (Eds.), *The effectiveness of student aid policies: What the research tells us* (pp. 159–187). Washington, DC: The College Board.

Dynarski, S. (2004). The new merit aid. In C.M. Hoxby (Ed.), *College choices: The economics of where to go, when to go, and how to pay for it* (pp. 63–100). Chicago, IL: University of Chicago Press.

Gladieux, L., & Perna, L. (2005). *Borrowers who drop out: A neglected aspect of the college student loan trend.* San Jose, CA: National Center for Public Policy and Higher Education.

Heller, D.E. (1997). Student price response in higher education: An update to Leslie and Brinkman. *Journal of Higher Education, 68,* 624–659.

Heller, D.E. (2008). The impact of student loans on college access. Chapter 3 in S. Baum, M. McPherson, & P. Steele (Eds.), *The effectiveness of student aid policies: What the research tells us.* Washington, DC: College Board.

Horn, L., & Kojaku, L. (2001). *High school academic curriculum and the persistence path through college.* (Report No. NCES 2001–163). Washington, DC: U.S. Department of Education, Office of Educational Research and Improvement.

Kane, T.J. (1999). *The price of admission: Rethinking how Americans pay for college.* Washington, DC: Brookings Institution Press.

Kim, D. (2004). The effects of financial aid on students' college choice: Differences by racial groups. *Research in Higher Education, 45*(1), 43–70.

Kirst, M.W., & Bracco, K.R. (2004). Bridging the great divide: How the K–12 and postsecondary split hurts students, and what can be done about it. In M.E. Kirst & A. Venezia (Eds.), *From high school to college: Improving opportunities for success in postsecondary education* (pp. 1–30). San Francisco, CA: Jossey-Bass.

Kirst, M.W., & Venezia, A. (2004). *From high school to college: Improving opportunities for success in postsecondary education.* San Francisco, CA: Jossey-Bass.

Lillis, M.P. (2008). High-tuition, high loan financing: Economic segregation in postsecondary education. *Journal of Educational Finance, 34,* 15–30.

Long, B.T. (2004). The impact of federal tax credits for higher education expenses. In C.M. Hoxby (Ed.), *College choices: The economics of where to go, when to go, and how to pay for it* (pp. 101–168). Chicago, IL: University of Chicago Press.

McDonough, P.M. (1997). *Choosing colleges: How social class and schools structure opportunity.* Albany: State University of New York.

McDonough, P.M. (2005). Counseling and college counseling in America's high schools. In D.A. Hawkins and J. Lautz (Eds.), *State of college admission* (pp. 107–121). Washington, DC: National Association for College Admission Counseling.

Mundel, D. (2008). What do we know about the impact of grants to college students? In S. Baum, M. McPherson, & P. Steele (Eds.), *The effectiveness of student aid policies: What the research tells us.* Washington, DC: The College Board.

National Association for College Admission Counseling. (2010). *2010 state of college admission.* Arlington, VA: Author.

National Center for Education Statistics (NCES). (2010). *Profile of undergraduate students: 2007–08* (Report No. NCES 2010–205). Washington, DC: Author.

National Center for Education Statistics (NCES). (2011). *The nation's report card: America's high school graduates* (Report No. NCES 2011–462). Washington, DC: Author.

National Center for Education Statistics (NCES). (2012a). *Digest of education statistics 2011.* Washington, DC: Author.

National Center for Education Statistics (NCES). (2012b). *The condition of education 2012.* Washington, DC: Author.

Pascarella, E.T., & Terenzini, P.T. (2005). *How college affects students, volume 2: A third decade of research.* San Francisco, CA: Jossey-Bass.

Perna, L.W. (2000). Differences in the decision to enroll in college among African Americans, Hispanics, and Whites. *Journal of Higher Education, 71*, 117–141.

Perna, L.W. (2002). Pre-college outreach programs: Characteristics of programs serving historically underrepresented groups of students. *Journal of College Student Development, 43*, 64–83.

Perna, L.W. (2005a). The key to college access: A college preparatory curriculum. In W.G. Tierney, Z.B. Corwin, & J.E. Colyar (Eds.), *Preparing for college: Nine elements of effective outreach* (pp. 113–134). Albany: State University of New York Press.

Perna, L.W. (2005b). A gap in the literature: The influence of the design, operations, and marketing of student aid programs on the formation of family college-going plans and resulting college-going behaviors of potential students. *Journal of Student Financial Aid, 35*(3), 7–15.

Perna, L.W. (2006). Studying college choice: A proposed conceptual model. In J.C. Smart (Ed.), *Higher education: Handbook of theory and research: Vol. 21* (pp. 99–157). The Netherlands: Springer.

Perna, L.W. (2008). Understanding high school students' willingness to borrow to pay college prices. *Research in Higher Education, 49*, 589–606.

Perna, L.W. (2010a). Toward a more complete understanding of the role of financial aid in promoting college enrollment: The importance of context. In J.C. Smart (Ed.), *Higher education: Handbook of theory and research: Vol. 25* (pp. 129–179). The Netherlands: Springer.

Perna, L.W. (Ed.). (2010b). *Understanding the working college student: New research and its implications for policy and practice.* Herndon, VA: Stylus Publishing, LLC.

Perna, L.W., Lundy-Wagner, V., Yee, A., Brill, L., & Teran, T. (2011). Showing them the money: The role of institutional financial aid policies and communication strategies in attracting low-income students. In A. Kezar (Ed.), *Recognizing social class and serving low-income students in higher education: Institutional policies, practices, and culture* (pp. 72–96). New York, NY: Routledge.

Perna, L.W., May, H., Yee, A., Ransom, T., Rodriguez, A., & Fester, R. (2012). *The potential role of the International Baccalaureate diploma programme in improving academic preparation for college for all students.* Manuscript submitted for publication.

Perna, L.W., Rowan-Kenyon, H., Bell, A., Thomas, S.L., & Li, C. (2008). A typology of federal and state programs designed to promote college enrollment. *Journal of Higher Education, 79*, 243–267.

Perna, L.W., Rowan-Kenyon, H.T., Thomas, S.L., Bell, A., Anderson, R., & Li, C. (2008). The role of college counseling in shaping college opportunity: Variations across high schools. *Review of Higher Education, 31*, 131–159.

Perna, L.W., & Steele, P. (2011). The role of context in understanding the contributions of financial aid to college opportunity. *Teachers College Record, 113*, 895–933.

Perna, L.W., & Thomas, S.L. (2009). Barriers to college opportunity: The unintended consequences of state-mandated tests. *Educational Policy, 23*(3), 451–479.

Perna, L.W., & Titus, M. (2004). Understanding differences in the choice of college attended: The role of state public policies. *Review of Higher Education, 27*(4), 501–525.

Perna, L.W., & Titus, M. (2005). The relationship between parental involvement as social capital and college enrollment: An examination of racial/ethnic group differences. *Journal of Higher Education, 76*, 485–518.

Reed, M. (2011). *Critical choices: How colleges can help students and families make better decisions about private loans.* Oakland, CA: The Institute for College Access & Success, Project on Student Debt.

Reschovsky, A. (2008). Higher education tax policies. In S. Baum, M. McPherson, & P. Steele (Eds.), *The effectiveness of student aid policies: What the research tells us* (pp. 69–100). Washington, DC: College Board.

Rethinking Student Aid Study Group. (2008). *Fulfilling the commitment: Recommendations for reforming federal student aid.* Washington, DC: College Board.

Roderick, M., Nagaoka, J., & Coca, V. (2009). College readiness for all: The challenge for urban high schools. *The Future of Children, 19*(1), 185–210.

Rowan-Kenyon, H., Bell, A., & Perna, L.W. (2008). Contextual influences on parental involvement in college-going: Variations by socioeconomic class. *Journal of Higher Education, 79*, 564–586.

Sokatch, A. (2006). Peer influences on the college-going decisions of low socioeconomic status urban youth. *Education and Urban Society, 39*(1), 128–146.

St. John, E.P. (2003). *Refinancing the college dream: Access, equal opportunity, and justice for taxpayers.* Baltimore, MD: Johns Hopkins University Press.

St. John, E.P., Musoba, G.D., & Chung, C.G. (2004). Academic access: The impact of state education policies. In E.P. St. John (Ed.), *Public policy and college access: Investigating the federal and state roles in equalizing postsecondary opportunity: Vol. 19* (pp. 131–152). New York, NY: AMS Press, Inc.

Stanton-Salazar, R.D. (1997). A social capital framework for understanding the socialization of racial minority children and youth. *Harvard Educational Review, 67*, 1–40.

Tierney, W.G., Bailey, T., Constantine, J., Finkelstein, N., & Hurd, N.F. (2009). *Helping students navigate the path to college: What high schools can do: A practice guide* (Report No. NCES 2009–4066). Washington, DC: National Center for Education Evaluation and Regional Assistance, Institute of Education Sciences, U.S. Department of Education. Retrieved from http://ies.ed.gov/ncee/wwc/publications/praticeguides/

Tierney, W.G., & Venegas, K.M. (2009). Finding money on the table: Information, financial aid, and access to college. *Journal of Higher Education, 80*(4), 363–388.

Titus, M.A. (2010). Understanding the relationship between working while in college and future salaries. In L.W. Perna (Ed.), *Understanding the working college student: New research and its implications for policy and practice.* Herndon, VA: Stylus Publishing, LLC.

U.S. Department of Education. (2011). *College Navigator.* Retrieved from http://nces.ed.gov/collegenavigator

U.S. Department of Education. (2012). *Upward Bound program eligibility.* Washington, DC: Author. Retrieved from http://www2.ed.gov/programs/trioupbound/eligibility.html

Valadez, J.R. (2008). Shaping the educational decisions of Mexican immigrant high school students. *American Educational Research Journal, 45*, 834–860.

Venezia, A., & Kirst, M. (2005). Inequitable opportunities: How current education systems and policies undermine the chances for student persistence and success in college. *Educational Policy, 19*, 293–307.

Zumeta, W., Breneman, D.W., Callan, P.M., & Finney, J.E. (2012). *Financing American higher education in the era of globalization.* Boston, MA: Harvard Education Press.

3

PATHWAYS TO COLLEGE FOR UNDERSERVED AND NONTRADITIONAL STUDENTS

Lessons from Research, Policy, and Practice

Debra D. Bragg

In President Obama's first term, he urged Congress to support college completion, noting "everyone" in the United States should "complete one year or more of higher education or advanced training in his or her lifetime" (Kanter, Ochoa, Nassif, & Chong, 2011, n.p.). Once near the top of the world ranking on college completion, the United States has fallen to 16th among the world's industrialized nations according to the Organisation for Economic Co-operation and Development (OECD) (2011). Forty-one percent of the U.S. population age 25 to 34 has attained an associate's, bachelor's, or graduate degree, compared to 63% for top-ranked Korea. Tying the goal of college completion to improving the nation's economy, President Obama, as well as U.S. Department of Education (ED) officials, assert that producing 10 million more 2- and 4-year college and university graduates above a projected enrollment growth of 2 million by 2020 will enable the nation to regain its top spot and stimulate economic recovery.

President Obama and ED officials are not alone. Numerous policymakers and higher education leaders have joined government officials in promoting the college completion agenda, although the notion of what constitutes college completion varies widely. Some contend college completion refers to the first bachelor's degree, whereas others count completion of any college credential, whether a certificate, associate's, or bachelor's degree. For example, the Lumina Foundation for Education (2009) has advocated for raising "the proportion of Americans with high-quality degrees and credentials to 60% by the year 2025" (p. 1). The strategic goals of numerous other organizations, including the Bill and Melinda Gates Foundation, also define completion to include sub-baccalaureate certificates and degrees (Hauptman, 2011).

A theme of numerous high-profile initiatives is that the country will not achieve any completion goal without addressing the postsecondary needs of nontraditional learners, including ethnic and racial minorities and low-income, first-generation college students. Typically, these student populations are described as historically "underrepresented" in U.S. higher education; however, I use the term "underserved" in this chapter because that notion acknowledges that at least as much responsibility for college enrollment rests with the higher education system as with the students themselves.

Nontraditional students are an enormously important subset of underserved learners who are defined by their age; background characteristics such as work, family, school, and culture; and at-risk factors for college noncompletion (Advisory Committee on Student Financial Assistance, 2012). The Advisory Committee has noted that the nontraditional student population is growing in America, making it more important than ever to understand the breadth of the college experience for this large and diverse population. Therefore, I adopt the definition for the nontraditional student used in the Advisory Committee's *Pathways to Success* report:

> any student who fails to fit the traditional student template, which generally refers to an 18- to 24-year-old full-time college student. Among the students included in the non-traditional definition are not only older students, but students who may face additional challenges or barriers, e.g., foster youth, veterans, men and women on active duty, and first-generation college students. (Advisory Committee on Student Financial Assistance, 2012, p. 3)

Recognizing the diversity of these students' needs, many organizations have worked to design pathways that provide clearly structured programs of study so that nontraditional students can understand, pursue, and complete college credentials that lead to family-wage[1] employment (Complete College America, n.d.).

This chapter examines collegiate options for nontraditional students and describes these students and the pathway programs that allow them to enter, progress through, and complete college programs with credentials valued in the labor market. Key questions that the chapter addresses are the following:

1. What are the characteristics of nontraditional students who might be important to target for the nation's college completion agenda?
2. What are the pathways to and through college for nontraditional students?
3. What theory and research exists on pathways and programs of study for nontraditional students?
4. What do we know about how nontraditional students access and use financial aid?
5. What further research would improve pathways to and through college for nontraditional students?
6. What should policymakers and institutional leaders do to improve pathways to and through college for nontraditional students?

Nontraditional Students and the College Completion Agenda

Demystifying college completion, credential attainment, and employment for students who have never thought of themselves as eligible or capable of attending college, or who started college but dropped out before acquiring a marketable credential, is important to the nation's economic recovery (ED, 2011). Over 60% of the U.S. population between 25 and 64 years of age lacks any postsecondary credential, and over 37 million Americans (more than 20% of the working adult population) desire to enroll in college (Lumina Foundation for Education, 2009). A primary target for the additional 10 million new college degrees needed to attain global competitiveness is the population of 24 million nontraditional students who currently lack a high school credential, including nearly 2.4 million who enroll in the adult education system (Office of Vocational and Adult Education [OVAE], 2011a). Most students who participate in federally subsidized adult education programs and services have not finished high school, although high school graduates whose functional level is below college may also qualify.

Nationally, adult education consists of three core programs: pre-high school level instruction in Adult Basic Education (ABE), accounting for 42% of total national enrollment in adult education programs; English as a Second Language (ESL), accounting for 44%; and Adult Secondary Education (ASE), accounting for 14% (OVAE, 2011a). Many participants in adult education programs are members of racial and ethnic minority groups who attend school while working full or part time, or when unemployed, participating in public assistance or prison, or engaging in other formal institutional (often health care-related) settings (OVAE, 2011a). Low levels of literacy among these program populations contribute to low levels of postsecondary enrollment and, for those who enroll in college, are associated with attrition.

A substantial number of these adults obtain a high school diploma and enroll in college but do not complete a college credential. Only about half of full-time enrolled college students finish a credential within six years, with only 2 in 10 receiving an associate's degree in three years (National Center for Higher Education Management Systems [NCHEMS] & Jobs for the Future [JFF], 2007). African Americans are more likely than individuals of other racial/ethnic groups to have accumulated some credits but no degree (Education Trust, 2010a, 2010b).

Misalignment of curriculum between the adult education system and postsecondary education also contributes to adults' struggles to navigate college and obtain credentials. As described in other chapters in this volume (see Conley; Long & Boatman), high rates of remediation contribute to high dropout rates among community college students (Bailey, Jeong, & Cho, 2010), and nontraditional students are overrepresented among incoming cohorts who receive remedial education. Attewell, Lavin, Domina, and Levey (2006) found that 60% of community college entrants are required to take one or more developmental courses, usually mathematics.

Numerous studies by Bailey and colleagues at the Community College Research Center (CCRC; see, for example, Bailey et al., 2010) conclude that underpreparation in foundational subjects, especially mathematics, has a detrimental impact on college performance. Illustrating this point, a national study conducted by Greene and Foster (2003) found that only 32% of all high school graduates demonstrated the basic skill level needed to enter college mathematics courses, and that African American and Hispanic students are "seriously underrepresented in the pool of minimally qualified college applicants" (p. 3). The most vulnerable of all entering adult students are members of the African American and Hispanic minority groups; students who do not speak English before entering school; and students who have multiple physical, mental, and emotional disabilities (Kirsch, Braun, Yamamoto, & Sum, 2007; Kirsch, Jungeblut, Jenkins, & Kolstad, 1993).

Pathways to and through College for Nontraditional Students

The notion of pathways emphasizes a clearly articulated and straightforward means for students with limited higher education experience to navigate to and through college to complete credentials that lead to family-wage employment. Many students want to know that a commitment of such a substantial portion of their personal time and resources will produce tangible benefits; that is, they see higher education as a consumable good (Levine & Cureton, 1998). They want to know what tangible outcomes a college education will buy them, including whether college will lead to a good job. Nontraditional students are especially aligned with this consumer vantage point (Advisory Committee on Student Financial Assistance, 2012).

For example, an ethnographic study by Cox (2009) revealed that all but a tiny fraction of the community college students enrolled in English composition courses describe their purpose for enrolling in college as "improving their occupational prospects" (p. 43). For these students, college completion is linked to employment, the goal of improving the standard of living for themselves and their families, and the "need to *be* [emphasis added] something" (Cox, 2009, p. 43). Her findings suggest many students perceive college as a necessary but painful experience. Getting through college in order to get a decent job is the end goal that enables them to endure the monetary and personal costs that disrupt their lives (Pusser et al., 2007).

From this perspective, the priority for getting on a pathway to and through college is placed on a structured, competency-based curriculum that is complemented with intensive student supports and high levels of program and student accountability. The literature tends to refer to pathways to college and careers, recognizing that a college education is requisite to higher-paying technical and professional jobs.

The federally sponsored Technical Workgroup for the Designing Instruction for Career Pathways Initiative (2011) uses a definition of adult career pathways initially authored by Jenkins (2006). Jenkins explains:

> a [adult] career pathway is a series of connected education and training programs and support services that enable individuals to secure employment within a specific industry or occupational sector, and to advance over time to successively higher levels of education and employment in that sector. Each step on a career pathway is designed explicitly to prepare the participant for the next level of employment and education. (p. 6)

This definition makes a clear link between education and employment, noting that

> [adult] career pathways target jobs in industries of importance to local economies. They are designed to create both avenues of advancement for current workers, jobseekers and new and future labor market entrants and a supply of qualified workers for local employers. As such, they also serve as a strategy for strengthening the "supply chains" that produce and keep a region's knowledge workforce up to date. (p. 6)

Consistent with these definitions, various models are emerging that emphasize completion of credentials, from certificates to the baccalaureate, for students who have accumulated some credits but fall short of a bachelor's degree (U.S. Department of Education, 2011).

Few studies exist that examine pathways and programs of study in a comprehensive education reform package. Alfeld and Bhattacharya (2011) and the Joint Technical Working Group on Programs of Study (2011) describe pathways beginning in high school for traditional-age learners, rather than nontraditional learners who enter pathways later in life. Research on career and technical education (CTE) has contributed some meaningful lessons, but its modest focus on nontraditional learners has left substantial questions about how these students participate in and benefit from programs of study (Stipanovic, Lewis, & Stringfield, 2012).

Moreover, few studies isolate the experiences and outcomes of minority and low-income learners on either the secondary or postsecondary level, with small enrollments cited as the reason to forego subgroup analysis (for example, Alfeld & Bhattacharya, 2011). As the number of students in career pathway programs grows, opportunities increase for collecting rigorous evidence for diverse populations. Mixed methods research by Rosenbaum, Deil-Amen, and Person (2006) points to the potential for tangible benefits of pathways for nontraditional students. Rosenbaum and colleagues compare the experiences and outcomes of nontraditional students attending open-access community colleges and for-profit postsecondary schools in a large urban area of the United States. Focusing on how nontraditional students navigate their college experience, their results show that giving students a "complete package" of educational programs and services, the strategy used by for-profit institutions, results in better college completion outcomes than the cafeteria-style approach that students receive in many community colleges.

Rosenbaum et al. (2006) contend that "complete packages"—closely related to the notion of "pathways" and "programs of study" advanced in this chapter—result in improved rates of college completion, particularly for nontraditional students. Elements include aligned curriculum between K–12 education and postsecondary education; integrated academic and occupational content; structured learning in meaningful settings, including the workplace; support services that facilitate retention, especially financial support; and stackable college credit-bearing credentials (i.e., programs of study organized to produce sequential, or "stackable," credentials).[2] These elements are critical to adult career pathway programs that integrate academic and social supports in ways that facilitate student completion of credentials leading to employment (Kozumplik, Nyborg, Garcia, Cantu, & Larsen, 2011).

In particular, stackable credentials may offer solutions for many nontraditional students, as these sequences begin even with short-term certificate completion. As Carnevale, Smith, and Strohl (2010) and Carnevale, Rose, and Hanson (2012) show, among the growing array of college credentials, certificates have a positive economic payoff for some student populations, particularly males.

Adult career pathways should provide a clear sequence of steps that move students into and through college, and to family-wage employment. To these ends, connections between adult education and postsecondary education should be defined and structured explicitly so that adults know what they need to do to be successful in these steps. Without such an understanding, adults may become lost in the maze of programs and services, get confused and frustrated, and ultimately question why they should continue to enroll. In essence, students who try out college without a clear sense of direction or a conviction to stay are especially vulnerable (Rosenbaum et al., 2006).

Research on Pathways for Nontraditional Students

The focus on policy and practice in this chapter reflects the relative absence of a theoretical conceptualization of pathways. Experimentation at the local level (sometimes encouraged by state policy) is the primary manner in which new pathways have emerged for nontraditional students. No doubt, program strategies have been drawn from past literature on college recruitment and access, curriculum and instructional reform, student development, and the like; however, theory has not been the predominant force shaping notions of pathways to and through college for nontraditional learners (OVAE, 2008).

The roots of current pathways and programs of study are tied to efforts to integrate occupational and technical education with general and liberal education that began more than a century ago (Bragg, 2012). Grubb and Lazerson (2005) contend that the focus on the new vocationalism begins at the K–12 level and extends to all aspects of higher education, leading them to tie vocationalism to what they call "the education gospel," that is, a pervasive approach to education that emphasizes utilitarian function over liberal studies. They argue that students who pursue postsecondary education are doing so to satisfy occupational goals—offering a similar point to Cox's (2009) study—but noting that students need a wide range of knowledge and skills to succeed in their personal lives and the workplace, and fulfill their civic responsibilities.

Contextualized curriculum and instruction is one approach to such integration, often beginning before college, when students learn foundational knowledge and skills in familiar contexts and are introduced to employment contexts (e.g., Perin, 2001, 2011). Contextualized instruction can also continue to credit-bearing courses where students acquire knowledge and skills in the context of the workplace. Occupational and technical fields such as health care, engineering, and others have long histories of encouraging and supporting learning by blending academic and technical instruction through internships, cooperative education, and other work-based learning. Nontraditional student enrollment in learning that naturally blends general education and technical education is often a priority of career pathways (Taylor et al., 2009).

Research on Adult Career Pathways

Pathways to and through college have been shaped by federal legislation on CTE such as the 2006 Carl D. Perkins Act. This support has generated lessons about integrating academic and occupational-technical curriculum and instruction for adults (Taylor et al., 2009). Particularly important are strategies to align and structure curricula from adult education or workforce training programs to postsecondary education. Making clear connections between college and occupational preparation is important for nontraditional learners whose immediate need is to obtain marketable credentials to secure family-wage employment (Stephens, 2009). The following section presents three prominent adult career pathway models that have received regional and national recognition.

The Integrated Basic Education and Skills Training (I-BEST) model integrates ABE and ESL with CTE (also called professional-technical education in the Northwest). The I-BEST model seeks to help low-skill students understand the relevance of education when linked to and taught in the context of CTE and leading to college credentials (Jenkins, Zeidenberg, & Kienzl, 2009). A primary method of delivery is co-teaching English literacy and workforce skills. Specifically, I-BEST pairs ABE and ESL instructors with CTE faculty to both develop curriculum and co-teach in the classroom. The I-BEST model strives for co-teaching for at least half of instructional time. Wachen, Jenkins, and Van Noy (2011) claim I-BEST creates a structured educational pathway that increases the rate at which low-skill adults transition to college-level programs and pursue credentials that provide living-wage employment. Colleges seeking to implement I-BEST courses must commit to implementing support services and a career pathway that leads to both a credential and employment.

Although no adult career pathway model has a long track record of empirical results, initial findings for I-BEST are the most robust and promising of any research conducted thus far. Jenkins et al. (2009) report that I-BEST students are more likely to complete CTE-related college certificates than adults enrolled in other basic skills courses. Zeidenberg, Cho, and Jenkins (2010) report results from a follow-up study of I-BEST students over a longer time period than earlier studies, and confirm that I-BEST students earn more college credit and certificates than other basic skills students.[3]

The second model, the Oregon Pathways for Adult Basic Skills (OPABS) Transition to Education and Workforce Initiative, introduces new curriculum and high-quality support services designed to facilitate the transition of Adult Basic Skills (ABS) students into postsecondary education and employment. Surveying adult career pathway programming nationally, ED observed that Oregon was advancing more rapidly than many other states in the development and implementation of curricula associated with adult career pathways that lead to employment (OVAE, 2011b).

Of the various adult career pathway models that are emerging nationwide, OPABS has been more deliberate than most at instructional design and curriculum development. OPABS emphasizes enhancements to learner orientation, assessment, and placement into classes; improved access to advising and support services; better connections of students to One-Stop Centers that are funded by the Workforce Investment Act (WIA); and increased transition options into postsecondary education. Instructional models that offer standardized basic skills courses with contextualized CTE content provide lesson plans, curriculum scope and sequence, and learner and teacher materials (Alamprese, 2010). Although available research does not control for self-selection into the programs, OVAE (2011b) reports "adults participating in OPABS academically enhanced basic skills courses can identify a career path, develop their basic skills, and transition to postsecondary transfer-credit courses at the same or faster rates as adults in non-OPABS courses" (p. 7). State staff report that students understand the pathways model and that the college and career awareness component is "critical to students' persistence in the program" (OVAE, 2011b, p. 7).

A third adult career pathways model is Shifting Gears, an initiative launched in 2007 by the Joyce Foundation, the primary goal of which is to increase the number of low-skill, low-income Midwest adults who obtain college-level occupational credentials that have value in the labor market (Bragg, Smith, & Dresser, 2012). This initiative assumes that postsecondary education that leads to industry-valued credentials can be a route to family-wage employment for adult workers who are unemployed or underemployed. Shifting Gears suggests that strategic funding and technical assistance can accelerate state policy that is necessary to create promising programs for low-skill adults (Taylor, 2009).

Four core strategies associated with Shifting Gears are (1) policy change by leveraging improvements in systems and institutional practice, (2) data utilization to foster improvements in policy and practice, (3) stakeholder engagement to generate ideas and buy-in for systems and institutional change, and (4) strategic communications to cultivate stakeholder support for systems and institutional change (Price & Roberts, 2009). Adult career pathways and bridge programs are primary strategies employed by the two Midwest states (Illinois and Wisconsin) that have used Shifting Gears to link education, training, and support services for low-skill adults.[4]

Though modest, research on pathway programs in Illinois and Wisconsin has begun to show how pathway programs serve nontraditional adults in meaningful ways. In Illinois, bridge programs that begin with adult education or developmental education are administered by the Illinois Community College Board, offering students team teaching, computerized and online instructional supports, contextualized and laboratory-based instruction, and cohorts and other strategies (Bragg, Harmon, Kirby, & Kim, 2009). Results of the first 10 sites funded in Illinois with Shifting Gears monies showed that nearly half of all adults completed the bridge programs, with 72% of students enrolled in developmental education bridges and 42% of adults enrolled in education bridges completing the prescribed course(s). More recent data show a much higher completion rate of 68% (Taylor & Bragg, 2012). Disaggregating by student characteristics shows significant positive results for (1) Older students, ABE and ESL students, African American and Hispanic/Latino students, and employed students on bridge completion; and (2) ABE and ESL students and not-employed and unemployed students on functioning education level gains based on the Test of Adult Basic Education (TABE), Basic English Skills Test (BEST), and Combined English Language Skills Assessment (CELSA) tests.

Shifting Gears in Wisconsin, called Regional Industry Skills Education (RISE), was administered by the Technical College System and the Workforce Development System. RISE is developing adult career pathways by engaging businesses in identifying and addressing the needs of key industry sectors (Bragg et al., 2012) and "developing cross-system career pathways designed to help adult learners with low basic skills progress, over time, to the receipt of employer-valued postsecondary credentials" (Center for Law and Social Policy [CLASP], 2012, n.p.). Descriptive research by CLASP shows bridge programs associated with RISE help low-skill adults access high-demand occupations and develop a skilled workforce for the state. Constituents who advocate for career pathways in Wisconsin contend that, when curriculum is aligned to careers, students are better able to navigate their educational experiences to advance their career goals. RISE also seeks to accelerate learning using contextualized learning that integrates occupational skills. Programs are expected to include industry engagement, career pathway instructional design, ABE and ESL bridge instructional design, support for lifelong learning, and systems and partnerships between education and employers. Thus far, 14 colleges in the Wisconsin Technical College System have developed career pathway bridges, each offering basic skills and occupational instruction that lead to stacked credentials awarded by the Technical College System. Other accomplishments include raising the level of awareness and professional knowledge of stakeholders about the career pathway models; conducting an adult learning pipeline analysis that seeks to understand where nontraditional learners enter and exit the P–20 (primary through grade 20) educational system; identifying policy challenges and beginning to develop policy solutions at the state and local levels; funding prototype career pathway and bridge curricula; and stimulating industry engagement (CLASP, 2012).

Research on Pathways to the Baccalaureate

The aforementioned pathways focus primarily on entry points into postsecondary education for nontraditional learners who have limited or no preparation for or experience with college. However, it is also important to consider pathways that move nontraditional learners beyond the community college to the baccalaureate level.

Lumina Foundation for Education (2009) reported that more than 22% of working adults in America (that is, 37 million Americans) have attended college but not completed any degree. Researchers have long reported retention problems during the freshman year or its equivalent (see, for example, Tinto, 2006–2007), yet Bowen, Chingos, and McPherson (2009) estimate that almost 45% of departures from college occur after the sophomore year, with the rate of departure highest among students attending less-selective institutions. Results of unpublished analyses conducted by Ruud (2012) using the National Center for Education Statistic's 2003–2009 Beginning Postsecondary Students (BPS) dataset demonstrate that over 50% who entered college in 2003 had not obtained a certificate or degree at any higher education institution in six years, a finding substantiated by analysis of the 2003–2004 BPS cohort by Skomsvold, Radford, and Berkner (2011). Furthermore, over 40% of students who had not obtained a degree had accumulated 46 college credits or more. These results suggest that a large number of students may have earned enough credits to warrant the award of a certificate or an associate's degree to mark their accomplishments.

Bragg, Cullen, Bennett, and Ruud (2011) examined efforts of higher education institutions and governments to help nontraditional students capitalize on such accumulated credits. Exactly where students with substantial accumulated credits go and whether they eventually capitalize on their college credits to secure a degree is difficult to ascertain (for a discussion of these issues, see the chapter by Hossler, Dundar, and Shapiro in this volume). Tracking students over time and across institutions using longitudinal data is critical to unpacking the "all or nothing" credit phenomenon (Bragg et al., 2011).

Bragg et al. (2011) identified three programmatic approaches to address the problem of students earning substantial college credits but no degree. The first approach is directed at baccalaureate-seeking students who have earned substantial credits, sometimes more than half the amount required, but not enough to earn the degree. The University-Awarded En-Route Degree and the Community College-Awarded En-Route Degree provide an avenue toward a credential for these students. The former depends on the university having associate degree-granting authority; the latter exists where universities are unable to grant the associate's degree but partner with community colleges who can. The City University of New York (CUNY) Staten Island awards an En-Route Associate's Degree to students in baccalaureate programs who complete the requirements for an Associate of Arts (AA), Associate of Science (AS), or Associate of Applied Science (AAS) degree while they work toward their end-point degree. West Virginia University-Parkersburg offers students associate's degrees en route to their bachelor's credentials.

The second approach is the Associate Completion Degree and the Baccalaureate Completion Degree. Whether operating at the two- or four-year level, this approach provides students a means of completing a general college degree (Bragg et al., 2011). The *Reach Higher, Oklahoma* program is a good example of a state advancing this model (Bragg et al., 2011). Although limited research has been conducted on the labor market value of associate's (or baccalaureate) completion degrees, descriptive data suggest that students average higher earnings when they obtain a general completion degree than when they obtain some college but no degree (Baum, Ma, & Payea, 2010; Carnevale et al., 2010).

The third approach includes the Transfer-Back Degree, the Dual Admission Degree, and the Traditional Associate Transfer (Bragg et al., 2011). Sam Houston State University's collaboration with community college partners is illustrative of the transfer-back model, and Iowa State University's Admissions Partnership Program illustrates the dual admission degree approach. These models facilitate degree attainment for community college students who matriculate to a university with the intention of earning the baccalaureate, but who leave prior to completion of the associate's degree. For these students, associate level credits are captured and converted to an associate's degree.

Bennett and Makela (2012) reanalyzed data collected by Bragg et al. (2011) and identified additional pathways to the baccalaureate (see Figure 3.1), including models operating in the United States and others operating in such international settings as Australia, Canada, the United Kingdom, and Sri Lanka. Bennett and Makela label the three pathways depicted in Figure 3.1 as Alternative Exit, Stepping Stone, and Nested Opportunity. As depicted in the figure, these models provide different ways for nontraditional students to access and utilize college credits.

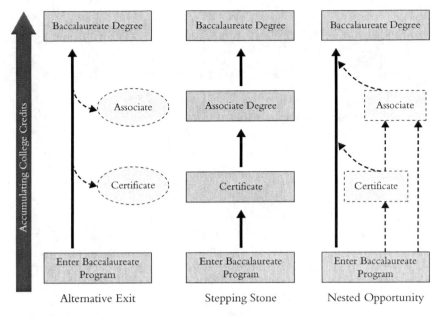

Figure 3.1 Three Conceptual Models of Mid-Point Credentials That Are Embedded Into Baccalaureate Degree Pathways
Source: Bennett and Makela (2012). University of Illinois, Office of Community College Research and Leadership. Reproduced with permission.

Finally, a national study by Bragg and Ruud (2011) shows how applied baccalaureate degrees are emerging to provide a pathway beyond the associate degree for students who seek to continue their education at the baccalaureate level. Similar to other pathways mentioned in this chapter, applied baccalaureate degree programs exhibit close ties between postsecondary institutions and employers and may also enhance transfer options for students moving between traditional associate, baccalaureate degree-granting institutions, and employment. For nontraditional students who are tied to a particular area by family and work, these degrees enhance geographic accessibility and make college a possibility.

Results of an online survey conducted by Bragg and Ruud (2011) showed patterns of applied baccalaureate degree[5] types by state, with the bachelor of applied science (BAS) being the predominant degree. The survey also revealed predominance in the fields of science, technology, engineering, and mathematics (STEM); in public service occupations such as public safety, criminal justice, and emergency management; and in business, administration, management, and supervision. Although certainly not the majority, some applied baccalaureate degrees are offered in general studies, liberal arts, and "applied liberal arts," suggesting the degrees are not always specific to a particular occupational field. Survey results also confirm that a preponderance of students participating in applied baccalaureate degrees are nontraditional students, including those who are employed part time or full time as well as unemployed or dislocated workers, active military personnel, and students with disabilities.

Research on Financial Aid to Assist Nontraditional Students

Nontraditional learners have some of the greatest reliance on financial aid programs of any student groups accessing higher education (Chao, DeRocco, & Flynn, 2007; Dougherty & Woodland, 2009). The focus on student aid is critical for low-income adults because they tend to have limited information about college funding options, and they tend to be loan averse (Chan & Cochrane, 2008). Nearly all adult career pathway models emphasize the importance of intensive services that facilitate nontraditional student enrollment, retention, and completion, including facilitating access to financial aid (see Bragg et al., 2012).

A cross-case analysis of pathway programs located in three states found numerous instances in which nontraditional students enrolling in college credit programs were unable to secure Pell grants to complete their programs of study (Bragg et al., 2007). Low-income students who are required to take two or more remedial courses prior to enrolling in college-level coursework are especially vulnerable to using a significant portion of their Pell Grant funding (Bragg et al., 2007). These qualitative data describe the detrimental effects of the time limitations of Pell on nontraditional students, especially for those who work and enroll in college simultaneously. Even when Pell grants are not depleted fully, student concerns about college payment options are detrimental to persistence and completion.

Nontraditional learners' patterns of college attendance, including part-time enrollment in college while working part or full time, create barriers to accessing financial aid. Cross (1981) identified institutional, situational, and dispositional barriers for nontraditional learners, and scores of researchers have extended Cross's work to show how these barriers continue to influence nontraditional student enrollment and college completion (see, for example, Spellman, 2007). For example, while full-time employment gives the appearance of adequate resources, often there is insufficient disposable income available to pay for tuition, especially when supporting a family (Hawley & Harris, 2005–2006; Spellman, 2007).

Kerouac and Badolato (2010) claim "research consistently demonstrates that educational costs, whether perceived or real, are a strong deterrent for adults who want to further their education" (p. 6). They recommend that two- and four-year colleges and universities offer financial support for part-time attendance to increase nontraditional student enrollment. Similarly, Lane, Michelau, and Palmer (2012) recommend allowing students to pay tuition and fees in affordable chunks rather than requiring full, up-front payment of tuition. They also contend that institutions reduce the use of financial holds[6] to help nontraditional students continue enrollment.

Recent changes in federal Pell grants threaten financial support for nontraditional learners who lack a high school diploma or a General Equivalency Degree

(GED). Beginning July 1, 2012, changes to the Pell Grant program disallow new students who lack these credentials from obtaining Pell grants awarded through the "ability to benefit" (ATB) program, designed for individuals who have not received a high school diploma or GED but have demonstrated capacity to benefit from postsecondary education. In the past, students who lacked a high school diploma or GED were able to qualify for student aid by passing a basic skills test or successfully completing six college credits. Estimates suggest about 836,000 individuals will be affected by the elimination of the ATB program, and that this change will have a disproportionately negative impact on older, low-income students and immigrants (Nelson, 2012).

Part of the federal government's concern in making this change is abuse of the ATB option (General Accounting Office [GAO], 2009). Shortly after GAO issued this report, Congress defunded the ATB option. This cut came at an unfortunate time, however, because new programs such as I-BEST built their models on ATB. In addition, Rhodes (2006) found that students who complete six college credit hours are as capable of succeeding in college (as defined by units attempted, units completed, and grade point average) as other college student groups, including students enrolled in college certificate or degree programs. Groups advocating for low-skill adults continue to seek the support of Congress to restore ATB on behalf of nontraditional students who require these funds to participate in college, and there is some indication that this change may happen (Choitz, Strawn, & Foster, 2012).

What Research Is Needed?

Research on nontraditional student use of pathways and programs of study is in its infancy. Substantial evidence suggests that the enrollment of nontraditional students is growing, yet less clear is the effectiveness of programs designed to structure these students' collegiate experiences, including ensuring that these students have adequate and sustained financial support to achieve their college completion and employment goals. More research on successful models is needed to inform policy and practice at the federal, state, and institutional levels. The following section puts forward some important questions.

How do nontraditional students participate in pathways and programs of study that are designed to structure and facilitate completion and transition to family-wage employment? Existing data systems do a poor job of identifying nontraditional students, so very little is known about when, where, and how these students access and participate in postsecondary education (Advisory Committee on Student Financial Assistance, 2012). Further, little is known about how pathway programs contribute to achievement of educational and employment goals. Descriptive research, qualitative case study research, and quantitative longitudinal research are needed to understand how nontraditional students participate in and benefit from pathway programs.

How does the nation's economic, social, and political climate influence student enrollment in pathways and programs of study? Current economic circumstances appear to be having a dramatic impact on nontraditional students' lives. Unemployment and underemployment are shaping decisions about college, but we know very little about college enrollment and completion for nontraditional students. Of those U.S. citizens who have lost jobs and subsequently enrolled in college, what factors influenced their decisions to enroll, and what experiences have determined whether they have been able to complete? To develop national policy, it is important to understand contextual factors related to the economy and the success of nontraditional students.

What changes are needed in measurement and data systems to determine whether nontraditional students are successful? Better understanding of outcomes at the local, state, and federal levels is needed, including measures associated with the Adult Education and Family Literacy Act, Titles I and II, which govern adult education and workforce training programs. Regardless of funding source, all programs need to document the short- and long-term education and employment outcomes for nontraditional students, analyzed by student subgroups (race/ethnicity, age, gender, income, etc.). This research needs to connect education and employment outcomes to students' competency gains so that student participation can be better understood.

How do nontraditional students benefit from programs of study and associated core components, such as structured curriculum, competence-based and contextualized instruction, and intensive support services? As Steve DesJardins and Allyson Flaster describe in their chapter in this volume, rigorous studies are needed, including studies that determine effects of particular program interventions.

What student financial aid policies, particularly grant aid programs, are most effective for nontraditional students, particularly those nontraditional students who struggle to maintain college enrollment while employed full time? Research is needed to better understand how student financial aid should be structured for such students. Furthermore, research should examine the roles employers could play in providing financial and other forms of support, including front loading or fully covering tuition, rather than reimbursing payments made for tuition by students whose income is so low that they are unlikely to make an initial investment in college.

How does implementation of these pathways on a national scale, such as the U.S. Department of Labor (DOL) and Trade Adjustment Assistance Community College and Career Training (TAACCCT) grant program, impact short- and long-term student outcomes, including completion of credentials, placement in family-wage employment, and employment retention? As pathways and programs of study become more commonplace in state and federal public policy that recognizes community colleges as the primary site for nontraditional enrollment, rigorous evaluation will be needed to provide evidence of the impact of pathways and programs of study on nontraditional students.

Recommendations for Federal, State, and Institutional Leaders

Policies and programs are needed to support nontraditional student enrollment in postsecondary pathways and programs of study that lead to employment.

For federal, state, and institutional leaders:

- Although the emphasis on college completion is important to students as well as the economy, prioritizing college completion may actually jeopardize college access if enrollment is restricted to only those students who are destined to complete. The nation will then fall short of its college completion goal. Ultimately, a strategy is needed that operates at all levels of government including at the level of the institution, which ensures that completion does not overshadow college access (Bragg & Durham, 2012). There are no easy solutions to this complex problem.

- All levels of the system need to work in concert if pathways and programs of study are to successfully promote enrollment and completion for nontraditional students. For example, better alignment is needed of multiple federal funding streams (e.g., CTE, Adult Education, Workforce Investment Act) with state funding for higher education, particularly community colleges. Colleges and universities need to understand how their policies and procedures must work in concert with federal and state policies. Changes at one level of the system may show incremental improvements.

- Substantial improvements are needed in data systems at all levels, particularly the state and local levels, in order to conduct rigorous research on nontraditional student matriculation from adult education to postsecondary education to employment. In addition, research is needed on how these students move back and forth between postsecondary education and employment as they progress through their careers. As Hossler, Dundar, and Shapiro argue in their chapter in this volume, few state or local systems have yet reached the level of sophistication that allows for strategic data tracking and subsequent outcomes evaluation, particularly for nontraditional students. Policymakers need to disaggregate measures by student subgroup to promote and sustain policies that promote access and completion. Without this, aggregate results will continue to mask deeper, structural inequities in student outcomes and success, and the system will not change in ways envisioned by policymakers counting on community colleges to increase the number of college completers.

For institutions:

- At the local institutional level, policies and programs seeking to enhance pathways and programs of study for nontraditional students should be structured to accommodate the personal lives and work schedules of prospective students, including the need to balance work, home, and school. Institutional leaders, faculty, support staff, students, and other stakeholders need to collaborate to design and implement programs of study. During implementation, data must be gathered that will inform decisions. Achieving the Dream (AtD), the Equity Scorecard™, and Pathways to Results™ are examples of initiatives that enroll nontraditional students and encourage and support data-driven decision making about program implementation to achieve equitable student outcomes (Bragg & Durham, 2012).

- Institutions can improve the financial landscape for nontraditional students by allowing students to pay tuition and fees in affordable chunks, as mentioned earlier (Lane, Michelau, & Palmer, 2012). Higher education institutions should also relieve the burden of institutional financial holds that prevent students from re-enrolling, as these contribute directly to attrition.

For states:

- States need to support innovations consistent with pathways and programs of study and disseminate promising programs and practices that show evidence of reaching nontraditional students. States should support descriptive and evaluative research to identify and disseminate promising practices that could be replicated on other college and university campuses. Understanding the curricular and instructional features of pathway programs requires qualitative research describing features such as contextualized curriculum and stackable credentials. Quantitative research is needed to measure the impact of programs of study on student outcomes associated with education and employment.
- In the past, states have complemented federal financial aid programs with need-based aid that has limited eligibility restrictions, which is more useful to nontraditional students. But state budget deficits have strained these resources, making it difficult to sustain adequate funding for nontraditional students at the same time this population is growing and needing support. State leaders should place a high priority on making need-based financial aid available to nontraditional students and eliminate barriers to nontraditional students' access to these programs (such as ensuring that information about the availability of and requirements for need-based financial aid is available to and understood by nontraditional students).

For the federal government:

- To address the nation's college completion agenda, pathways and programs of study must be supported with adequate financial resources. These programs require consistent, adequate funding to engage in the delivery of instruction, and also the provision of intensive support services, in order to advance students toward college and employment. Federal cuts to adult education and other workforce programs that target nontraditional learners (Foster & McLendon, 2012) present enormous barriers to students.

- If nontraditional students are to enroll in and complete college, a strong federal role is needed in the provision of financial aid. Recent changes to the ATB option demonstrate how the lack of federal aid may negatively affect nontraditional students. The federal government should also encourage states to use need-based financial aid programs to serve nontraditional students. Types of financial aid that incentivize enrollment in pathways and programs of study that show favorable educational and employment outcomes are especially important.

In conclusion, pathways and programs of study that prepare and support nontraditional student enrollment in college and preparation for employment are becoming more commonplace, but more research is needed to understand how these students enroll in and complete these programs. In addition, pathways and programs of study need to be adequately funded to enable nontraditional students to complete college and assume family-wage employment, if the nation is to fulfill the president's college completion agenda (Foster & McLendon, 2012).

Notes

1. In this chapter, I distinguish "family wage"—meaning a wage sufficient to support raising a family—from "living wage"—meaning a wage sufficient to support a single individual.
2. The U.S. Department of Labor (DOL) Trade Adjustment Assistance Community College and Career Training (TAACCCT) grant program may shed light on underserved learner progression through programs of study that provide stackable credentials. These start with short-term certificates and extend to the associate degree and even higher levels; however, data from these TAACCCT grants will not be available for at least one or two more years (U.S. Department of Labor, 2012).
3. Zeidenberg and colleagues obtained their results using statistical methods that permit causal inference, meaning the results can be attributed to I-BEST rather than other factors that might explain different outcomes for the student groups. Both studies cited in this paragraph (Jenkins, Zeidenberg, & Kienzl, 2009; Zeidenberg, Cho, & Jenkins, 2010) note that students taking basic skills courses included those students taking at least one college-level CTE course.
4. These two states are using pathways and bridge programs to bolster the foundational competencies of adults by linking ABE and English Language Learning (ELL) instruction with occupationally focused postsecondary education. The pathways provide sequential curriculum and instruction that enable adults to progress from one level of education to the next, offering industry-recognized credentials at critical milestones (Foster, Strawn, & Duke-Benfield, 2011).
5. Applied baccalaureate degrees are offered primarily by universities, often regional ones, but also community colleges located in states that have authorized the awarding of baccalaureate degrees by institutions that have historically awarded associate's degrees as the highest level of credential.
6. Lane, Michelau, and Palmer (2012) define financial holds as "the practice of prohibiting a potential student from reenrolling if he or she owes the institution money from fines, fees, or defaulted loans" (p. 29).

References

Advisory Committee on Student Financial Assistance. (2012, February). *Pathways to success: Integrating learning with life and work to increase college completion.* Washington, DC: Author. Retrieved from http://www2.ed.gov/about/bdscomm/list/acsfa/ptsreport2.pdf

Alamprese, J. (2010). *Oregon pathways for adult basic skills transition to education and work: Initiative description.* Bethesda, MD: Abt Associates.

Alfeld, C., & Bhattacharya, S. (2011). *Mature programs of study: A postsecondary perspective—Year 3 technical report.* Louisville, KY: National Research Center for Career and Technical Education, University of Louisville. Retrieved from http://136.165.122.102/mambo/content/view/45/54/

Attewell, P., Lavin, D., Domina, T., & Levey, T. (2006). New evidence on college remediation. *Journal of Higher Education, 77*(5), 886–924.

Bailey, T., Jeong, D.W., & Cho, S.-W. (2010). Referral, enrollment, and completion in developmental education sequences in community colleges. *Economics of Education Review, 29*(2), 255–270.

Baum, S., Ma, J., & Payea, K. (2010). *Education pays 2010: The benefits of higher education for individuals and society.* New York, NY: College Board. Retrieved from http://trends.collegeboard.org/downloads/Education_Pays_2010.pdf

Bennett, S., & Makela, J. (2012). *Pathways to college completion: Credentialing models for students who stop short of a bachelor's degree.* Urbana: Office of Community College Research and Leadership, University of Illinois. Retrieved from http://occrl.illinois.edu/update-newsletter-spring-2012/

Bowen, W.G., Chingos, M.M., & McPherson, M.S. (2009). *Crossing the finish line: Completing college at America's public universities.* Princeton, NJ: Princeton University Press.

Bragg, D.D. (2012). Career and technical education. In J.S. Levin & S.T. Kater (Eds.), *Understanding community colleges* (pp. 187–202). New York, NY: Routledge.

Bragg, D.D., Bremer, C. D., Castellano, M., Kirby, C., Mavis, A., Schaad, D., et al. (2007). *A cross-case analysis of career pathway programs that link low-skilled adults to family-sustaining careers.* St. Paul, MN: National Research Center for Career and Technical Education, University of Minnesota.

Bragg, D.D., Cullen, D., Bennett, S., & Ruud, C.M. (2011). *All or nothing: Midpoint credentials for students who stop short of the baccalaureate degree.* Champaign: Office of Community College Research and Leadership, University of Illinois at Urbana-Champaign. Retrieved from http://occrl.illinois.edu/publication/1071

Bragg, D.D., & Durham, B. (2012). Perspectives on access and equity in the era of (community) college completion. *Community College Review, 40*(2), 106–125.

Bragg, D.D., Harmon, T., Kirby, C., & Kim, S. (2009). *Initial results of Illinois' Shifting Gears pilot demonstration evaluation.* Champaign: Office of Community College Research and Leadership, University of Illinois at Urbana-Champaign. Retrieved from http://occrl.illinois.edu/files/Projects/shifting_gears/Report/SG_Eval_Report%20PRINT.pdf

Bragg, D.D., & Ruud, C. (2011). *The adult learner and the applied baccalaureate: Lessons from six states.* Champaign: Office of Community College Research and Leadership, University of Illinois. Retrieved from http://occrl.illinois.edu/publication/906

Bragg, D.D., Smith, W., & Dresser, L. (2012). Leveraging workforce development and postsecondary education for low-skill, low-income workers: Lessons from the Shifting Gears Initiative. *New Directions for Community Colleges, 153*, 53–66.

Carnevale, A., Rose, S., & Hanson, A. (2012). *Certificates: Gateway to gainful employment and college degrees.* Washington, DC: Center on Education and the Workforce, Georgetown University. Retrieved from http://cew.georgetown.edu/certificates/

Carnevale, A., Smith, N., & Strohl, J. (2010). *Help wanted: Projections of jobs and education requirements through 2018.* Washington, DC: Center on Education and the Workforce, Georgetown University. Retrieved from http://cew.georgetown.edu/jobs2018/

Center for Law and Social Policy (CLASP). (2012). *Working better together: How states are using cross-system approach to improve outcomes for lower-skilled adults in the Shifting Gears initiative.* Washington, DC: Author.

Chan, D., & Cochrane, D. (2008). *Paving the way: How financial aid awareness affects college access and success.* Oakland, CA: The Institute for College Access and Success. Retrieved from http://projectonstudentdebt.org/fckfiles/Paving_the_Way.pdf

Chao, E., DeRocco, E. S., & Flynn, M. (2007). *Adult learners in higher education: Barriers to success and strategies to improve results.* Boston, MA: Jobs for the Future. Retrieved from http://www.jff.org/publications/education/adult-learners-higher-education-barriers/157

Choitz, V., Strawn, J., & Foster, M. (2012). *Ability to benefit FAQs.* Washington, DC: Center for Law and Social Policy.

Complete College America. (n.d.). *Restructure delivery for today's students.* Washington, DC: Author. Retrieved from http://www.completecollege.org/docs/CCA Essential Steps Restructure for Today's Students.pdf

Cox, R. (2009). *The college fear factor.* Cambridge, MA: Harvard University Press.

Cross, K.P. (1981). *Adults as learners.* San Francisco, CA: Jossey-Bass.

Dougherty, C., & Woodland, R. (2009). Understanding sources of financial aid to support adult learners. *The Journal of Continuing Higher Education, 57,* 181–186.

Education Trust. (2010a). *Big gaps, small gaps: Some colleges and universities do better than others in graduating African-American students.* Washington, DC: Author. Retrieved from http://www.edtrust.org/dc/publication/big-gaps-small-gaps-in-serving-african-american-students

Education Trust. (2010b). *Big gaps, small gaps: Some colleges and universities do better than others in graduating Hispanic students.* Washington, DC: Author. Retrieved from http://www.edtrust.org/dc/publication/big-gaps-small-gaps-in-serving-hispanic-students

Foster, M., & McLendon, L. (2012). *Sinking or swimming: Findings from a survey of state adult education tuition and financing policies.* Washington, DC: Center for Law and Social Policy. Retrieved from http://www.clasp.org/admin/site/publications/files/Sinking-or-Swimming-State-Adult-Education-Tuition-and-Financing-Policies.pdf

Foster, M., Strawn, J., & Duke-Benfield, A.E. (2011). *Beyond basic skills: State strategies to connect low-skilled students to an employer-valued postsecondary education.* Washington, DC: Center for Law and Social Policy, Center for Postsecondary Education and Employment Success. Retrieved from http://www.clasp.org/admin/site/publications/files/Beyond-Basic-Skills-March-2011.pdf

General Accounting Office. (2009). *Proprietary schools: Stronger Department of Education oversight needed to help ensure only eligible students receive federal financial aid* (Report No. GAO-09–600). Washington, DC: Author.

Greene, J., & Foster, G. (2003). *Public high school graduation and college readiness rates in the United States* (Education Working Paper No. 3). New York, NY: Manhattan Institute, Center for Civic Information. Retrieved from http://www.manhattan-institute.org/html/ewp_03.htm

Grubb, W.N., & Lazerson, M. (2005). *The education gospel: The economic power of schooling.* Cambridge, MA: Harvard University Press.

Hauptman, A. (2011). *Increasing higher education attainment in the United States: Challenges and opportunities.* Paper presented at the American Education Enterprise Institute Conference, Washington, DC.

Hawley, T.H., & Harris, T.A. (2005–2006). Student characteristics related to persistence for first-year community college students. *Journal of College Student Retention, 7*(1–2), 117–142.

Jenkins, D. (2006). *Career pathways: Aligning public resources to support individual and regional economic advancement in the knowledge economy.* Barrington, RI: Workforce Strategy Center. Retrieved from http://www.workforcestrategy.org/images/pdfs/publications/WSC_pathways8.17.06.pdf

Jenkins, D., Zeidenberg, M., & Kienzl, G. (2009). *Building bridges to postsecondary training for low-skill adults: Outcomes of Washington State's I-BEST program. CCRC Brief,* No. 42. New York, NY: Community College Research Center, Teachers College, Columbia University.

Joint Technical Working Group on Programs of Study. (2011, July). *Programs of study: Year 3 joint technical report.* Louisville: National Center for Research in Career and Technical Education, University of Louisville, KY. Retrieved from http://136.165.122.102/UserFiles/File/Tech_Reports/POS_Year_3_Joint_Technical_Report.pdf

Kanter, M., Ochoa, E., Nassif, R., & Chong, F. (2011, July). *Meeting President Obama's 2020 college completion goal.* Washington, DC: U.S. Department of Education. Retrieved from http://www.completionmatters.org/resource/meeting-president-obama%E2%80%99s-2020-college-completion-goal%0B

Kerouac, P., & Badolato, V. (2010). *Recommendation ten: Adult education.* New York, NY: The College Board.

Kirsch, I., Braun, H., Yamamoto, K., & Sum, A. (2007). *A perfect storm.* Princeton, NJ: Educational Testing Service.

Kirsch, I.S., Jungeblut, A., Jenkins, L., & Kolstad, A. (1993). *Adult literacy in America: A first look at the findings of the national adult literacy survey.* Washington, DC: National Center for Education Statistics. Retrieved from http://nces.ed.gov/ pubs93/93275.pdf

Kozumplik, R., Nyborg, A., Garcia, D., Cantu, L., & Larsen, C. (2011). *Career pathways toolkit: Six key elements for success.* Oakland, CA: Social Policy Research Associates.

Lane, P., Michelau, D.K., & Palmer, I. (2012). *Going the distance in adult college completion: Lessons from the Non-traditional No More project.* Boulder, CO: Western Interstate Commission for Higher Education (WICHE).

Levine, A., & Cureton, J.S. (1998). Student politics: The new localism. *The Review of Higher Education, 21*(2), 137–150.

Lumina Foundation for Education. (2009). *Lumina Foundation's strategic plan: Goal 2025.* Indianapolis, IN: Author. Retrieved from http://www.luminafoundation.org/goal_2025/goal2.html

National Center for Higher Education Management Systems, & Jobs for the Future. (2007). *Adding it up: State challenges for increasing college access and success.* Boulder, CO: National Center for Higher Education Management Systems. Retrieved from http://www.cpec.ca.gov/CompleteReports/ExternalDocuments/Adding_It_Up.pdf

Nelson, L. (2012, March 20). No diploma, no GED, no aid. *Inside Higher Ed.* Retrieved from http://www.insidehighered.com/news/2012/03/20/colleges-worry-about-end-federal-aid-based-ability-benefit

Office of Vocational and Adult Education (OVAE). (2008). *Bridges to opportunity: Federal adult education programs for the 21st century, Report to the President on Executive Order 13445.* Washington, DC: Author, U.S. Department of Education. Retrieved from http://www2.ed.gov/about/offices/list/ovae/pi/AdultEd/topics.html

Office of Vocational and Adult Education (OVAE). (2011a). *Adult Education and Family Literacy Act of 1998: Annual report to Congress, program year 2008–09.* Washington, DC: Author, U.S. Department of Education.

Office of Vocational and Adult Education (OVAE). (2011b). *Promoting college and career readiness: Bridge programs for low-skill adults.* Washington, DC: Author, U.S. Department of Education.

Organisation for Economic Co-operation and Development (OECD). (2011). *Education at a Glance 2011: OECD Indicators.* Paris, France: OECD Publishing. Retrieved from http://dx.doi.org/10.1787/eag-2011-en

Perin, D. (2001). Academic-occupational integration as reform strategy for the community college: Classroom perspectives. *Teachers College Record, 103*(2), 303–335.

Perin, D. (2011). Facilitating learning through contextualization: A review of evidence. *Community College Review, 39*(3), 268–295.

Price, D., & Roberts, B. (2009). *Educating adult workers: The Shifting Gears approach to systems change.* Chicago, IL: The Joyce Foundation.

Pusser, B., Breneman, D.W., Gansneder, B.M., Kohl, K.J., Levin, J.S., Milam, J.H., & Turner, S.E. (2007). *Returning to learning: Adults' success in college is key to America's future.* Indianapolis, IN: Lumina Foundation for Education. Retrieved from http://www.lumina foundation.org/publications/researchreports.html

Rhodes, D. (2006). *Analysis of the experimental sites initiative, 2006–07 award.* Washington, DC: Federal Financial Aid, U.S. Department of Education. Retrieved from https:// experimentalsites.ed.gov/exp/pdf/0607ExSitesReportFINAL.pdf

Rosenbaum, J., Deil-Amen, R., & Person, A.R. (2006). *After admission: From college access to college success.* New York, NY: Russell Sage Foundation.

Ruud, C. (2012). [The midpoint credential]. Unpublished raw data.

Skomsvold, P., Radford, A.W., & Berkner, L. (2011). *Six-year attainment, persistence, transfer, retention, and withdrawal of students who began postsecondary education in 2003–04.* Washington, DC: Institution of Education Sciences, U.S. Department of Education. Retrieved from http://nces.ed.gov/pubs2011/2011152.pdf

Spellman, N. (2007). Enrollment and retention barriers adult students encounter. *The Community College Enterprise, 13*(1), 63–79.

Stephens, R.P. (2009). *Charting a path: An exploration of the statewide career pathway efforts in Arkansas, Kentucky, Oregon, Washington and Wisconsin.* Seattle, WA: Seattle Jobs Initiative.

Stipanovic, N., Lewis, M.V., & Stringfield, S. (2012). Situating programs of study within current and historical career and technical education educational reform efforts. *International Journal of Educational Reform, 21*, 80–97.

Taylor, J. (2009). Year three of the Shifting Gears initiative: An interview with Whitney Smith from the Joyce Foundation. *Update on Research and Leadership, 21*(1), 1–3. Retrieved from http://occrl.illinois.edu/Newsletter/2009/fall/1

Taylor, J., & Bragg, D.D. (2012). *Participation and immediate outcomes of Illinois bridge programs.* Champaign: Office of Community College Research and Leadership, University of Illinois at Urbana-Champaign.

Taylor, J.L., Kirby, C.L., Bragg, D.D., Oertle, K.M., Jankowski, N.A., & Khan, S. (2009). *Illinois program of study guide.* Champaign: Office of Community College Research and Leadership, University of Illinois at Urbana-Champaign. Retrieved from http://occrl. illinois.edu/node/431

Technical Workgroup for the Designing Instruction for Career Pathways Initiative. (2011). *U.S. Departments of Labor and Education Partner on Career Pathways Technical Assistance Initiative, 1*(1), p. 2. Retrieved from http://www.acp-sc.org/vol1issue1.html

Tinto, V. (2006–2007). Research and practice of student retention: What next? *Journal of College Student Retention, 8*(1), 1–19.

U.S. Department of Education. (2011). *College completion tool kit.* Washington, DC: Author. Retrieved from http://www.ed.gov/college-completion/governing-win

U.S. Department of Labor. (2012). *Trade Adjustment Assistance Community College and Career Training Grant Program.* Washington, DC: Author. Retrieved from http://www.doleta.gov/taaccct/

Wachen, J., Jenkins, D., & Van Noy, M. (2011). Integrating basic skills and career-technical instruction: Findings from a field study of Washington State's I-BEST model. *Community College Review, 39*(2), 136–159.

Zeidenberg, M., Cho, S., & Jenkins, D. (2010, September). Washington State's Integrated Basic Education and Skills Training Program (I-BEST): New evidence of effectiveness. CCRC Working Paper No. 20. New York, NY: Community College Research Center, Teachers College, Columbia University.

4

PROFICIENCY APPROACHES FOR MAKING MORE STUDENTS COLLEGE AND CAREER READY

David T. Conley

Most students do not enter postsecondary education fully ready or prepared to succeed. Existing measures of college readiness, such as courses taken and grades received, and placement and admissions tests, have predictive power (Belfield & Crosta, 2012; Farrington et al., 2012), but do not sufficiently gauge the proficiency level students must reach in many areas in order to be ready for college-level courses (Conley, 2000; Garb, 1998). Using admission test scores as a measure of readiness, three-quarters of high school students are not fully prepared for college (ACT, 2011, 2012). Although 31 states require students to pass exit exams to earn a diploma, few use these test results as college readiness indicators (Dietz, 2011). As described by Long and Boatman in their chapter in this book, as well as other sources (Adelman, 1999, 2006; California State University System, 2009), significant numbers of students require remediation, including many who meet all admission requirements. Nationally, 36% of first-year undergraduates and 42% of students at public two-year institutions enroll in at least one remedial course (Aud et al., 2011). Many of these students take multiple remedial courses (Bailey, Jeong, & Cho, 2010), and those who do are far less likely to succeed (Adelman, 1999).

Students with the lowest college academic readiness attend high schools with large concentrations of racial/ethnic minority students, low-income students, and those who would be first-generation college students: groups who tend to be underrepresented across the full spectrum of postsecondary education (Bowen, Chingos, & McPherson, 2010). These students may take courses with titles that reflect college admission requirements and receive acceptable grades, but they still arrive at college unprepared (Venezia, Kirst, & Antonio, 2004). For example, researchers examining North Carolina high school students found that only 14% of those attending the least rigorous high schools earned a bachelor's degree in six years compared to 34% of students attending the most rigorous schools. This gap was evident even among students who had a 4.0 GPA and attended a selective college. Those who attended a rigorous high school had a college graduation rate 8% higher than those who attended high schools classified as least rigorous (Bowen et al., 2010).

These data suggest that some schools hold students to a different and lower standard than students at other schools, even when courses taken have comparable titles. Comparisons indicate that "B" students in high-poverty schools have about the same National Education Longitudinal Study of 1988 (NELS:88) test scores as do students receiving a "D" or lower in schools with the lowest concentrations of poor students. The "C" students in the poorest schools have approximately the same test scores as failing students in the most affluent schools (Office of Educational Research and Improvement, 1994). Additionally, evidence suggests that high school grades have been increasing, particularly at and above the "B" (3.0) level, without concomitant increases on independent measures of achievement such as admissions exam scores (Ziomek & Svec, 1995).

Because the challenge levels of high school courses vary so widely, the grades students receive in classes labeled "college preparatory" are not a reliable indicator of readiness to engage in college-level studies. The net effect is that students taking less-rigorous classes are disadvantaged, even though the course titles meet college entrance requirements. Students may become less confident and less inclined to apply either to college itself or to the most challenging postsecondary programs for which they are eligible, a phenomenon Bowen et al. (2010) described as "undermatching," found more commonly among African American students than White students and also highly correlated with socioeconomic status.

If postsecondary certificates and degrees had not taken on tremendous significance as gateways to most career pathways and professions, most of this would not be a serious problem. However, as described in the introduction and conclusion to this volume, the economy places an ever-greater value on formal education credentials, particularly postsecondary certificates and degrees. Simultaneously, the cost burden for postsecondary education has been shifted to the individual, which magnifies the need for college readiness and program completion in a timely fashion without the need for remediation. Seeking to address these phenomena, one goal of current national education policy is to include more academically prepared students from historically underrepresented groups in a broad range of postsecondary programs (U.S. Department of Education, 2010).

Theoretical and Conceptual Framework of the Proficiency Approach

These changing dynamics set the stage for a new conceptual model of college and career readiness, one based on demonstrated proficiency that either replaces or supplements traditional measures of course title, grades, and admissions tests (Conley, 2004). A proficiency model details what colleges expect of entering students and how these expectations differ from what high schools do to prepare students for postsecondary education (Conley, 2003, 2005, 2010). Research over the past 20 years has found that college and career readiness is much more complex than previously thought and that many of the key skills necessary for college success are overlooked or underdeveloped in secondary schools today. A college-ready student is able to, first and foremost, engage with and comprehend challenging course content, apply knowledge in novel and nonroutine ways, use a variety of learning skills and techniques, and successfully transition from secondary to postsecondary learning (Conley, 2003, 2005).

A proficiency approach is grounded in competency models of learning, the roots of which can be traced back to the mastery learning concept of the late 1970s and early 1980s (Block, 1971, 1980; Bloom, 1971; Guskey, 1980a, 1980b). Mastery learning relies on, first, diagnosing individual performance on specific skills and, subsequently, teaching to provide students with additional explanation or practice in skill areas not yet mastered. All students are tested on the same content knowledge, and subsequent lessons are adapted to focus on skill areas until mastery is demonstrated. All students work toward the goal of demonstrating mastery on key content, even if they do so at different rates.

Mastery learning was applied primarily in reading and mathematics, reaching its practical limits as academic skills were deconstructed into smaller and smaller pieces. For example, the complexity of tracking hundreds of individual skill areas became daunting. More importantly, as knowledge was broken down into ever-smaller bits, overall understanding of the structure of knowledge in a subject area became less clear and more difficult to measure. As mastery learning became less functional, new brain-based, cognitive models of learning emerged (Bransford, Brown, & Cocking, 2000; National Research Council, 2002; Willingham, 2009) emphasizing contextualization of knowledge within disciplinary structures and the retention of knowledge through activities with meaning beyond completion of worksheets or drill-and-practice materials. Also gaining prominence was the notion of learning progressions (Heritage, 2008) in which students progress from novice toward expertise by developing knowledge and skills in a logical sequence dictated by the structure of knowledge under study.

Competency-based approaches differ from mastery learning in the aggregation level of skills that comprise a competency. Learning progressions support competency-based models because they allow for assessment of larger constellations of knowledge and skill, and the reporting of results along a novice-expert continuum. Competency-based learning has become more prevalent in primary and secondary education with the advent of K–12 academic content standards. However, the approach is becoming incorporated more and more in postsecondary settings. Rather than consisting of dozens of components, a competency is more integrated and reflects the ways that knowledge and skills are actually utilized by people in real-world settings. Competencies are generally better measures of readiness because they align more closely with the actual task performed. The

Western Governors University (WGU) is an example of a competency-based degree program designed around relevant competencies as defined and organized by faculty and professional organizations. These competencies create a framework for the development of course pre-assessments, individualized plans of study, curriculum design, and progress monitoring, culminating in performance-based and traditional demonstrations of course competencies (Case, 2008; Mendenhall, 2012; Nicastro & Moreton, 2008; Zane, 2008).[1]

At the heart of the proficiency approach is the idea that key knowledge and skills must be identified, taught, mastered, and demonstrated (Conley, 2004). Reading and writing, in particular, can be demonstrated through a range of projects and products that are carefully calibrated against the actual expectations students will encounter in postsecondary courses, such as the ability to analyze literature, read informational texts, conduct research reviews, and write expository papers. Mathematics proficiency requirements can be designed so that students demonstrate understanding of mathematical concepts, as well as content, and that they can apply mathematics to other subject areas, such as science and social sciences, something that is not easily done on a state test.

A proficiency approach as applied to postsecondary readiness first identifies what students need to know and be able to do to succeed after high school and then assesses them as directly as possible to determine if their performance is at the level of postsecondary readiness. Proficiency evidence can come from a variety of sources, including classroom assignments, tests, performance tasks, as well as external exams aligned with college readiness. One development that encourages wider use of proficiency-based admissions models at the present time is a much greater understanding of the nature and content of college courses and the expectations of college instructors, a result of a large body of research on the topic over the past decade (Conley, 2003; Conley, Aspengren, Gallagher, & Langan, 2006; Conley, Aspengren, Gallagher, & Nies, 2006; Conley, Aspengren, Stout, & Veach, 2006; Conley, Drummond, DeGonzalez, Rooseboom, & Stout, 2011; Conley, McGaughy, Brown, van der Valk, & Young, 2009; Conley et al., 2008, 2009). An overview of findings from this body of work is presented later in the chapter.

Proficiencies, thus, need to be developed and defined by high school and college instructors working together, as occurred in Texas, where the Higher Education Coordinating Board sponsored a joint development process with "vertical teams" of high school and college faculty, which led to the creation and subsequent adoption of the Texas College and Career Readiness Standards (Texas Higher Education Coordinating Board & Educational Policy Improvement Center, 2009).[2]

Students who are able to demonstrate proficiency in specific areas while still in high school receive the message that they may be college ready in those areas. This message may encourage them to explore college-level courses, whether those be Advanced Placement®, concurrent enrollment courses that offer college credit at their high school, or a course offered on a local college campus or online. The net effect is that more students get more college-level experiences before they leave high school, a critical factor in improving subsequent success in college. Many of these students also start to receive college credit while in high school, which decreases their time to degree or certificate completion and reduces the cost of college, increasingly important goals, particularly for first-generation college attendees and those from low-income family backgrounds.

The use of competency approaches in postsecondary education generally, and the rapid increase in online courses in particular, suggests that proficiency-based admissions may become feasible in the near future. Adoption of proficiency-based college admissions may create clearer signals and closer alignment between secondary and postsecondary education by making explicit the knowledge and skills high school students must acquire by college entrance. When necessary knowledge and skills are specified, postsecondary institutions are more accountable for the alignment of entry-level courses with stated college readiness criteria. Proficiency models are much more compatible with online learning models that specify the content to be learned and assess student performance against competency criteria. In addition, a proficiency approach may reduce substantially the number of students entering college who lack basic academic skills that require remedial or developmental education. This approach also helps students, who may then avoid the frustrating, expensive, and ineffective experience of being placed in remedial courses (Bailey, 2009).

A proficiency-based college and career readiness system can serve to raise academic expectations across all high school classes by making explicit the standards to reach and addressing any gap that may exist between a student's performance and what is necessary for college readiness (U.S. Department of Education, 2002). A proficiency model also provides students clearer, earlier, and more frequent feedback on where they stand relative to the goal of postsecondary readiness. In the current prevailing approach, a score on a high school-level state test or admissions exam may come too late for the student to close the gap or may give the student an erroneous read on readiness, particularly on state tests with lower challenge levels (Olson, 2002).

Background and Context of the Proficiency Approach

The proficiency approach to postsecondary readiness was first put forward in the 1990s (Conley, 1996a, 1996b) and was designed to capitalize on the development of K–12 academic content standards, which delineated what students must know and be able to do to be judged well educated by the state. No state created a set of exit standards that defined college readiness at that time, although most states had standards extending through 10th grade. The K–12 standards movement also encouraged schools to explore different forms of organization and instruction, including block scheduling, integrated curriculum, project-centered learning, and school-to-work programs, the results of which did not align well with college admissions requirements based on subjects and credits (Conley, 1999).

It was left to higher education systems to develop college readiness standards that defined the knowledge and skills students should demonstrate by the end of high school. Initial exploration and implementation of competency-based admissions systems in higher education followed on the heels of state adoption of standards. By 1997, 11 states were examining a competency-based approach to college admissions (Russell, 1998).

By the late 1990s, proficiency-based systems were piloted in five states, including Colorado (Conley, 1999), Washington (Conley, 1999; Sherman & Scrima, 1997), Wisconsin (Conley, 1998; Garb, 1998), Oregon (Conley, 1998; Oregon University System, 2001), and Georgia (University System of Georgia, 2002), and steps toward such an approach were taken by others. Each state pursued its own approach, and each faced unique challenges. With its tradition of strong local control, the Colorado Commission on Higher Education functioned as a facilitating body to develop the College-Level Entrance Competencies and assisted with district standards development. In Washington and other states, legislative frameworks encouraged partnerships between higher education agencies and state K–12 departments to implement standards-based reforms, an example of which is Washington's Basic Education Act. Georgia developed standards and proficiency assessments but faced inconsistent participation by teachers, limiting full implementation (Venezia, Callan, Kirst, & Usdan, 2006). Other states, including California and Nebraska, developed college readiness standards but did not link them to admissions directly (Intersegmental Committee of the Academic Senates [ICAS], 2002, 2010; University of Nebraska, 1993). Such readiness standards were often used in discussions of systems alignment or to inform development of high school tests.

Few studies directly compared the postsecondary success of students who participated in proficiency standards and assessments to students who completed a traditional grade-based system. In states that conducted pilots, the following findings were suggested based upon available evidence: that students who participated in proficiency approaches performed at least as well in college as students admitted on the basis of traditional measures, that proficiency scores correlated well with then-current state test scores and national admissions examinations, and that a wide range of high schools are capable of implementing proficiency-based programs successfully (Conley, 1998, 2000, 2002; Garb, 1998; Tell & McDonald, 2003). Two states, Wisconsin and Oregon, conducted some of the earliest and most extensive tests of proficiency-based admissions, gathering the most evidence of its effects.

In Wisconsin, students admitted based on American College Testing (ACT) scores and a proficiency-based Supplemental Reporting Profile (SRP), instead of standard transcripts, had slightly higher college retention rates and grade point averages by their second and third semesters (Garb, 1998). High school competency scores were as effective as traditional admissions criteria, such as high school grades, in predicting first-term performance and more strongly correlated with ACT subject scores. Oregon's Proficiency-based Admission Standards System (PASS), which aligned proficiency benchmarks in grades 3, 5, 8, and 10 with college entry, showed similar close alignment between performance on the 10th grade benchmark and freshman year college GPA (Oregon University System, 2003).

The first national set of college readiness standards was developed in 2003 by Standards for Success, sponsored by the Association of American Universities (Conley, 2003). Soon after, in 2004, another set of readiness standards, the American Diploma Project, were also widely distributed and promoted (Achieve, The Education Trust, & Thomas B. Fordham Foundation, 2004). Standards for Success and the American Diploma Project served as forerunners for other systems, such as those developed by ACT (2005) and the College Board (2006), and, subsequently, state-level standards, such as the Texas College and Career Readiness Standards (Texas Higher Education Coordinating Board & Educational Policy Improvement Center, 2009).

Currently, proficiency approaches to college and career readiness are again under examination, partly due to the release in 2010 of the Common Core State Standards (Council of Chief State School Officers & National Governors Association, 2010), which culminate with proficiency standards for the college and career level, thereby creating a universal target for college readiness. As of the fall of 2012, 45 states and 3 territories had adopted the Common Core State Standards (National Governors Association & Council of Chief State School Officers, 2012). In a recent survey of these states regarding implementation plans, 26 out of 31 states indicated they will create formal partnerships among the higher education agency or institutions and the state education agency, while 16 out of 29 planned to align undergraduate admissions requirements or first-year undergraduate core curriculum with the Common Core State Standards (Kober & Rentner, 2012). Many states appear to be committed to the Common Core State Standards, as indicated by the fact that 28 out of 34 states planned to require district implementation, 27 out of 31 planned to have specific initiatives to ensure full implementation in the lowest-performing schools, and 15 of 31 planned to require districts to develop long-term plans for local implementation (Kober & Rentner, 2012).

At the present time, several states use these standards as a framework for a competency demonstration system that can extend from kindergarten through exit from high school. New Hampshire, for example, piloted competency-based approaches a decade ago and then implemented an academic year 2008–2009 deadline for schools to begin awarding credit on competency, instead of seat time (Gewertz, 2012). In 2002, Oregon's State Board of Education new policy allowed students to receive credit for proficiency in lieu of Carnegie units as a means of meeting state graduation requirements (Oregon Department of Education, 2011), and the Oregon University System continues to honor admission through the PASS, developed in the 1990s.

Significant work is currently taking place to improve existing college readiness measures and develop new ones. Most notably, the work of two state consortia created entirely new assessments of the Common Core State Standards (Partnership for Readiness for College and Careers, 2012; Smarter Balanced Assessment Consortium, 2012). With funding from the U.S. Department of Education, these consortia are developing new assessments from scratch to be delivered online and to include a variety of new and novel item types; new performance tasks taking several hours or more to complete; and a new emphasis on reading informational texts, writing, research, speaking, and listening. The assessments will delve more deeply into student understanding of mathematical concepts, including knowledge of algorithms.

These emerging assessments promise to yield much more information than current state tests generate, information that could demonstrate college and career readiness in more sophisticated ways and measure that information against competency standards. These could conceivably serve as the foundation for a proficiency-based system in which consortia data could be combined with information generated in classrooms, such as more extensive research papers, along with measures of noncognitive skills, such as persistence, goal focus, and effort, also important to postsecondary success. The resulting profile of student readiness would help students and colleges understand where individuals stand relative to college and career readiness and how best to improve the success of the incoming class each year.

Key Proficiency Areas for Postsecondary Readiness

A student who is ready for college and career can qualify for and succeed in entry-level, credit-bearing college courses leading to a baccalaureate degree or certificate, or in career pathway-oriented training programs, without the need for remedial or developmental coursework. However, different postsecondary pathways require proficiency in different areas. The National Postsecondary Education Cooperative (NPEC) differentiated between competencies and other commonly interchanged terms and in so doing described their hierarchical interrelationship that results in different outcomes for different students. For example, *traits and characteristics* are described as innate attributes, upon which learning experiences build *skills, abilities, and knowledge*, which bundle in relation to tasks at hand to become *competencies* (U.S. Department of Education, 2002). Competence not only reflects interactions among knowledge, skills, and attributes, but within a specific context (Gonczi & Hager, 2010; U.S. Department of Education, 2002). NPEC states: "Competency-based initiatives seek to insure that students attain specific skills, knowledge, and abilities considered important with respect to whatever they are studying or the transitions for which they are preparing" (U.S. Department of Education, 2002, p. 9). This description corresponds with an integrated conception approach that "views competence in terms of knowledge, abilities, skills, and attitudes displayed in the context of a carefully chosen set of realistic professional tasks which are of an appropriate level of generality" (Gonczi & Hager, 2010, p. 405).

A student's interests and post–high school aspirations influence the precise knowledge and skill that students need to be ready for postsecondary studies. Judging a student's readiness and preparation for college based on a single threshold score from a test given to high school students does not take into account the match between knowledge and skills on the one hand; and aspirations, goals, and plans on the other. Therefore, a secondary school program of instruction should be designed to equip all students with sufficient knowledge and skill as follows: the measure of success should be readiness to engage in entry-level postsecondary courses. Measuring this outcome requires an assessment strategy more specialized and adapted than can be achieved with a single cut score on a single test.

College and career readiness consist of four key areas identified by researchers who analyzed the content of entry-level college courses and queried college instructors regarding expectations and requirements (Conley, 2005; Conley, Aspengren, Gallagher, & Langan, 2006; Conley, Aspengren, Gallagher, & Nies, 2006; Conley, Aspengren, & Stout, 2006; Conley, Aspengren, Stout, & Veach, 2006; Conley et al., 2011; Conley, McGaughy, Cadigan, et al., 2009). Students are considered ready to the degree to which they have mastered all four. As shown in Figure 4.1, the four key areas are: cognitive strategies, content knowledge, learning skills and techniques, and transition knowledge and skills.

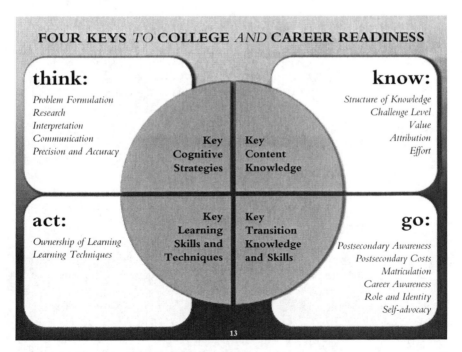

FIGURE 4.1 The Four Keys for College and Career Readiness
Source: Conley (2012). Copyright 2012. Education Policy Improvement Center. Reproduced with permission.

Key cognitive strategies are modes of thinking necessary for college-level work. These include formulating hypotheses and developing problem-solving strategies, identifying sources and collecting information, analyzing and evaluating findings or conflicting viewpoints, organizing and constructing work products in a variety of formats, and monitoring and confirming the precision and accuracy of all work produced. Some examples of readiness measures for cognitive strategies include

- Reading a range of materials, with an emphasis on informational texts.
- Interpreting tables, graphs, charts, and pictures as they relate to content contained in text.
- Demonstrating fluency in several modes of writing, most notably expository and descriptive, and not just narrative or opinion.
- Showing quantitative literacy based on an understanding of measurement and number systems and their application through the level of foundational concepts of algebra and geometry.
- Being able to locate, organize, understand, and interpret a wide range of types of data through a series of methods that include basic statistics and other means for displaying data.

Key content knowledge refers to foundational content and "big ideas" from core subjects that all students must know well, as well as an understanding of the structure of knowledge in core subject areas, which enables students to gain insight and retain learning. This key also contains the technical knowledge and skills associated with career aspirations, including ways in which students interact with content knowledge, its perceived value to them and the effort they are willing to expend to learn necessary content, and their explanations of why they succeed or fail in mastering this knowledge. Some examples of readiness measures for content knowledge include

- Understanding the scientific method and possessing insight regarding the big ideas and organization of knowledge in the sciences.
- Possessing awareness of how social systems operate and how they are studied, how history is studied, and some of the major trends and organizers used to describe history.
- Engaging in career planning through career exploration and the development of career management skills.
- Demonstrating some proficiency in a second language and showing awareness that languages reflect cultures.
- Having experiences in and appreciation of creative and expressive arts.

Key learning skills and techniques consist of two broad categories: student ownership of learning, which includes attribution, goal setting, persistence, self-awareness, motivation, progress monitoring, help seeking, and self-efficacy; and specific learning techniques, such as time management, study skills, strategic reading, memorization techniques, collaborative learning, technology skills, and self-monitoring. Some examples of readiness measures for learning skills and techniques include

- Speaking clearly and concisely in front of groups, listening with care to instructors and peers, and being able to recall what was said and retain what was important.
- Managing the learning process by organizing time properly, using effective study techniques, and persisting with challenging tasks.
- Setting and achieving learning goals in classes, seeking help when necessary, and self-advocating as appropriate.
- Using technology proficiently, efficiently, and appropriately in a variety of ways in the learning process.

Key transition knowledge and skills are necessary to navigate successfully the transition to life beyond high school. As Laura Perna and Elizabeth Kurban describe in their chapter, this information is often privileged knowledge not equally accessible to all students. Students from families and communities historically underrepresented in higher education or certain career pathways are least likely to have this information. The key includes knowing which courses to take in high school in order to be admitted to an appropriate postsecondary program, understanding financial aid options and procedures, being focused on a career pathway or major, understanding college-level and workforce norms and expectations, and knowing how to be a self-advocate within the institutional framework of postsecondary programs. Some examples of readiness measures for transition knowledge and skills include

- Describing a career aspiration and goal, and then demonstrating behaviors consistent with achieving that goal.
- Understanding application requirements for postsecondary programs and financial aid.
- Knowing that the role of the learner in college is different than in high school in many important ways and recognizing that ownership for learning is shifted toward the learner post-high school.

Figure 4.1 provides a graphical representation of these four keys to college and career readiness. Being on the path to college and career readiness means that students can demonstrate proficiency in all key areas, as detailed above.

Implementing a Proficiency Approach

Implementing a proficiency approach to college and career readiness requires quality control of assessment methods. Two basic models exist. If the postsecondary institutions to which students are applying are of low selectivity, the technical demands are less stringent, and a less centralized, standardized model may be acceptable. When proficiency results are used for institutions with higher selectivity or for any of a range of higher stakes decisions, such as financial aid eligibility, demands for greater reliability and consistency of scoring, along with assurances of the nature of the evidence, increase. These contingencies require a greater reliance on the first model described below. Proficiency evidence may be new and unusual to some postsecondary institutions, and their admissions and placement staff may not know how to interpret such information or have great faith in it.

In the first model, the criteria for proficiency are consistent statewide, as are the scoring criteria and methods. Teachers or others who score proficiency evidence are trained to ensure that judgments made are reliable and credible. Students across all high schools in the state are subject to very similar processes and standards. This approach has the advantage of producing consistent scores statewide; however, training teachers to score consistently and reliably requires more work and removes the option for educators to develop local criteria and scoring guides.

The second and more common approach relies on locally developed standards, criteria, and scoring methods. Using this approach, teachers at a high school work together or with local postsecondary faculty to develop proficiency statements and, in some cases, assessment guidelines. Each teacher is then free to assign activities and score student work products independently. While potentially leading to greater variation in scoring consistency, this approach is easier to implement into existing classroom practices and allows teachers greater latitude to develop activities consistent with their teaching style and instructional methods. This approach is generally cheaper as well because fewer activities are managed centrally. The costs incurred are borne locally and may end up becoming components of the instructional process rather than stand-alone expenses in a line-item budget.

While a proficiency-based system creates a wealth of information about a student's performance in authentic contexts, the source information itself, as noted above, cannot currently be used effectively or efficiently by colleges. Multiple platforms have been developed that allow for the storage, transmission, and use of student portfolios, but none have yet been linked successfully or on a large scale to the admissions process in ways that allow records of large numbers of students to be reviewed and evaluated or in ways that allow the possibility of using proficiency products themselves in admissions processes, such as student essays, research papers, projects, and demonstrations.

Next Steps in the Development of Proficiency Models

A proficiency approach creates the potential for much more evidence to be brought to bear on admissions, placement, and financial aid decisions in the near future, once transmission and storage systems are developed, and new interfaces are created that allow college staff to make decisions efficiently and equitably using this larger dataset. For students, this proficiency profile can inform areas of strength and flag clearly those in need of improvement. Students can be provided links to resources that corresponded to profile categories where they need assistance, such as tutorials or videos on content topics, or online modules on time management or study skills, for example.

When aggregated at the institutional level, student proficiency information can yield an admissions picture of the entering class that reveals its strengths and weaknesses, a profile that can be used to allocate resources to support students. Such information can also be shared with faculty so they might understand and even anticipate potential issues with incoming students, incorporating supports to help students succeed, whether they be content knowledge, cognitive strategies, learning techniques, or even knowledge of the culture of a college classroom. College instructors could for the first time adapt instruction based on a profile of student knowledge and skill. In addition to classroom-generated information, proficiency evidence can be gathered from a wide variety of assessments—some high stakes, some low stakes—which are then combined with classroom-based judgments. The results can be used for multiple purposes, including placement and advising.

Future research regarding proficiency models should investigate whether this approach, as opposed to traditional measures of grades and test scores, identifies more students or different students as college ready. If proficiency demonstration results in different students being identified as college ready, how are these students different from those identified via traditional means? Does the approach result in the identification of more students who have the potential to succeed in college, but who did not fare well on traditional measures? Do they persist past the first year of college at a greater rate? Perhaps most relevant to this discussion is how students from groups historically underrepresented in college fare under such a system. Is a proficiency approach a better way to ensure more students from underrepresented groups are ready to succeed in postsecondary education than the use of traditional state tests, admissions exams, teacher grades, and placement scores?

Policy Recommendations to Promote Proficiency Approaches

Although evidence on the effectiveness of proficiency-based systems is still emerging, what is clear is that student college readiness has not increased significantly during the era of state standards and assessments. For example, SAT scores in 1991, at the beginning of the standards era, were 499 in critical reading and 500 in mathematics. In 2011, scores were 497 and 514, respectively (College Board, 2012), although more students were taking the SAT in 2011 than in 1991, which could depress means marginally. Scores on the National Assessment of Educational Progress (NAEP) during the past 20 years have shown gains at 4th and 8th grades, but 2008 12th grade scores are similar to or lower than they were in 1990. The mean mathematics score in 1990 was 305, and in 2008, it was 306. Reading scores declined from 290 in 1991 to 286 in 2008 (NAEP, 2012). Remediation rates have also proven to be stubbornly steady, even in states such as California that have strong standards-based programs, vigorous state testing programs, and an early assessment of college readiness (California State University System, 2006; Kurlaender, Howell, & Salvetti, 2008).

Available evidence suggests that, while state standards and assessments may have been effective in focusing elementary instruction on key literacy and numeracy skills, particularly for students at the lowest achievement levels, they have not had the same effect on secondary school students and their postsecondary readiness. Furthermore, the number of students enrolled in degree-granting undergraduate education programs has increased from 7 million in 1970 to 18 million in 2010, and is projected to grow to 20 million by 2020 (National Center for Education Statistics, 2012). As noted earlier, national education policy is becoming increasingly focused on raising college completion numbers (U.S. Department of Education, 2010). Thus, designing and implementing new ways to ensure that more students are academically prepared to succeed appears to be an important and pressing national priority.

Proficiency-based college readiness systems may be a way to enable more students to succeed in postsecondary education. Federal, state, and local policymakers can help advance their development with some strategic actions.

Federal Policy Recommendations

- Create incentives for states, postsecondary institutions, and local high schools to pilot proficiency approaches and to compare the effectiveness of proficiency models with current admissions models to determine under which circumstances each is most effective.
- Require that any ongoing or future revisions of state K–12 or postsecondary data systems incorporate the means to transmit student proficiency scores and profiles directly from high schools to colleges in a form that can be easily understood, analyzed, and used by postsecondary institutions.
- Craft federal education policy to allow states to experiment with proficiency approaches to college and career readiness, which will require a much wider range of performance measures and assessments than are allowed under current law, including classroom-based evidence of proficiency. The waiver process under the No Child Left Behind Act represents an applicable model. However, readiness measures will need to be expanded beyond English and math scores to include more complex academic products as indicators, such as research papers.
- Ensure financial aid eligibility accommodates students, especially those from underrepresented groups, who exhibit proficiency. Use an expanded set of readiness indicators for which proficiency can be demonstrated to allow more students from these groups to show readiness across more dimensions and in more ways.

- Encourage local high school–college collaborations and partnerships for the purpose of aligning expectations and encouraging student participation in postsecondary experiences while in high school.

State Policy Recommendations

- Create a state-level governance structure to coordinate K–12 and postsecondary education with a specific focus on systems alignment. This can be accomplished via joint commissions or committees among governing boards, interagency task forces, and/or joint meetings of boards of education. The goal is policy coordination involving the issues of college and career readiness and simplification of high school to college transition.
- Include measures of college and career readiness within the state accountability system. Establish some measures of proficiency: for example, the proportion of students reading college-level informational texts, the number of students receiving passing scores on Advanced Placement tests, or the number of students placing into remedial courses.
- Support the use of a wide range of information about types of assessments of college and career readiness. Additional information could include measures of involvement, persistence, effort, and the ability to set and achieve goals. Encourage the reporting of this information to students and parents, and to postsecondary institutions for use in student support, rather than for high stakes decisions.

Local (High School) Policy Recommendations

- Connect with local postsecondary institutions to identify ways to improve student readiness for and success in college. Focus on knowledge and skills, and behaviors and attitudes.
- Expect all students to complete complex projects and papers that require research and synthesis of information.
- Ensure that all courses designated as college preparatory meet high, consistent standards that ensure students who take such classes are truly ready for college.
- Design down from the college- and career-ready level of the Common Core State Standards such that the K–12 instructional program is fully aligned with the development of knowledge and skills necessary for pursuit of postsecondary studies.

Proficiency-based college admission systems bear close examination in an era where greater emphasis is given to competency demonstration in a wide variety of contexts, including online courses. Increasingly, learning is parsed into coherent groupings, and learners are recognized when they exhibit competency with an integrated set of knowledge and skills. Allowing individual or separate recognition of competence in specific areas (i.e., "badges") is one example of a movement away from all-or-nothing determinations, such as a high school diploma or bachelor's degree, in favor of fine-grained, contextualized determinations of mastery of the precise knowledge and skills needed for a particular purpose, alternative program, or individualized course of study.

Although two decades ago schools led the pioneering of proficiency demonstration systems, that lead has been surrendered to other sectors, such as high tech, where competence has been clearly defined in many areas and appropriate assessments developed and implemented, generally online. Education can take advantage of experience gained in previous proficiency-based initiatives, new competency assessments applied in learning settings outside of schools, the clarity of the Common Core State Standards, and the increased body of knowledge concerning college and career readiness requirements. Such knowledge, resources, and research can assist the establishment of proficiency approaches that enable all students to improve their odds of success in postsecondary settings. Furthermore, this work will help to ensure that more students from groups underrepresented in postsecondary education develop college and career readiness.

Notes

1. In surveys, employers of WGU graduates gave high ratings to the academic excellence (88%), workforce contribution (88%), and preparation of students (93%) (Mendenhall, 2012). During a span of less than 10 years, WGU enrollment has increased from 500 to over 30,000 students, and state-branded WGUs have been established and recognized by state governments of Indiana, Washington, and Texas (Mendenhall, 2012). Carnegie Mellon's Open Learning Initiative takes a similar approach to learning as WGU, but in nondegree courses of study. Open learning projects are growing rapidly, including the Massachusetts Institute of Technology's MITx and Mozilla's Open Badges Initiative, which utilize competency-based models of instruction in open access, nondegree postsecondary courses (Soares, 2012).
2. These standards became the legal reference point for college and career readiness that the K–12 system used when developing high school end-of-course examinations that were required to be able to generate a college readiness score in addition to one for high school graduation (Texas Education Agency, 2012).

References

Achieve, The Education Trust, & Thomas B. Fordham Foundation. (2004). *The American Diploma Project: Ready or not: Creating a high school diploma that counts.* Washington, DC: Achieve.

ACT. (2005). *College Readiness Standards.* Iowa City, IA: Author.

ACT. (2011). *The Condition of College & Career Readiness.* Retrieved from http://www.act. org/readiness/2011

ACT. (2012). *The Condition of College & Career Readiness.* Retrieved from http://www.act. org/research/policymakers/cccr12/index.html

Adelman, C. (1999). *Answers in the tool box: Academic intensity, attendance patterns, and bachelor's degree attainment.* Washington, DC: U.S. Department of Education.

Adelman, C. (2006). *The tool box revisited: Paths to degree completion from high school through college.* Washington, DC: U.S. Department of Education.

Aud, S., Hussar, W., Kena, G., Bianco, K., Frohlich, L., Kemp, J., & Tahan, K. (2011). *The condition of education 2011.* (Report No. NCES 2011–033). Washington, DC: U.S. Department of Education, National Center for Education Statistics.

Bailey, T. (2009). Challenge and opportunity: Rethinking the role and function of developmental education in community college. *New Directions for Community Colleges, 145,* 11–30.

Bailey, T., Jeong, D.W., & Cho, S.-W. (2010). Referral, enrollment, and completion in developmental education sequences in community colleges. *Economics of Education Review, 29*(2), 255–270.

Belfield, C.R., & Crosta, P.M. (2012). *Predicting success in college: The importance of placement tests and high school transcripts.* New York, NY: Community College Research Center, Teachers College, Columbia University.

Block, J.H. (1971). *Mastery learning: Theory and practice.* New York, NY: Holt, Rinehart, & Winston.

Block, J.H. (1980). Promoting excellence through mastery. *Theory into Practice, 19*(1), 66–74.

Bloom, B. (1971). *Mastery learning.* New York, NY: Holt, Rinehart, & Winston.

Bowen, W.G., Chingos, M.M., & McPherson, M.S. (2010). *Crossing the finish line.* Princeton, NJ: Princeton University Press.

Bransford, J.D., Brown, A.L., & Cocking, R.R. (Eds.). (2000). *How people learn: Brain, mind, experience, and school: Expanded Edition.* Washington, DC: U.S. National Academy of Sciences' National Academies Press.

California State University System. (2006). *Early assessment program.* Retrieved from http://www.calstate.edu/eap/

California State University System. (2009). *Fall 2009 regularly admitted first-time freshmen remediation systemwide.* Retrieved from http://www.asd.calstate.edu/remediation/09/Rem_Sys_fall2009.htm

Case, R.E. (2008). Independent learning and test question development: The intersection of student and content. *Assessment Update: Progress, Trends, and Practices in Higher Education, 20*(1), 5–7.

College Board. (2006). *Standards for college success.* New York, NY: Author.

College Board. (2012). *Mean SAT scores of college-bound seniors, 1972–2011.* Retrieved from http://professionals.collegeboard.com/data-reports-research/sat/cb-seniors-2011/tables

Conley, D. (1996a). Daddy, I'm scared: A prophetic parable. *Phi Delta Kappan, 78*(4), 290–297.

Conley, D. (1996b). Where's Waldo? The conspicuous absence of higher education from school reform and one state's response. *Phi Delta Kappan, 78*(4), 309–314.

Conley, D. (1998, April). *Early research on proficiency-based college admissions: The cases of Oregon and Wisconsin.* Paper presented at the annual meeting of the American Educational Research Association, San Diego, CA.

Conley, D. (1999). *Statewide strategies for implementing competency-based admissions standards.* Denver, CO: State Higher Education Executive Officers & ACT.

Conley, D. (2000, April). *Who is proficient: The relationship between proficiency scores and grades.* Paper presented at the annual meeting of the American Educational Research Association, New Orleans, LA.

Conley, D. (2002, January–February). *Proficiency-based admissions.* Paper presented at the College Board Invitational Conference, Washington, DC.

Conley, D. (2003). *Understanding university success*. Eugene, OR: Center for Educational Policy Research.

Conley, D. (2004). Proficiency-based admissions. In W.J. Camara & E.W. Kimmel (Eds.), *Choosing students: Higher education tools for the 21st century* (pp. 313–330). Mahwah, NJ: Lawrence Erlbaum Associates.

Conley, D. (2005). *College knowledge: What it really takes for students to succeed and what we can do to get them ready*. San Francisco, CA: Jossey-Bass.

Conley, D. (2010). *College and career ready: Helping all students succeed beyond high school*. San Francisco, CA: Jossey-Bass.

Conley, D. (2012). *A complete definition of college and career readiness*. Eugene, OR: Education Improvement Policy Center. Retrieved from http://epiconline.org/publications/index.dot

Conley, D., Aspengren, K., Gallagher, K., & Langan, H. (2006). *College Board Curriculum Study in Science*. Eugene, OR: Educational Policy Improvement Center.

Conley, D., Aspengren, K., Gallagher, K., & Nies, K. (2006, April). *College Board validity study for math*. Paper presented at the the the annual meeting of the American Educational Research Association, San Francisco, CA.

Conley, D., Aspengren, K., & Stout, O. (2006). *Advanced Placement best practices study: Biology, chemistry, environmental science, physics, European history, US history, world history*. Eugene, OR: Educational Policy Improvement Center.

Conley, D., Aspengren, K., Stout, O., & Veach, D. (2006). *College Board Advanced Placement best practices course study report*. Eugene, OR: Educational Policy Improvement Center.

Conley, D., Drummond, K.V., DeGonzalez, A., Rooseboom, J., & Stout, O. (2011). *Reaching the goal: The applicability and importance of the common core state standards to college and career readiness*. Eugene, OR: Educational Policy Improvement Center.

Conley, D., McGaughy, C., Brown, D., van der Valk, A., & Young, B. (2009). *Texas career and technical education career pathways analysis study*. Eugene, OR: Educational Policy Improvement Center.

Conley, D., McGaughy, C., Cadigan, K., Flynn, K., Forbes, J., & Veach, D. (2008). *Texas college readiness initiative phase II: Examining the alignment between the Texas college and career readiness standards and entry-level courses at Texas postsecondary institutions*. Eugene, OR: Educational Policy Improvement Center.

Conley, D., McGaughy, C., Cadigan, K., Flynn, K., Forbes, J., & Veach, D. (2009). *Alignment of the Texas college and career readiness standards with entry-level general education courses at Texas postsecondary institutions*. Eugene, OR: Educational Policy Improvement Center.

Council of Chief State School Officers, & National Governors Association. (2010). *Common core state standards for English language arts & literacy in history/social studies, science, and technical subjects*. Retrieved from http://www.corestandards.org/assets/CCSSI_ELA Standards.pdf

Dietz, S. (2011). *State high school tests: Changes in state policies and the impact of the college and career readiness movement*. Washington, DC: Center on Education Policy.

Farrington, C.A., Roderick, M., Allensworth, E., Nagaoka, J., Keyes, T.S., Johnson, D.W., & Beechum, N.O. (2012). *Teaching adolescents to become learners. The role of noncognitive factors in shaping school performance: A critical literature review*. Chicago, IL: University of Chicago Consortium on Chicago School Research.

Garb, F. (1998). University of Wisconsin competency based admissions pilot project spring 1998: Final report. Madison, WI: University of Wisconsin System.

Gewertz, C. (2012). N.H. schools focus on competency. *Education Week, 31*(20), 1–16.

Gonczi, A., & Hager, P. (2010). The competency model. In P. Peterson, E. Baker, & B. McGaw (Eds.), *International encyclopedia of education: Vol. 8* (pp. 403–410). Oxford, UK: Elsevier.

Guskey, T.R. (1980a). Mastery learning: Applying the theory. *Theory into Practice, 19*(2), 104–111.

Guskey, T.R. (1980b). What is mastery learning? And why do educators have such hopes for it? *Instructor, 90*(3), 80–82, 84, 86.

Heritage, M. (2008). *Learning progressions: Supporting instruction and formative assessment.* Los Angeles, CA: National Center for Research on Evaluation, Standards, and Student Testing (CRESST), UCLA Graduate School of Education and Information Studies.

Intersegmental Committee of the Academic Senates. (2002). *Academic literacy: A statement of competencies expected of students entering California's public colleges and universities.* Sacramento: Intersegmental Committee of the Academic Senates of the California Community Colleges, the California State University, and the University of California.

Intersegmental Committee of the Academic Senates. (2010). *Statement on competencies in mathematics expected of entering college students.* Sacramento: Intersegmental Committee of the Academic Senates of the California Community Colleges, the California State University, and the University of California.

Kober, N., & Rentner, D.S. (2012). *Year two of implementing the common core state standards: States' progress and challenges.* Washington, DC: Center on Education Policy. Retrieved from http://www.cep-dc.org/displayDocument.cfm?DocumentID=391

Kurlaender, M., Howell, J., & Salvetti, J. (2008). *Postsecondary preparation and remediation: Examining the effects of the Early Assessment Program at California State University.* Davis: School of Education, University of California, Davis.

Mendenhall, R.W. (2012). Western Governors University. In D.G. Oblinger (Ed.), *Game changers: Education and information technologies* (pp. 115–132). Louisville, CO: EDUCAUSE.

National Assessment of Educational Progress. (2012). *2008 long-term trend top stories.* Retrieved from http://nationsreportcard.gov/ltt_2008/

National Center for Education Statistics. (2012). *Condition of education 2012.* Washington, DC: U.S. Department of Education.

National Governors Association & Council of Chief State School Officers. (2012). *Common core state standards initiative: In the states.* Retrieved from http://www.corestandards.org/in-the-states

National Research Council. (2002). *Learning and understanding: Improving advanced study of mathematics and science in U.S. high schools.* Washington, DC: National Academy Press.

Nicastro, G., & Moreton, K.M. (2008). Development of quality performance tasks at Western Governors University. *Assessment Update: Progress, Trends, and Practices in Higher Education, 20*(1), 8–9.

Office of Educational Research and Improvement. (1994). *What do student grades mean? Differences across schools* (Education Research Report). Washington, DC: U.S. Department of Education.

Olson, L. (2002). A "proficient" score depends on geography. *Education Week, 21*(23), 1–15.

Oregon Department of Education. (2011). *Proficiency-based teaching and learning in Oregon: An evolution from state policy to practice.* Salem, OR: Author.

Oregon University System. (2001). *An introduction to the Proficiency-based Admission Standards System (PASS).* Eugene: Oregon University System.

Oregon University System. (2003). *Aligning public university admission with K–12 student learning.* Eugene, OR: Office of Academic Affairs. Retrieved from http://www.ous. edu/sites/default/files/state_board/jbac/files/Aligning-w-K–12.pdf

Partnership for Readiness for College and Careers. (2012). *Home.* Retrieved from http:// www.parcconline.org/

Russell, A.B. (1998). *Statewide college admissions, student preparation, and remediation policies and programs.* Boulder, CO: State Higher Education Executive Officers.

Sherman, J.C., & Scrima, D.P. (1997, March). *Competency-based admissions standards in Washington: A status report.* Paper presented at the annual meeting of the American Educational Research Association, Chicago, IL.

Smarter Balanced Assessment Consortium. (2012). *Home.* Retrieved from http://www. smarterbalanced.org/

Soares, L. (2012). *A "disruptive" look at competency-based education: How the innovative use of technology will transform the college experience.* Washington, DC: Center for American Progress.

Tell, C.A., & McDonald, D. (2003, November). *The first year: Students' performance on 10th grade standards and subsequent performance in the first year of college (2001–02).* Paper presented at the annual meeting of the Association for the Study of Higher Education, Portland, OR.

Texas Education Agency. (2012). *STAAR resources.* Retrieved from http://www.tea.state. tx.us/student.assessment/staar/.

Texas Higher Education Coordinating Board & Educational Policy Improvement Center. (2009). *Texas College and Career Readiness Standards.* Austin, TX: Authors.

University of Nebraska. (1993). *University of Nebraska subject matter competencies: Preparation of students for admission to the university* (Working paper). Lincoln: University of Nebraska.

University System of Georgia. (2002, June). *PACTS: Performance Assessment for Colleges and Technical Schools.* Retrieved from http://www.usg.edu/p16/pacts/

U.S. Department of Education. (2002). *Defining and assessing learning: Exploring competency-based initiative* (Report No. NCES 2002–159). Prepared by E.A. Jones and R.A. Voorhees, with K. Paulson, for the Council of the National Postsecondary Education Cooperative Working Group on Competency-Based Initiatives. Washington, DC: Author.

U.S. Department of Education. (2010). *Blueprint for reform: The reauthorization of the Elementary and Secondary Education Act.* Washington, DC: Author.

Venezia, A., Callan, P.M., Kirst, M.W., & Usdan, M.D. (2006). *The governance divide: The case study for Georgia.* San Jose, CA: The National Center for Public Policy and Higher Education.

Venezia, A., Kirst, M., & Antonio, A. (2004). *Betraying the college dream: How disconnected K–12 and postsecondary systems undermine student aspirations.* San Francisco, CA: Jossey-Bass.

Willingham, D.T. (2009). *Why don't students like school: A cognitive scientist answers questions about how the mind works and what it means for the classroom.* San Francisco, CA: Jossey-Bass.

Zane, T.W. (2008). Domain definition: The foundation of competency assessment. *Assessment Update: Progress, Trends, and Practices in Higher Education, 20*(1), 3–4.

Ziomek, R.L., & Svec, J.C. (1995). *High school grades and achievement: Evidence of grade inflation.* Iowa City, IA: American College Testing Program.

5

THE ROLE OF REMEDIAL AND DEVELOPMENTAL COURSES IN ACCESS AND PERSISTENCE

Bridget Terry Long and Angela Boatman

Over the past 20 years, increasing numbers of students have entered and returned to college underprepared for college-level coursework (Strong American Schools, 2008). Recent estimates suggest that only one-quarter to one-third of America's high school students are at least minimally prepared for college academically, and this proportion is even smaller among Black and Hispanic students (20% and 16%, respectively) (Chen, Wu, & Tasoff, 2010; Greene & Forster, 2003).[1] In addition, wide variation exists in the types of courses students take in high school and how well they perform, two important predictors of future college success (Adelman, 1999, 2006). As such, academically underprepared students enrolling in college are frequently required to enroll in remedial and developmental courses that offer material below "college-level."[2] Estimates suggest that around 40% of all first-year students in college today are taking some form of remedial coursework; however, this figure can be as high as 6 out of 10 students at some postsecondary institutions (Bailey, 2009; Bettinger & Long, 2009b; National Center for Education Statistics [NCES], 2003).

Traditionally, the purpose of developmental education has been to address whatever was missed in high school (Education Commission of the States, 2012). The general purpose of these courses is to provide academically underprepared students with the skills they need to succeed in college and the labor market. Upon enrolling in college, however, students are often surprised to learn they need to take such courses, thereby illuminating an important disconnect between secondary (K–12) and postsecondary education. As David Conley describes in his chapter in this volume, many students and families believe that meeting high school graduation requirements will adequately prepare them for college, but in reality, to avoid remedial college coursework, students often need to take a more rigorous, demanding secondary school curriculum than that required by the district or state. A lack of alignment between the K–12 and postsecondary education systems frequently results in confusing messages to students and their parents about how and what students should do to be able to enter and succeed in college (Venezia, Kirst, & Antonio, 2003).

While remediation plays an increasingly important role in the lives of students and the colleges and universities they attend, debates are growing about its effectiveness and how it should be delivered. Debate over who should offer remediation (high schools, two-year colleges, or four-year colleges) and how it should be offered, if at all, are important questions for policymakers struggling to address college access and success, particularly for underrepresented groups. Proponents of remediation at the postsecondary level assert that helping students to accumulate skills they either missed or forgot in high school should allow them to persist through to graduation when they might not otherwise have done so. The academic supports commonly offered in remedial courses may help integrate students into their academic environment, leading to higher rates of persistence and completion of their degrees. Theories of student integration and engagement suggest that students who feel connected to their institution (either academically, socially, or both) are more likely to stay enrolled than those that feel disconnected (Astin, 1993; Kuh et al., 1991; Tinto, 1975). Critics, however, argue that college is fundamentally not the place to be focusing on skills not learned in high school and that remedial courses may negatively impact college major choice, persistence, and completion, particularly given that remedial courses rarely count toward a student's graduation requirements.

In this chapter, we describe the current landscape of remedial and developmental education in America's colleges and detail what is known from existing research about the best ways to address the needs of academically underprepared students. We also discuss the limitations of this knowledge when it comes to creating policy and outline the need for future research on remedial and developmental programs, including the use of more rigorous research designs to better target causal impact, ways to utilize existing data for such analyses, and the roles governments and institutions should take in addressing the needs of underprepared students.

The Problem: Underprepared Students in Higher Education

Nonselective public institutions provide the bulk of remediation, as they serve as the point of entry for 80% of four-year students and virtually all two-year students (Bettinger & Long, 2009b). In addition to recent high school graduates, a substantial number of adult students, including recent immigrants or workers displaced by structural shifts in the labor market, enroll in remedial and developmental courses.

Descriptive studies suggest that students placed into remedial courses have lower persistence rates than students placed into college-level courses (Adelman,

2006; Bailey, 2009; Bettinger & Long, 2005; Complete College America, 2012). Typically, students are placed into remedial courses in math, English, or writing based on an exam or assessment taken when a student first arrives on campus. Colleges then assign students to a specific course, oftentimes a remedial course, based on their scores on the placement exam.[3] The vast majority of institutions require students to complete their remedial courses before they are allowed to enroll in college-level courses (NCES, 2003). Thus, for students in need of multiple remedial courses in the same subject, this could mean over a year of course taking before the remedial requirements are fulfilled. However, less than 50% of students referred to remediation actually complete the entire sequence to which they are referred (Bailey, Jeong, & Cho, 2010). This percentage is even lower for men, older students, African American students, part-time students, and students in vocational programs. The students assigned to the lowest levels of math remediation are the least likely to advance into college-level courses, with only 10% of this group ever completing a college-level math course (Bailey et al., 2010).

These low rates of college persistence can be explained by the numerous challenges facing academically underprepared students, both inside the classroom and out. Academic difficulties are often discouraging, leading students to become frustrated and daunted by the whole package of academic, social, and financial adjustments to college (Raab & Adam, 2005). Students struggling in the classroom may also experience an attached stigma of not being as "smart" or college ready as their peers, potentially leading to lower self-esteem, higher frustration, and higher dropout rates (Bettinger & Long, 2009a; Jacob & Lefgren, 2004). Remedial and developmental courses may also slow students' progress toward a degree, and factors that lengthen time to degree likely reduce the probability of degree completion (Bailey, 2009).

The Costs of Remediation

In 2006, the Alliance for Excellent Education estimated that the cost of the delivery of remediation nationwide was $1.4 billion in the form of direct costs to students and institutions. Additionally, there may be further costs associated with the lost earning potential for those remedial students who drop out of college without completing a degree. Another recent study estimated the annual cost of remediation at $1.9 to $2.3 billion at community colleges and another $500 million at four-year colleges (Strong American Schools, 2008). Several states report costs of tens to hundreds of millions of dollars annually to support remedial programs (Collins, 2009). Additionally, students must shoulder the tuition costs of the courses. In most postsecondary institutions, remedial and developmental courses are typically offered for credit and will count toward a student's overall GPA, but rarely are they counted toward graduation requirements. While expensive, however, it may be relatively less expensive for institutions to provide remedial courses compared to nonremedial ones. Two primary reasons for the cost differences are larger class sizes and the higher prevalence of lower-paid adjunct instructors in remedial courses (Phipps, 1998).

Addressing the Problem: Remedial and Developmental Education

The Challenges of Comparing Remedial to Nonremedial Students

While remedial courses are offered at the overwhelming majority of postsecondary institutions in the United States, states and colleges know little about whether their remediation programs are successful. Because students who are placed in remedial courses differ from those who are not placed into remediation, one would expect these students to be less likely to persist and complete a degree even in the absence of remediation. Therefore, one must develop a way to separate the effects of lower preparation from the effects of being placed in a remedial course. As Stephen DesJardins and Allyson Flaster describe in their chapter in this volume, simply contrasting the average outcomes of these two different groups ignores the problem of selection and tells us nothing about whether differences in outcomes are *caused* by students' enrollment in remedial classes, or whether these differences are instead explained by lower levels of academic preparation prior to ever enrolling in remedial courses. Fortunately, the recent availability of new data sources has prompted several large-scale studies that attempt to address these selection problems.

Does Remediation Work for Those on the Margin of Needing the Courses?

Mixed results from prior research suggest that the causal effect of remediation on student outcomes is not yet fully understood. While some studies find negative effects from being placed into a remedial course on a student's educational progress and degree attainment, other studies find no effect or even slightly positive effects. These inconsistent findings may be explained partly by the fact that much of this previous research has focused on students just on the margin of needing remedial courses (i.e., scoring just below the cutoff on the placement test required for college-level courses). By focusing on these marginal students, researchers are better able to isolate the causal effects of remedial courses on student academic outcomes through the use of quasi-experimental research designs. For example, Bettinger and Long (2009b) examine the effects of remediation in Ohio. By exploiting institutional variation in placement policies and using distance from a student's home to the nearest four-year college as an instrument for college choice (and thereby placement), the authors compare academically similar students who had different experiences with remedial courses. The authors find that remedial students at Ohio colleges were more likely to persist in college and complete a bachelor's degree than students with similar test scores and backgrounds who were not required to take the courses.[4] Alternatively, Attewell and colleagues (2006) use propensity-score matching, another quasi-experimental research technique (see the chapter by DesJardins and Flaster in this volume for more information on this technique), to estimate the effects of remediation on student outcomes. This study uses national data from the National Education Longitudinal Study of 1988 (NELS:88) to compare observationally similar students, half of whom had taken remedial courses and half of whom had not. Their results suggest that, on average, students in remedial courses were less likely to receive a bachelor's degree but no less likely to receive an associate's degree or certificate.

Because students are typically assigned to remedial courses based on place-ment exam scores, a popular quasi-experimental research method used in studies of remedial education is a regression discontinuity (RD) design. Assuming that students who score just above and below the preset cutoff on a remedial place-ment exam have similar ability, one can obtain a causal estimate of the effects of remedial placement on subsequent outcomes for those students at the margins of passing (Shadish, Cook, & Campbell, 2002). Calcagno and Long (2008) use this strategy to examine the effects of remediation in Florida. The results suggest that remediation might promote early persistence in college, but does not necessar-ily help community college students make long-term progress toward a degree. More specifically, students on the margin of requiring math remediation were slightly more likely to persist to their second year of college than their nonre-medial peers. However, students in need of reading remediation were slightly less likely to pass subsequent college-level English composition than their peers who did not require a remedial reading course. Martorell and McFarlin (2011) use a similar method to examine the impact of remediation in Texas; during the time period of their study, Texas had a single placement exam and cutoff score. The au-thors find that remediation had little effect on persistence, degree completion, or a range of other educational outcomes. They also find no effect on labor market earnings. Generally, their estimates were small and statistically insignificant.

How Do the Effects of Remediation Differ by Type of Student?

The mixed results from prior studies suggest that the causal effects of remedial courses on student outcomes are mixed at best for students at the margin of re-mediation. Little is known about how these effects might vary by age, gender, or prior academic preparation. Additional work by Long and Calcagno (2010) focus-ing on Florida finds that the effects of remediation differ by student background and demographics. Women experienced more positive effects from remedial placement than men. This gender difference is consistent with other studies that have found females to be more positively influenced by interventions (Belfield, Nores, Barnett, & Schweinhart, 2006).

Interestingly, in Florida, older students placed into remediation realized more positive effects in a host of outcomes in comparison to younger students (Long & Calcagno, 2010). One potential explanation is that older students are more focused or ready to take advantage of "refresher" courses. It may also be the case that older students have a greater need for developmental courses because they have been out of high school for a longer period. Therefore, older students who score high enough on the placement exam to just barely pass out of remediation might actually benefit from taking the courses anyway, regardless of placement status.

Family income also appears to be related to the effectiveness of remediation. In Florida, Pell grant recipients in remediation experienced more negative outcomes than their peers in remediation not receiving Pell grants in terms of persistence, associate degree completion, transfer rates, and credits earned (Long & Calcagno, 2010). Because income is often highly correlated with high school quality, the underlying cause of these differences may be academic preparation. Lower-income students are more likely to attend high schools with less rigorous college preparatory curricula. However, affordability may interact with performance in remediation and subsequent college coursework. While low-income students receive the Pell grant, the Pell grant usually does not cover the full costs of their education. The patterns suggest the need for further investigation of the interaction of financial need and experiences within and after remediation.

How Do the Effects of Remediation Differ by Level of Prior Preparation?

The aforementioned studies were limited to students just on the margin of needing remedial courses, and so little is known about the effects of remediation on students with much lower levels of preparation. Research by Boatman and Long (2010) expands the literature by examining the impact of remedial and developmental courses on the academic outcomes of students with varying preparation levels. They focus on students who began at a public college or university in Tennessee in fall 2000. Due to the state's multitiered system, in which students may be assigned into one of four levels of math and one of three levels of reading or writing, the effects of multiple levels of remediation, from students who need only one course to those who need several courses, is examined.

The results suggest that the impact of remedial and developmental courses on student outcomes varies based on the level of student preparation (Boatman & Long, 2010). The largest negative effects were found for students on the margin of remediation: in comparison to their peers placed in college-level courses, students assigned to the highest-level remedial math, reading, and writing courses were less likely to complete a college degree in six years compared to their peers assigned to college-level courses. However, for students assigned to the lowest-level remedial courses, the negative effects of remediation were much smaller and sometimes positive compared to their peers assigned to the next highest course. For example, students placed in the lowest levels of remedial writing persisted through college and attained a degree at higher rates than their peers who started in the next-highest-level course (Boatman & Long, 2010).

In summary, these results suggest the effects of remediation differ by preparation level, and that more, rather than less, remediation may be beneficial for students with weaker academic preparation. This study, along with others (e.g., Bettinger & Long, 2009b), also suggests that writing (or English) remediation may have more positive effects on student outcomes than math remediation. The skills obtained through remedial writing courses may be so fundamental to success in other courses that the acquisition of these skills improves academic performance and persistence in the long term.

Redesigning How Remediation Is Offered

Given the growing numbers of students in need of remediation and the small, mixed academic success of students in these courses, an increasing number of institutions are beginning to rethink the ways that they offer and teach their remedial and developmental courses. Redesigning developmental courses can take a number of purposes and forms. Rutschow and Schneider (2011) distill the multitude of redesign efforts into four types of interventions: (a) strategies targeted to students *before* they enter college; (b) interventions that shorten the timing or content of remedial courses; (c) programs that combine basic skill attainment with college-level coursework (mainstreaming); and (d) supplemental programs such as tutoring, advising, or participation in targeted sections outside of class. One program, for example, that combines basic skill attainment with college-level coursework is Washington State's Integrated Basic Education and Skills Training (I-BEST) Program. While Debra Bragg's chapter in this volume points to this program as an exemplar in promoting educational pathways for nontraditional students, others have frequently cited this program as an example of a highly successful innovation in developmental education. The I-BEST program combines instruction in basic skills with college-level material, all taught jointly by remedial instructors and college-level faculty. Evaluations of the I-BEST program show higher rates of credit accumulation among recipients over time, as well as higher rates of persistence to the second year (Jenkins, Zeidenberg, & Kienzl, 2009). These positive early findings have helped make the I-BEST program a model that other institutions are beginning to alter and adopt for their campuses.

In the last several years, a host of states and individual institutions have received financial support from government and private sources to provide incentives for redesigning and assessing alternative approaches to remedial and developmental education (Carnegie Foundation for the Advancement of Teaching, 2012; Couturier, 2011; Zachry & Schneider, 2010). Traditionally, remedial courses are structured in a 15-week, semester-long lecture or seminar format in which a student takes one remedial course in a given subject before moving on to the next course in the sequence. An increasing number of redesign efforts now incorporate into the classroom the use of innovative learning technology, such as self-directed learning labs and online learning models, and use high-tech classrooms (Epper &

Baker, 2009). These newer models of remediation attempt to better target students' academic needs and help them to move more quickly through their remedial courses. Research suggests that students enrolled in condensed courses, self-paced courses, and/or mainstreamed developmental courses show higher rates of persistence than students taking traditional developmental courses, yet causal questions about the effects of these programs on student outcomes remain unanswered (Edgecombe, 2011; Epper & Baker, 2009; Jenkins, Speroni, Belfield, Jaggars, & Edgecombe, 2010; Zachry, 2008).

Other institutions have tried overhauling the entire structure and curriculum of their remedial courses. In 2007–2008, the Tennessee Board of Regents implemented a redesign of remediation at four public college campuses using grants from the National Center for Academic Transformation (NCAT), with the goal of decreasing the time students spend in remedial courses and ultimately improving persistence rates. While the details of each institution's course redesign efforts differed, chief among the changes was a shift to using learning technology, both in and out of the classroom, to enable students to work at their own pace and focus their attention specifically on the particular skills in which they were deficient (Twigg, 2009). Boatman (2012) employs a regression discontinuity research design to provide causal estimates of the effects of the redesigned courses on the subsequent academic outcomes of students placed in remediation. She concludes that students exposed to redesigned developmental mathematics courses had more positive outcomes than similar students from both non-redesign institutions and from prior cohorts at the same institutions. The largest positive effects on persistence occurred at Austin Peay State University, which eliminated its developmental math courses entirely and created two core college-level courses, Fundamentals of Mathematics and Elements of Statistics, which were linked to additional tutoring workshops. The results of this research suggest that the instruction and delivery methods of remedial courses may actually *cause* student academic outcomes to improve.

In recent years, additional states have begun to consider redesigning their developmental courses, although these redesign efforts have yet to be evaluated. For example, in July 2011, Georgia received a $1 million Completion Innovation Challenge Grant to pilot innovative remediation programs at four state institutions. These new courses will use computer-based assessments to refine placement into remedial courses, modularize the curriculum, and provide learning supports for students requiring remediation.

Other Efforts to Address the Needs of Academically Underprepared Students

While remedial and developmental courses are the most prominent tool currently used to improve college success for academically underprepared students, other increasingly popular strategies focus on mentoring and advising models, financial incentives, partnerships with students' current employers, and child care/transportation support. The key idea behind these supports is that these students face not only academic barriers, but also barriers that transcend the basic academic skills upon which remediation focuses.

The research on many of these support programs remains mixed, suggesting small positive effects in the short term, but few lasting long-term impacts. A number of random assignment evaluations of educational interventions have focused on enhancing student services. In one such study, students randomly assigned to receive financial incentives and increased availability to academic counseling were slightly more likely to stay in school into the second semester and more likely to register for school once these supports had ended, but did not realize any long-run benefits after the first year (Scrivener & Weiss, 2009). A second study focused on students randomly assigned to participate in a "student success course" designed to provide college information, time management, motivation, and study skills (Weis et al., 2011). In the short run, the program helped students to exit probation and acquire more credits. However, after four years, there did not appear to be any significant improvement in students' academic outcomes (Weiss et al., 2011).

Avoiding the Need for Remediation

Another tactic some states and institutions are taking is trying to avoid the need for remediation altogether through the use of early placement testing. Such programs administer remediation placement exams to high school students in order to provide them with early signals that they may lack competencies critical to success in college. Most often this testing is done during the 10th or 11th grade year. As David Conley describes in his chapter in this volume, such tests are designed to improve the information high school students have regarding their preparation for college and encourage those who fall short to take additional coursework in their senior year. With assistance from their teachers, counselors, and parents, students can then determine what courses to take while still in high school in order to avoid college remediation.

In California, the Early Assessment Program (EAP) provides high school juniors with information about their academic readiness for coursework at California State University campuses. A recent evaluation of the program found that participation in the EAP reduced a student's probability of needing remediation in college by 6.2 percentage points in English and 4.3 percentage points in math (Howell, Kurlaender, & Grodsky, 2010). The authors conclude that EAP increased students' academic preparation in high school but did not discourage poorly prepared students from applying to college. This research suggests the promise of early assessment programs in reducing the need for remediation.

What Is Not Known

The existing research suggests that the effects of remediation are considerably nuanced: remedial courses appear to help or hinder students differentially by state, institution, background, and level of academic preparedness. The mixed conclusions of the existing research present an interesting puzzle about why remediation can have such different effects. Future research needs to systematically explore the effects of remedial programs on subpopulations of students, particularly by age and level of prior academic preparation. Only by first identifying those subgroups of students for whom remedial programs appear to be helping or hindering can administrators, practitioners, and policymakers begin to better design and implement effective remediation programs more broadly. Additionally, the research literature needs more examples of successful remedial interventions at both the institutional and state level in order to better identify those policies and practices that produce the largest learning and persistence gains for students. Much more research is needed to determine the most promising, cost-effective ways to improve remediation.

What Are the Best Practices for Colleges and Universities?

While the studies cited in this chapter give a general sense of the impact of remediation, certain types of instruction and supports may be more beneficial than others. Innovative approaches in the instruction and delivery of remedial courses, such as those described earlier, are among the more promising trends in higher education today. Further research is needed to identify which of these practices are the most effective in remediation programs. The literature highlights factors that *might* matter in the success of a remediation program, but few studies use rigorous methods to document best practices. Some suggest that the most promising strategies are those that help students build their skills in high school, integrate remedial students into college-level courses, and provide opportunities for the development of skills for the workforce through contextualized learning programs (Zachry & Schneider, 2010). Others assert more work is needed to compare the relative effectiveness of different models of delivery (Parker, Bustillos, & Behringer, 2010).

More research is also needed on the placement process itself. There is a lack of consensus on what it means to be prepared for college-level work, and as such, there are differing views of what would necessitate remedial or developmental course placement. Among two-year colleges, 92% of institutions use some kind of standardized placement exam to assign students to remedial or developmental courses (Parsad, Lewis, & Greene, 2003), but the exact cutoffs and tests used differ widely.[5] As discussed, remedial courses may be more or less effective for students depending on the severity of their academic needs. Furthermore, recent research indicates that these college placement tests have little correlation with students' future academic success, raising serious questions of how then to assess remedial needs (Burdman, 2012). Several states, such as California, are moving to the use of placement tests to assess the needs of students who are still in high school. Wyoming recently adopted a measure calling for the development of a computer-adaptive college placement exam to be given to all those in grades 11 and 12, which will help students identify and address their academic needs before arriving at college (Wyoming Accountability in Education Act, 2012).

More information is also needed to understand how instructors are used in remedial and developmental courses, including adjunct faculty, as well as the use of professional development for instructors (Zachry & Schneider, 2010). Remedial courses tend to be less costly than college-level classes because adjunct instructors, who cost less than full-time faculty, are more likely to be assigned to teach remedial courses. Additionally, class sizes in developmental courses have traditionally been larger than college-level courses. However, some research suggests that, among all college students, those who have adjuncts as instructors do worse in terms of educational outcomes (Bettinger & Long, 2010). Moreover, larger class sizes, especially for underprepared students who have already had past trouble engaging with material, may be detrimental to progress. Increasingly, institutions are beginning to think much more deliberately about how remedial courses are offered and conducted, in terms of instruction, pedagogy, format, and size.

Where Should Remediation Happen? State Policy Questions

Given that states differ in terms of which public institutions offer remedial courses and how remediation is structured and delivered, little consensus exists as to which institutions are most effective. While many states offer remedial courses at both two- and four-year institutions, an increasing number limit classes to only two-year institutions. Although Florida first limited remediation at public colleges and universities to its two-year schools in 1985 (with the exception of historically black colleges), other states have only more recently adopted a policy shift of this type. New York's decision to phase out most remedial education within the City University of New York's (CUNY) four-year system in 1999 generated a great deal of attention. Students are granted provisional admission to a CUNY four-year institution based on high school grades and other non-test measures, but are required to demonstrate "skills proficiency" with scores on either the SAT or the state-administered Regents exam. Students who are unable to pass this hurdle are not accepted until they complete remedial coursework at a community college and ultimately pass the CUNY/ACT Basic Skills Tests (Parker & Richardson, 2005).

More recently, states such as Indiana, South Carolina, and Tennessee have all prohibited their in-state public universities from offering remedial education. In Virginia, community colleges are primarily responsible for remedial education. Beginning in fall 2012, public four-year institutions in the University of Tennessee system will no longer offer remedial courses and are expected to make arrangements with community colleges to handle remediation of students accepted for admission. Over the past decade, North Carolina has restricted schools within the University of North Carolina (UNC) system from offering remedial education. Instead, universities were originally encouraged to refer students to nearby community colleges to complete their remedial coursework (University of North Carolina Board of Governors, 1992). When California moved toward concentrating remediation in the community college system in the late 1990s, several University of California (UC) campuses contracted or folded their remedial classes into regular courses (Breneman, Costrell, & Haarlow, 1998).

The California State University (CSU) system has made several efforts to reduce the need for remedial education. These efforts include offering more summer remedial education programs, trying to strengthen teacher preparation, and attempting to set clearer standards and better communicate these to students, parents, and schools to ensure that high school graduates meet university admission requirements. The goal is to require recent high school graduates to demonstrate college-level skills in English and mathematics as a condition of admission (Moore, Shulock, Ceja, & Lang, 2007). Additionally, California encourages students to complete remediation at two-year colleges before entering the four-year system. Other states continue to debate the possible benefits of limiting remediation at public institutions to the two-year colleges.

Recently, Connecticut took an even bolder move by choosing to eliminate remedial and developmental courses altogether. In May 2012, both houses of the Connecticut legislature passed a bill requiring the state's public institutions to eliminate noncredit remedial classes by fall 2014 (Act Concerning College Readiness and Completion, 2012). Under the policy, students in need of remedial or developmental courses are to be placed into college-level courses and receive "embedded remedial support" in the form of access to additional office hours and academic support centers. They would also be required to attend an "intensive college readiness" program to learn basic study skills and strategies before the semester begins. This policy decision has initiated an important debate surrounding the sweeping nature of the policy. Currently 70% of students in Connecticut's 12 community colleges take at least one remedial class during their first year of enrollment, and critics are concerned these students will fail to make academic progress and may ultimately drop out without the aid of any remedial and developmental courses.

The movement away from four-year institutions offering remediation raises important questions about the effects on student outcomes of restricting remedial services to community colleges. By shifting the locus of remediation, states could change enrollment patterns, and eventual degree completion could fall as a result: research suggests community college students do not perform as well as their peers who initially enter four-year institutions, perhaps due to a lack of institutional resources and support (Long & Kurlaender, 2009).

Should States Limit or Shift the Costs of Remediation?

Just as states may debate where remedial courses should be offered, how states should control the costs of these efforts is an additional question. Some states limit the percentage of students who need remedial courses that can be accepted by an institution. Other states and institutions impose limits on the amount of time students have to complete the remediation or the number of times a student can repeat a remedial course. In 2012, seven states (South Dakota, Colorado, Missouri, Nevada, Ohio, Oklahoma, Utah) were restricting or had eliminated state funding for remedial courses at some of their four-year colleges, thereby forcing these institutions to fund remedial courses strictly through the use of tuition and fees (Smith, 2012). While the effects of these limitations are not yet known, they may have important implications for students' access to and progress through college.

Massachusetts is an example of a state that has chosen to limit the number of students with remedial needs who can be admitted to a public university. In 1998, the Massachusetts Board of Higher Education imposed a 5% cap on the enrollment of freshmen in remedial courses. The Board of Higher Education raised the cap to 10% in recent years; students above that percentage are referred to community colleges to complete their remedial coursework. A recent bill passed into law in Maine requires public higher education system leaders to publically report the number of students enrolled in remedial courses, and to provide recommendations to the legislature as to how they will reduce the number of students requiring remedial education (Act to Require, 2012).

Some institutions and states impose time limits for remedial education courses. Texas limits both the amount of development credits that students can take and how many levels of remediation an institution can offer. The Texas Success Initiative states that legislative appropriations may not be used for developmental coursework taken by a student in excess of "(1) 18 semester credit hours, for a general academic teaching institution; and (2) 27 semester credit hours, for a public junior college, public technical institute, or public state college" (Texas Higher Education Coordinating Board, 2008, p. 1).

Other states limit the number of remedial courses that may be taken. At California community colleges, there is a limit of 30 semester or 45 quarter credits of "pre-collegiate basic skills" courses, except for ESL students or those with "verified learning disabilities" (James, Morrow, & Perry, 2002). In Georgia, students who do not meet the minimum standards for college-level work within the University of Georgia system are placed into Learning Support classes. However, students may only take a maximum of one Learning Support class in English language arts and have only two attempts to pass the course. Students may only take two Learning Support classes in math and must pass these courses in three attempts, with no appeals (Georgia Board of Regents, 2010).

Efforts to limit remediation, either in where it is offered or how much is allowed, may have the effect of pressuring high school students to prepare better for college while pushing programs and college students to be more effective with their time. However, limiting remediation could have potentially harmful effects on student success. Students in need of remediation may become overwhelmed as they try to navigate the fulfillment of both their remedial and college-level requirements under a more restrictive timeline or across multiple institutions. Therefore, while policymakers lament the need for remediation and how to diminish it, many of the efforts described above do little to reduce remediation rates or improve programs. Instead of moving forward the conversation on how to "fix" remediation through research and practice, the policies being debated are focused almost entirely on how to manage it.

Conclusions and Implications for Policymakers and Institutional Leaders

The big question policymakers and institutions wrestle with today concerns whether remediation is worth the costs. Given that much recent evidence suggests that remedial education and other support programs are having only small effects—positive or negative—on student outcomes, are remediation efforts worth it? However, as discussed earlier in this chapter, these limited benefits may be explained by differences in student background or prior levels of academic preparation, suggesting that targeting remediation efforts to the students most in need may improve student learning and long-term outcomes. In essence, remedial and developmental courses appear to help or hinder students differently by state, institution, background, and level of academic preparedness. Therefore, states and schools need not treat remediation as a singular policy but instead should consider it as an intervention that might vary in its impact according to student needs. Understanding differences in student needs could spur some insight into how to make *all* developmental and remedial courses more effective.

On the other hand, the negative effects found for students at the margin of remediation may suggest that it is not needed for as many students as are currently placed. If the method used to assign students to remedial courses is flawed or unreliable, then students near the cutoff for assignment to these courses may be able to succeed in college-level courses without remediation if given the opportunity (Hughes & Scott-Clayton, 2010). A more accurate placement system could lead to a reduction in the number of difficulties students face in the classroom as a result of improper placement. Prince (2005) summarizes arguments for more standardized and consistent testing instruments and cutoff scores. He asserts that policies that are "more consistent and predictable" would help to "establish a common definition of academic proficiency ... which could accelerate the alignment of secondary and postsecondary academic requirements and expectations and enable colleges to send clear signals to high schools about the preparation students need to be college-ready" (p. 2). In addition, he argues that doing so would improve states' ability to track and evaluate their programs. Having a mandatory policy might also help facilitate transfer, as students would be able to avoid duplication and arbitrary placement if moving to another institution within the state. However, even if standardization is preferred, it is not clear which assessment(s) should be used and where the threshold for remediation should be drawn.

Finally, campus administrators and policymakers should be aware that remediation efforts need not focus solely on the skills students did not learn in the past, but can instead attempt to identify and provide the skills students will need for a future career or academic major. Efforts to redesign the ways in which remediation is offered should be focused much more explicitly on the areas in which students most need improvement. By redefining developmental education as an academic support rather than a curricular burden, colleges and universities will be much more effective in helping underprepared students succeed. Future policy changes should continue this focus on differentiated delivery based on student skill and placement level as more institutions look to customize instruction to address specific student deficiencies.

Notes

1. The National Center for Education Statistics (NCES) defines "high-level" high school academic coursework as four years of English, three years of mathematics (including at least one year of a course higher than algebra II), three years of science, three years of social studies, and two years of a single non-English language (Chen et al., 2010). Similarly, Greene and Forster (2003) define being minimally "college ready" as (a) graduating from high school; (b) having taken four years of English, three years of math, and two years of science, social science, and foreign language; and (c) demonstrating basic literacy skills by scoring at least 265 on the reading National Assessment of Educational Progress (NAEP).
2. In an effort to avoid possible negative connotations associated with the term "remedial," practitioners often use the term "developmental education" to describe the courses and services offered to students below college level (Bailey et al., 2010); however, the terms "remedial" and "developmental" are often used interchangeably in the literature, and as such, throughout this chapter.
3. Placement into mathematics remediation is more common than placement into English (i.e., reading and/or writing) remediation, but participation in English remediation may be more serious as some evidence suggests that reading and writing deficiencies have more negative effects on a student's success (Bailey et al., 2010).
4. Bettinger and Long (2009b) focuses on degree-seeking, traditional-age, full-time undergraduates in Ohio's public colleges who were at the margins of placement into remediation.
5. The most widely used placement exams are the Computerized Adaptive Placement Assessment and Support Systems (COMPASS) and the Assessment of Skills for Successful Entry and Transfer (ASSET), each published by ACT, Inc., and the ACCUPLACER published by the College Board.

References

Act Concerning College Readiness and Completion. Connecticut Public Act No. 12–40 (Senate Bill No. 40). (2012). Retrieved from http://cga.ct.gov/2012/ACT/PA/2012PA-00040-R00SB-00040-PA.htm

Act to Require the Maine Community College System, the University of Maine System and the Maine Maritime Academy to Report the Number of Students Enrolled in Remedial Courses. Maine S.P. 544—L.D. 1645. (2012) Retrieved from http://www. mainelegislature.org/legis/bills/getPDF.asp?paper=SP0544&item=4&snum=125

Adelman, C. (1999). *Answers in the toolbox: Academic intensity, attendance patterns, and bachelor's degree attainment.* Washington, DC: U.S. Department of Education.

Adelman, C. (2006). *The toolbox revisited: Paths to degree completion from high school through college.* Washington, DC: U.S. Department of Education.

Alliance for Excellent Education. (2006, August). *Paying double: Inadequate high schools and community college remediation* (Issue Brief). Washington, DC: Author. Retrieved from http://www.all4ed.org/files/remediation.pdf

Astin, A.W. (1993). *What matters in college: Four critical years revisited.* San Francisco, CA: Jossey-Bass.

Attewell, P., Lavin, D., Domina, T., & Levey, T. (2006). New evidence on college remediation. *Journal of Higher Education, 77*(5), 886–924.

Bailey, T. (2009). Challenge and opportunity: Rethinking the role and function of developmental education in community college. *New Directions for Community Colleges, 145,* 11–30.

Bailey, T., Jeong, D.W., & Cho, S.-W. (2010). Referral, enrollment, and completion in developmental education sequences in community colleges. *Economics of Education Review, 29*(2), 255–270.

Belfield, C., Nores, M., Barnett, S., & Schweinhart, L. (2006). The high/scope perry preschool program: Cost–benefit analysis using data from the age-40 followup. *Journal of Human Resources, 41*(1), 162–190.

Bettinger, E., & Long, B.T. (2005). Remediation at the community college: Student participation and outcomes. *New Directions for Community Colleges, 129,* 17–26.

Bettinger, E., & Long, B.T. (2009a). Remedial and developmental courses. In S. Dickert-Conlin & R. Rubenstein (Eds.), *Economic inequality and higher education: Access, persistence, and success* (pp. 69–100). New York, NY: Russell Sage Foundation.

Bettinger, E., & Long, B.T. (2009b). Addressing the needs of underprepared students in higher education: Does college remediation work? *Journal of Human Resources, 44*(3), 736–771.

Bettinger, E., & Long, B.T. (2010). Does cheaper mean better? The impact of using adjunct instructors on student outcomes. *Review of Economics and Statistics, 92*(3), 598–613.

Boatman, A. (2012). *Evaluating institutional efforts to streamline postsecondary remediation: The causal effects of the Tennessee developmental-course redesign initiative on early student academic success.* (An NCPR Working Paper). New York, NY: National Center for Postsecondary Research.

Boatman, A., & Long, B.T. (2010). *Does remediation work for all students? How the effects of postsecondary remedial and developmental courses vary by level of academic preparation* (An NCPR Working Paper). New York, NY: National Center for Postsecondary Research.

Breneman, D.W., Costrell, R., & Haarlow, W. (1998). *Remediation in higher education: A symposium.* Washington, DC: Thomas B. Fordham Foundation.

Burdman, P. (2012). *Where to begin: The evolving role of placement exams for students starting college.* Boston, MA: Jobs for the Future.

Calcagno, J.C., & Long, B.T. (2008). *The impact of postsecondary remediation using a regression discontinuity approach: Addressing endogenous sorting and noncompliance* (NBER Working Paper No. 14194). Cambridge, MA: National Bureau of Economic Research.

Carnegie Foundation for the Advancement of Teaching. (2012). *Homepage.* Retrieved from http://www.carnegiefoundation.org/

Chen, X., Wu, J., & Tasoff, S. (2010). *Academic preparation for college in the high school senior class of 2003–04.* Washington, DC: U.S. Department of Education, National Center for Education Statistics.

Collins, M.L. (2009). *Setting up success in developmental education: How state policy can help community colleges improve student outcomes* (An *Achieving the Dream* Policy Brief). Boston, MA: Jobs for the Future.

Complete College America. (2012). *Remediation: Higher education's bridge to nowhere.* Washington, DC: Author. Retrieved from http://www.completecollege.org/docs/CCA-Remediation-final.pdf

Couturier, L.K. (2011). *Scaling and sustaining: State progress in the developmental education initiative* (A Policy Brief). Boston, MA: Jobs for the Future. Retrieved from http://www.jff.org/sites/default/files/ATD_ScalingSustaining_100311.pdf

Edgecombe, N. (2011). *Accelerating the academic achievement of students referred to developmental education* (CCRC Working Paper No. 30, Assessment of Evidence Series). New York, NY: Columbia University, Teachers College, Community College Research Center.

Education Commission of the States. (2012). *Instructional delivery.* Retrieved from http://gettingpastgo.org/policy-levers/instructional-delivery/

Epper, R.M., & Baker, E. (2009). *Technology solutions for developmental math: An overview of current and emerging practices.* Report prepared with funding from the William and Flora Hewlett Foundation and the Bill & Melinda Gates Foundation.

Georgia Board of Regents. (2010). *Board of regents policy manual.* Section 4.2.1.1: Freshman Admission Requirements. Atlanta: University System of Georgia. Retrieved from http://www.usg.edu/student_affairs/students/admissions_enrollment/ls_requirements

Greene, J.P., & Forster, G. (2003). *Public high school graduation and college readiness rates in the United States* (Education Working Paper No. 3). New York, NY: Manhattan Institute for Policy Research, Center for Civic Innovation.

Howell, J.S., Kurlaender, M., & Grodsky, E. (2010). Postsecondary preparation and remediation: Examining the effect of the Early Assessment Program at California State University. *Journal of Policy Analysis and Management, 29*(4), 726–748.

Hughes, K.L., & Scott-Clayton, J. (2010). *Assessing developmental assessment in community colleges: A review of the literature* (Working Paper No. 19). New York, NY: Community College Research Center, Teachers College, Columbia University.

Jacob, B.A., & Lefgren, L. (2004). Remedial education and student achievement: A regression-discontinuity analysis. *Review of Economics and Statistics, 86*(1), 226–244.

James, J., Morrow, V., & Perry, P. (2002, July). *Study session on basic skills.* A presentation to the board of governors at the California Community Colleges, Sacramento, CA.

Jenkins, D., Speroni, C., Belfield, C., Jaggars, S.S., & Edgecombe, N. (2010). *A model for accelerating academic success of community college remedial English students: Is the Accelerated Learning Program (ALP) effective and affordable?* (CCRC Working Paper No. 21). New York, NY: Columbia University, Teachers College, Community College Research Center.

Jenkins, D., Zeidenberg, M., & Kienzl, G.S. (2009). *Building bridges to postsecondary training for low-skill adults: Outcomes of Washington State's I-BEST program* (CCRC Brief No. 42). New York, NY: Columbia University, Teachers College, Community College Research Center.

Kuh, G.D., Schuh, J.H., Whitt, E.J., Andreas, R.E., Lyons, J.W., Strange, C.C., . . . MacKay, K.A. (1991). *Involving colleges: Successful approaches to fostering student learning and development outside the classroom.* San Francisco, CA: Jossey-Bass.

Long, B.T., & Calcagno, J.C. (2010). *Does remediation help all students? The heterogeneous effects of postsecondary developmental courses.* (An NCPR Working Paper). New York, NY: National Center for Postsecondary Research.

Long, B.T., & Kurlaender, M. (2009). Do community colleges provide a viable pathway to a baccalaureate degree? *Educational Evaluation and Policy Analysis, 31*(1), 30–53.

Martorell, P., & McFarlin, I., Jr. (2011). Help or hindrance? The effects of college remediation on academic and labor market outcomes. *The Review of Economics and Statistics, 93*(2), 436–454.

Massachusetts Board of Higher Education. (1998, September 16). *Academic and Campus Affairs Meeting, No. ACA 99-02.*

Moore, C., Shulock, N., Ceja, M., & Lang, D. (2007). *Beyond the open door: Increasing student success in the California community colleges.* Sacramento: Institute for Higher Education Leadership and Policy, California State University.

National Center for Education Statistics. (2003). *Remedial education at degree-granting postsecondary institutions in fall 2000.* Washington, DC: U.S. Department of Education.

Parker, T.L., Bustillos, L.T., & Behringer, L.B. (2010). *Remedial and developmental education policy at a crossroads.* Boston: University of Massachusetts Boston.

Parker, T.L., & Richardson, R.C. (2005). Ending remediation at CUNY: Implications for access and excellence. *Journal of Educational Research & Policy Studies, 5*(2), 1–22.

Parsad, B., Lewis, L., & Greene, B. (2003). *Remedial education at degree-granting postsecondary institutions in fall 2000* (Report No. NCES 2004–101). Washington, DC: U.S. Department of Education, National Center for Education Statistics.

Phipps, R.A. (1998). *College remediation: What it is, what it costs, what's at stake.* Washington, DC: Institute for Higher Education Policy.

Prince, H. (2005). *Standardization vs. flexibility: State policy options on placement testing for developmental education in community colleges* (Policy Brief). Boston, MA: Jobs for the Future.

Raab, L., & Adam, A.J. (2005). The university college model: A learning-centered approach to retention and remediation. *New Directions for Institutional Research, 125*(2), 86–106.

Rutschow, E.Z., & Schneider, E. (2011). *Unlocking the gate: What we know about improving developmental education.* New York, NY: MDRC.

Scrivener, S., & Weiss, M. (with Teres, J). (2009). *More guidance, better results? Three-year effects of an enhanced student services program at two community colleges.* New York, NY: MDRC.

Shadish, W., Cook, T., & Campbell, D. (2002). *Experimental and quasi-experimental designs for generalized causal inference.* Boston, MA: Houghton-Mifflin.

Smith, M. (2012). *Choosing who delivers: The impact of placing limits on the delivery of remedial education at four-year institutions.* Denver, CO: Education Commission of the States.

Strong American Schools. (2008). *Diploma to nowhere.* Washington, DC: Author.

Texas Higher Education Coordinating Board. (2008) *Overview: Developmental education.* Retrieved from http://www.thecb.state.tx.us/reports/PDF/1592.PDF?CFID=32298254&CFTOKEN=29824613

Tinto, V. (1975). Dropout from higher education: A theoretical synthesis of recent research. *Review of Educational Research, 45*(1), 89–125.

Twigg, C. (2009). *Developmental courses: An oxymoron?* Saratoga Springs, NY: National Center for Academic Transformation. Retrieved from http://www.thencat.org/NCAT Plans/Dev%20Courses%20An%20Oxymoron.htm

University of North Carolina Board of Governors. (1992). *The UNC Policy Manual.* Guideline 400.1.11[G] Adopted July 9, 1992. Retrieved from http://intranet.northcarolina.edu/docs/legal/policymanual/400.1.11%5Bg%5D.pdf

Venezia, A., Kirst, M., & Antonio, A. (2003). *Betraying the college dream: How disconnected K–12 and postsecondary education systems undermine student aspirations.* Stanford, CA: Stanford Institute for Higher Education Research.

Weiss, M., Brock, T., Sommo, C., Rudd, T., & Turner, M.C. (2011). *Serving community college students on probation: Four-year findings from Chaffey College's opening doors program.* New York, NY: MDRC.

Wyoming Accountability in Education Act. Enrolled Act No. 65 (2012). Retrieved from http://legisweb.state.wy.us/2012/Enroll/SF0057.pdf

Zachry, E. (with Schneider, E.). (2008). *Promising instructional reforms in developmental education: A case study of three Achieving the Dream colleges.* New York, NY: MDRC.

Zachry, E., & Schneider, E. (2010). *Building foundations for student readiness: A review of rigorous research and promising trends in developmental education.* Paper presented at the National Center for Postsecondary Research Developmental Education Conference, New York, NY.

6

THE ROLE OF FINANCES IN POSTSECONDARY ACCESS AND SUCCESS

Donald E. Heller

Higher education has long been seen as a vehicle for economic growth and development, both for individuals and for society as a whole. Economists describe the former as private returns to postsecondary education and the latter as public, or social returns.[1] As individuals invest in schooling beyond high school, they reap benefits in the form of higher wages and access to better careers (that is, careers with not just higher wages, but more job autonomy, better benefits, and better working conditions). These individual investments benefit society through higher levels of economic growth, higher levels of tax collections (assuming progressive income tax structures), and lower levels of what are categorized as socially negative behaviors such as crime and reliance on public assistance.

In recent decades, discussions of the returns to postsecondary education have focused primarily on the higher wages earned by college graduates (Goldin & Katz, 2008; Heller, 2011b; Levy & Murnane, 1992; Murnane, Willett, & Levy, 1995). The college wage premium—the additional amount earned by those with a college degree compared to those entering the labor force with only a high school diploma—has increased during this period, thus making the need for some form of postsecondary training even more important. Figure 6.1 shows the earnings premium of college-educated men over those men with no education beyond a high school diploma, or high school dropouts. While a major portion of this increasing premium is due to a decline in the absolute wages of those with less than a baccalaureate degree rather than more rapidly increasing wages for those with a college diploma, the benefits of investing in postsecondary education have received much attention from policymakers, the media, and students themselves. Earnings patterns for women are similar.

Since the report of the Truman Commission on Higher Education in 1947, the federal government has articulated the goal of promoting access to higher

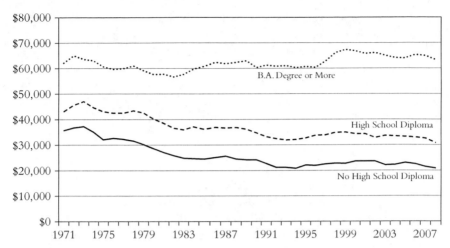

FIGURE 6.1 Median Income of Men Age 25 and Older by Educational Attainment, 1971–2008 (constant 2008 dollars)
Source: Heller (2011b).

education for all students qualified to benefit from a college degree, regardless of whether they have sufficient resources to pay for it. For example, volume II of the report (President's Commission on Higher Education, 1947) stated:

> It is the responsibility of the community, at the local, State, and National levels, to guarantee that financial barriers do not prevent any able and otherwise qualified young person from receiving the opportunity for higher education. There must be developed in this country the widespread realization that money expended for education is the wisest and soundest of investments in the national interest. The democratic community cannot tolerate a society based upon education for the well-to-do alone. If college opportunities are restricted to those in the higher income brackets, the way is open to the creation and perpetuation of a class society which has no place in the American way of life. (p. 23)

It was almost two decades before this goal was legislated through passage of the Higher Education Act of 1965 (HEA). Title IV of the act, which created the federal financial aid programs, opens by stating:

> It is the purpose of this part to provide, through institutions of higher education, educational opportunity grants to assist in making available benefits of higher education to qualified high school graduates of exceptional financial need, who for lack of financial means of their own or of their families would be unable to obtain such benefits without such aid. (HEA, 1965)

This same goal of ensuring that financial barriers do not prevent students from benefiting from a postsecondary education has been adopted by many states through creation of their own financial aid programs.

Microeconomic theory also helps us understand the process through which students make decisions about whether to invest in college (Baum, McPherson, & Steele, 2008; Heller, 1997; Kim, 2010; Leslie & Brinkman, 1988). Like most goods, college attendance is a normal good—as incomes rise, individuals desire to, and are more likely to, consume more of it. From the perspective of markets, the ability of higher-income students to access higher education might not be an issue. But the positive relationship between enrollment and income does conflict with long-standing public policy goals in the United States.

Although long in place, the ability of policies—particularly federal, state, and institutional financial aid programs—to achieve the goal of equal access in higher education has been highly compromised. Even though federal and state governments and colleges and universities, along with private organizations, provided over $175 billion in financial aid (grants, loans, work study wages, and tax benefits) to undergraduate students in the 2010–2011 academic year, access to higher education for students from low- and moderate-income families—those historically underrepresented in American higher education—has been constrained in the face of tuition price increases that have exceeded three times the rate of growth in inflation and family incomes over the last four decades (Heller, 2011b).

In this chapter, I begin by examining the status of college participation in the United States, followed by an analysis of historical trends in tuition prices and financial aid. I then describe what existing theory and research tells us about the effectiveness of financial aid policies on the college participation of students. I close the chapter with an analysis of how this information should inform federal, state, and institutional policy to develop strategies to help reduce inequities and stratification in college-going across income groups.

The State of College Participation

As referenced in the introductory chapter to this volume, the Obama administration has recognized the importance of postsecondary education through its goal that the United States will once again have the highest postsecondary attainment rate of any country in the world. A generation ago, the nation did enjoy this standing, having a proportion of adults with college degrees higher than almost any other country. Over the last three decades, however, other countries have also recognized the relationship between postsecondary training and economic growth, and they have invested in higher education to the extent that many have eliminated the gap in educational attainment with the United States, and in some cases, have even exceeded American levels.

Figure 6.2 shows the proportion of the population in two age cohorts that has some form of postsecondary credential, including bachelor's degrees and

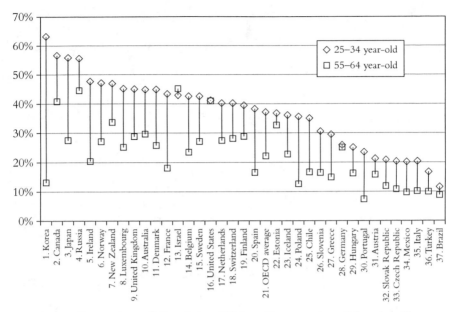

FIGURE 6.2 Proportion of Population With a Postsecondary Education Degree, 25–34-year-old and 55–64-year-old Age Cohorts
Source: Organisation for Economic Co-operation and Development (2010).

associate's (or two-year) degrees. In the United States, both age cohorts—the 25- to 34-year-olds and the 55- to 64-year-olds—have approximately the same attainment rate, 41%. Among the older cohort, the United States is surpassed only by Israel; among the younger cohort, 15 countries have rates greater than that of the United States. It is this trend—that other countries are making more progress in increasing postsecondary attainment rates than is our nation—that is the driving force behind the Obama administration's goal.

Postsecondary attainment rates are a function of two factors: (1) how many students enter college, and (2) how many persist to complete a degree. While there are some economic returns to those students who enter college and leave without a credential, the largest returns accrue to those who complete a degree (Carnevale, Rose, & Cheah, 2012). While the United States has long had relatively high college access rates, it is in this latter measure, persistence to degree attainment, where the United States has lagged behind the performance of other nations.

Figure 6.3 shows the postsecondary enrollment rates of students from five family-income quintiles over a 25-year period beginning in 1984. The rates shown are the proportion of each income group that enrolled in some form of postsecondary education within 12 months of high school graduation. The trend is positive; all groups increased their college entry rates during the period, and the lower-income groups gained more than the higher-income groups, helping to close the

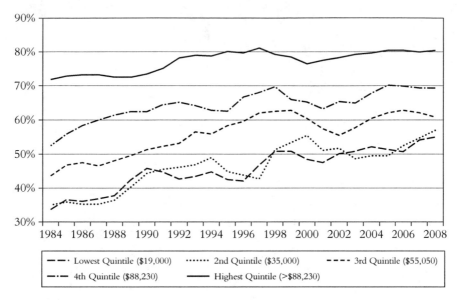

FIGURE 6.3 Postsecondary Enrollment Rates of Recent High School Graduates by Family Income, 1984–2008.
Note: Income limits of quintiles shown in parentheses.
Source: Baum, Ma, & Payea (2010).

gap in college participation—a goal, as noted earlier, of federal and state postsecondary policy. And these gains occurred in the face of tuition prices that rose far faster than did the ability of students and their families to pay (Heller, 2011b).

This good news masks other trends, however, that are detrimental to the goal of equality of postsecondary education opportunity. First, as Laura Perna and Elizabeth Kurban describe in their chapter, although lower-income students have seen faster gains in college enrollment, their rates still lag those of the highest-income group by 20 to 25 percentage points. Second, lower-income students are less likely to be enrolled in four-year institutions, and are also less likely to be enrolled in college full time—two characteristics of enrollment that have been shown to be critical to the goal of completing a bachelor's degree (Adelman, Daniel, & Berkovits, 2003; Wei & Horn, 2002). In the 2007–2008 academic year, while 54% of students from the top family-income quartile were enrolled full time in a four-year institution, only 33% of those in the bottom income quartile followed this enrollment pattern (Heller, 2012).

Lower-income students also stay enrolled in college and persist to completion at lower rates than do their higher-income peers. Research demonstrates that college access is not just a function of financial factors, but academic and social factors as well (Advisory Committee on Student Financial Assistance, 2001, 2002, 2006; Perna, 2010). So to understand the role that finances alone contribute to

TABLE 6.1 College Entry and Bachelor's Degree Attainment Rates by Academic and Socioeconomic Status Quartile, 1992 High School Graduates

			Socioeconomic Status	
			Lowest quartile	Highest quartile
Academic achievement, 8th-grade reading and math tests	Lowest quartile	Percent attending college by 1994	36	77
		Percent earning BA degree by 2000	7	27
	Highest quartile	Percent attending college by 1994	78	97
		Percent earning BA degree by 2000	43	77

Source: Heller (2012).

the access and attainment gaps, it is necessary to try to isolate these different conceptual factors.

One way to understand the role of finances is to examine the educational pathways of students who are similar in terms of one characteristic, such as academic performance, but differ in terms of another, such as financial resources. In an earlier study (Heller, 2012), I used data from a longitudinal survey of the U.S. Department of Education to conduct such an analysis. This survey, the National Education Longitudinal Study of 1988 (NELS:88), tracked a nationally representative cohort of students who were in the eighth grade in 1988, and whose normal high school graduation date would have been in 1992.

In order to separate the effect of academic factors from financial and social factors on the college access and completion decisions of high school graduates, I divided the students in the study into quartiles based on two measures: (1) their performance on reading and math achievement tests given to the students when they were in the eighth grade; and (2) their family's socioeconomic status, which is a composite of their family income and their parents' education and occupation. Table 6.1 shows the proportion entering college and completing a bachelor's degree in the top and bottom quartiles of each group.

Looking first at the students performing in the bottom quartile of academic achievement on the eighth grade reading and math tests, only 36% of the students from families in the bottom socioeconomic quartile entered college within two years of graduating high school, while 77% of their more well-off peers did. For the higher-achieving students, 78% of the students in the bottom quartile of socioeconomic status entered some form of postsecondary education, while 97% of those from high socioeconomic status families did.

What is striking about these numbers is they demonstrate that the odds of attending college were roughly the same—about 77% or 78%—if you were a high-achieving, yet poor, student, as they were if you were a lower-achieving, yet wealthier, student. Another way to compare these results is by noticing the roughly 20 percentage point gap in college entry between high-achieving, yet poor, students, compared to their more well-off peers. It is fair to conclude that a large proportion of this gap is due to the financial and social advantages that the students from the higher socioeconomic status families enjoy.

Turning to the measure of bachelor's degree attainment, we see that the gaps between the social classes are even greater than the gaps in college entry. Looking again at the higher-achieving students, the gap in attainment grows to 34 percentage points—43% for the lower-class students versus 77% for the higher-class students. This gap is an indication not just of the social and financial advantages of these higher social class students, but also a sign that these advantages persist and increase through students' college careers.

The impact of these advantages throughout the educational pipeline can be seen in Figure 6.4. Data from the NELS:88 survey were used here also to examine the attitudes and behavior of students from eighth grade through approximately age 26. The data in this figure were restricted to those students who were

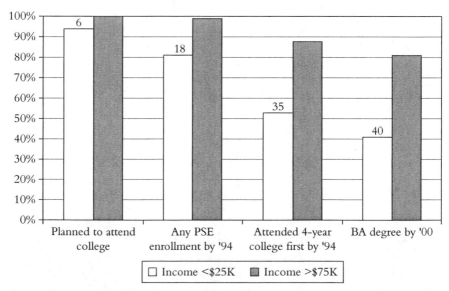

FIGURE 6.4 Proportion of Lower- and Upper-Income College-Qualified Students at Various Stages of the Educational Pipeline

Note: The numbers above the bars are the percentage point gaps between the two income groups.

Source: Heller (2012).

identified as being at least minimally qualified for entry into a four-year college or university. This identifier was based on the following student characteristics:

- Class rank in their senior year of high school
- Cumulative high school grade point average
- SAT or ACT test scores
- Score on the NELS:88 reading and math tests (National Center for Education Statistics, 2012)

This restriction allows us to compare students who have taken the minimal steps necessary in preparing for enrollment in a four-year postsecondary institution. These college-qualified students were then further restricted to those in two income groups: those with a family income during their eighth grade year of less than $25,000, and those from families with income above $75,000. This figure then provides another comparison of the impact of family finances on educational decision making.

The first pair of bars indicates the percentage of students in the two income groups who during the eighth grade indicated that they planned on attending college. Very high proportions of both groups of college-qualified eighth graders—94% for the poorer students and 100% of the wealthier students—indicated they planned on going to college after graduating from high school. By 1994, or two years after high school graduation, 99% of the upper-income students were enrolled in some form of postsecondary education, while 81% of the lower-income students were so enrolled.

Research has demonstrated that a critical factor in predicting whether a student will ever receive a bachelor's degree is initial postsecondary attendance at a four-year institution (Adelman, 2006; Heller, 2001). While some students who start their postsecondary careers at a community college are successful in transferring to a four-year institution and completing a bachelor's degree, the path to a bachelor's degree is easier for those starting at the four-year institution. In examining the initial college enrollment of the lower-income students in the NELS:88 survey, only 53% had their first postsecondary experience at a four-year institution—even though they had taken the steps necessary to qualify themselves for entry into one. Among their wealthier peers, 88% had their first experience in a four-year institution.

The final step in the educational pipeline shown in Figure 6.4 is the proportion who received a bachelor's degree by the year 2000, or within approximately eight years of high school graduation. The gap between the rich and poor students has grown once again, now to a level of 40 percentage points. Thus, Figure 6.4 demonstrates that the gaps in educational participation and attainment grow as the students move through the pipeline.

Trends in Tuition Prices and Financial Aid

As mentioned earlier, tuition prices in American universities have risen at rates far in excess of inflation or average incomes in the country over the last three decades.

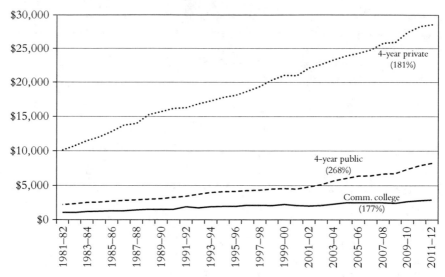

FIGURE 6.5 Changes in Tuition Prices by Sector (constant 2011 dollars)
Note: Increase over the period shown in parentheses.
Source: College Board (2011a).

Figure 6.5 shows this growth in constant dollars, after adjusting for inflation (based on the consumer price index). In each sector, average tuition prices grew by at least 177% above inflation over the three decades from 1981 to 2011, with the highest growth in the four-year public university sector, where prices increased from an average of $2,242 in 1981 (in constant 2011 dollars) to $8,244 in 2011. These are tuition prices alone, which do not include room and board charges.

While these rising prices affected all students attending college, the impact was not uniform across income groups. Family income, which determines how affordable tuition prices are, changed at varying rates for different groups during this period. Table 6.2 shows that families in the bottom quintile, or the bottom 20% of all families in the income distribution, saw their average income decrease by 4% in real terms between 1981 and 2010, and families in the middle income quintile saw growth of just 16%. At the other end of the income distribution, the top 1/20th of all families saw an increase of 83% in their average income. So the rising tuition prices shown above had the largest impact—decreasing affordability the most—for poorer families, although the tuition price increases in every sector far outstripped growth in income.

The reasons behind these tuition increases have been well documented (Clotfelter, 1996; Cunningham, Wellman, Clinedinst, & Merisotis, 2001; Ehrenberg, 2000; Heller, 2011b; Mumper, 2011). Increasing competition for star faculty, an arms race in student amenities, the need for more student services to meet the demands of an increasingly diverse student body, the use of technology—all have been substantiated as helping to drive increases in college costs and, thus, prices.

TABLE 6.2 Changes in Mean Family Income, 1981–2010 (constant 2010 dollars)

	First (bottom) quintile	Second quintile	Third quintile	Fourth quintile	Fifth (top) quintile	Top 5%
Mean income (1981)	$15,649	$34,030	$52,049	$73,076	$122,612	$171,330
Mean income (2010)	$14,991	$37,066	$60,363	$91,991	$187,395	$313,298
Percent change	−4	9	16	26	53	83

Source: U.S. Census Bureau (2012).

In the public sector, however, the primary driver of tuition price increases has been slow growth (or even cuts) in state appropriations. There is a very strong linkage between the change in state appropriations to higher education in a given state and the subsequent change in tuition prices at public sector institutions (Cunningham et al., 2001; Heller, 2004). A study of tuition price increases conducted by the U.S. Department of Education at the request of Congress in its passage of the 1998 reauthorization of the HEA concluded that, "For the public four-year institutions, the single most important factor associated with tuition increases was decreasing revenue from government appropriations, with state appropriations making up the majority of such revenue" (Cunningham et al., 2001, p. 132).

Tuition prices alone, of course, are not the only factor in determining what students pay to attend college. Undergraduate students in the 2010–2011 academic year received over $175 billion in financial aid, and some forms of financial aid have kept pace with increases in tuition prices (College Board, 2011a, 2011b). Figure 6.6 shows the change in major categories of financial aid as compared to increases in tuition prices over the last two decades. Tuition prices at four-year public universities more than doubled in real terms (discounting for inflation) during the period, while prices in private four-year institutions and community colleges increased 75% and 80%, respectively.

Figure 6.6 also shows the large increase in borrowing by students over the last 20 years. The increase in average borrowing in the federal student loan programs far outpaced the growth in grants or tuition prices, increasing 200% over the period. The impact of increases in the amounts that students were allowed to borrow in the federal loan programs, implemented in the 1992 and 2008 reauthorizations of the HEA, can clearly be seen in the higher slope of the curve in the years following those reauthorizations.

The good news from this chart is that the increase in average grants per student (federal, state, and institutional combined) outpaced the growth in tuition prices at private institutions and community colleges, and fell just below the growth in prices at public four-year universities. So grants have helped to cushion the impact of the increasing prices faced by students.

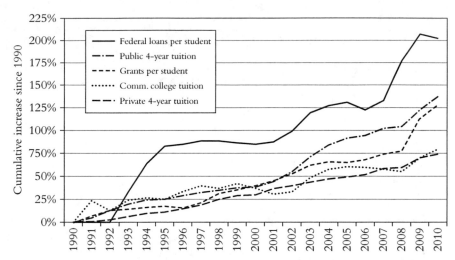

FIGURE 6.6 Change in Grants, Loans, and Tuition Prices for Undergraduate Students, 1990–2010 (constant 2010 dollars)

Note: Increase over the period shown in parentheses.

Source: College Board (2011a, 2011b).

But, the change in grant aid shown in Figure 6.6 masks an important trend that impacts access to and persistence in higher education for students from low- and moderate-income families. While historically most grant aid was provided based on the financial need of the student and her parents, in recent years there has been a shift toward providing more aid using merit criteria, rather than need (Heller, 2011a). In 1990, over 90% of all state grant dollars provided to undergraduate students were awarded through some form of means testing. By 2010, this proportion had been reduced to 70% (National Association of State Student Grant & Aid Programs, 2012).

A similar trend has occurred in how higher education institutions award their own grant aid. In the 1995–1996 academic year, 65% of all institutional grant dollars awarded to undergraduates were need-based grants; by the 2007–2008 year, the percentage of need-based grant awards dropped to 45% (author's calculations from National Center for Education Statistics, 2005, 2010).

Research on financial aid shows that merit grants, whether provided by state grant agencies or institutions, tend to be awarded disproportionately to wealthier students than are need-based grants, because of the more narrow targeting of the latter (Ehrenberg, Zhang, & Levin, 2005; Heller & Marin, 2002, 2004). The reason for this difference is that the measures typically used as the criteria for awarding merit grants—most often grades or standardized test scores—are highly correlated with income.

Because of this relationship between academic merit and social class, students from poorer families are less likely to be awarded merit grants. In an earlier study

(Heller, 2011a), I analyzed the proportion of students in different groups receiving state and institutional need-based and merit grants. The study found that while students in the bottom half of the income distribution were much more likely to receive need-based grants—because the target population is the lower-income student—students from the top half of the income distribution were more likely to be awarded merit grants.

Improving the Effectiveness of Financial Aid to Promote College Access

The hundreds of studies[2] that have been conducted on financial aid provide a very clear picture of the impact of financial aid on the college participation of low- and moderate-income students. The following conclusions may be drawn from this body of research:

- Lower-income students are more sensitive to tuition prices and are more likely to decide not to enroll in college when faced with price increases than are their wealthier peers (Heller, 1997).
- Grants have been shown to be much more effective in promoting college participation than are student loans. While loans have become an important tool for those from middle- and upper-income families, poorer students have been shown to be more averse to borrowing to finance their college education. They instead will often choose to enroll only part time and work more hours, behaviors that we know are detrimental to completing a bachelor's degree program. Thus, grant aid is particularly critical for ensuring access to and progress through postsecondary education for lower-income students (Baum et al., 2008).
- There is an asymmetry between increases in tuition prices and concomitant increases in grant aid. In other words, a $1,000 increase in the tuition price is more likely to have a negative impact on the enrollment decision of a poor student, even if the increase is accompanied by a $1,000 increase in grant aid. This is because low-income students base their college-going decisions primarily on the posted sticker price of college, rather than the net price after grants (Heller, 1999).

This information provides guidance in crafting principles for the design of financial aid policies to promote college access and success for poorer students, which in turn will help close the gap in higher education participation between the income groups. If the United States is to achieve the goal of regaining the leadership in educational attainment among developed countries, we are going to have to focus attention and energy on the population of students—those from poor and moderate-income families—who are on the margins of going to college and staying enrolled once there.

Institutions need to hold poorer students harmless when tuition prices are raised. Tuition price increases are a fact of life. As shown in Figure 6.5, prices have increased steadily over the last three decades, and while the rate of change may vary, there is little hope that prices will be reduced, even in real terms. Thus, as prices increase, poorer students need to be protected so that their ability to enroll and persist in college is not diminished even further.

Short of implementing income-based pricing schemes, where the sticker price students pay would be based on their ability to pay—a system that no institution has evidently been willing to explore—the best mechanism to ensure these students can afford college is to increase their grant aid as tuition prices rise. Well-targeted grant aid awarded based on the ability of students and their families to pay for college has been shown to be the best form of financial aid to help offset price increases (Baum et al., 2008).

Federal, state, and institutional financial aid programs need to be simple to understand, easily accessible, and provide information early enough in students' lives so that they and their families can make good decisions about preparing for college both financially as well as academically. Much has been written about the complexity of the financial aid system in our country, and how difficult it is for students to gather good information about aid and apply for it (Advisory Committee on Student Financial Assistance, 2005; Dynarski & Scott-Clayton, 2008; Scott-Clayton & Dynarski, 2007). While the sticker price of college is readily accessible through viewbooks, college websites, and U.S. Department of Education websites, information about the net prices students will pay is much harder to come by. The Free Application for Federal Student Aid (FAFSA) is still a complex process containing well over 100 questions that form the gateway to all federal financial aid, as well as most state and institutional aid. For students who are the first in their family to go to college, completing the FAFSA can be a daunting task.

One of the biggest problems is that most students do not find out to any degree of certainty exactly how much it will cost them to attend college until the latter half of their senior year—after they have applied to college, been admitted, and been provided with a financial aid offer. Thus, many poorer students may be discouraged earlier in their lives from even thinking about going to college if all they can respond to are sticker prices.

Some steps have been taken to try to address this issue. As Laura Perna and Elizabeth Kurban discuss in their chapter, the last reauthorization of the HEA, passed by Congress and signed into law by former President George Bush in 2008, mandated that colleges create websites that allow students to receive an estimate of their net cost of college based on financial characteristics of themselves and their families. Although a step in the right direction, there are still limitations to the accuracy of this information, because the regulations only require that colleges include in these net price calculators those grant programs that are mandatory or entitlements. In addition, the calculators often include only estimates, if any information at all, for state grants. And the websites still require students to input much of the same information that they need to include on their FAFSA, so the process of getting the financial aid estimate can be quite complex (The Institute for College Access and Success, 2011).

Approximately 50 colleges in recent years have implemented "no-loan" financial aid policies, where they guarantee that students from below a designated income level will be able to attend the institution and receive enough grant aid (from federal, state, and institutional sources) to allow them to graduate without having to incur any borrowing. While each university's program has somewhat different characteristics, they show some promise in helping to promote college access and success for lower-income students, as long as the programs can be proactively and effectively communicated to the target population (Perna, Lundy-Wagner, Yee, Brill, & Tadal, 2011).

Another promising strategy in helping to overcome the limitations of the current financial aid system is the early financial aid commitment program. Many of these are privately run programs based on the model developed by businessman Eugene Lang and his I Have a Dream Foundation, in which individuals or organizations "adopt" a class of elementary or middle school students with the promise of paying for their college educations ("I Have a Dream" Foundation, 2012). More recently, foundations and other organizations in some cities, including Kalamazoo, Michigan, and Pittsburgh, Pennsylvania, have provided similar guarantees of funding for college for all graduates of the local public schools.

Although there have been few rigorous evaluations of these private programs, some of their principles have been included in the design of state programs like the Indiana 21st Century Scholars program and the Oklahoma Promise program (Heller, 2006). In these two, students as early as the 7th grade who meet income eligibility requirements are provided with a promise of full tuition payment at a public institution in their state when they graduate from high school and enroll in college. Evaluations show that the Indiana program has had a positive impact on the college participation of lower-income students in that state (St. John, 2004, 2011; St. John, Musoba, Simmons, & Chung, 2002). Other states should consider implementing programs similar to Indiana's and Oklahoma's, in order to provide students with a guarantee of funding for college earlier in their careers.

Federal, state, and institutional grant programs need to be focused on helping financially needy students. As described earlier, over the last two decades, state and institutional grant programs have seen a shift toward more grants being awarded without consideration of financial need. While the federal government has largely resisted this trend, states and institutions are also a critical source of grant aid for students. In the 2010–2011 academic year, federal Pell grants provided $34.8 billion to undergraduates, while states and institutions together awarded $38.8 billion (College Board, 2011b). Thus, in order to ensure that the $75 billion in grants are used most effectively to promote increased postsecondary participation and attainment, this aid needs to be focused on students who would not be able to enroll and persist in higher education—or be able to afford only a community college—without it.

A recent report on state grant programs from the Brookings Institution recommended that

> To maximize the impact of their financial aid programs, states should do a better job of targeting aid dollars at students whose potential to succeed is most constrained by limited resources. Students whose options are constrained by limited resources are most likely to be affected by state grant awards—in terms of both their ability to attend college and the likelihood that they will graduate. (Baum et al., 2012, p. 2)

As noted earlier, almost 30% of state grant dollars provided to undergraduate students are made without consideration of financial need; this money goes disproportionately to higher-income students. Refocusing these $2.6 billion on students with financial need will help promote college access and persistence for this underrepresented group of students.

A disproportionate number of institutional grants are also being awarded without means testing. In an earlier study, Callender and I (2010) examined the distribution of institutional grant dollars by income group, using data from the National Postsecondary Student Aid Study of 2008. We found that 63% of institutional merit-grant awards were going to students in the top half of the income distribution, that is, those from families with incomes above $67,755, in 2006. As with state merit grants, the over $7 billion being awarded to students without consideration of their financial aid would be better spent on financially needy students, if we are to hold higher education institutions accountable for helping to achieve the national goal of increasing postsecondary educational attainment.

Conclusion

Gaps in college participation between rich and poor students in the United States have persisted over the five decades since the passage of the HEA, even though one of the primary goals of the act was to eliminate financial barriers to postsecondary education. These gaps have persisted even in the face of almost $2.5 *trillion* in financial aid provided to students since passage of that legislation (College Board, 2011b). Research has shown that these gaps are due in part to academic and social factors, and not just to financial barriers (Baum et al., 2008; Perna & Kurban, this volume). But we know that finances do pose important obstacles, particularly as tuition prices continue to rise at rates far outpacing the ability of families to pay for postsecondary education. These gaps prevent students from low- and moderate-income families from reaping the benefits of a college degree, and they also rob the nation of the social benefits that accrue from higher levels of postsecondary attainment.

Research also informs us which financial aid policies and programs are most effective in helping students from low- and moderate-income families attend college and stay enrolled. It is not a lack of knowledge that prohibits us from helping to address the financial barriers contributing to the gaps in college participation. We know what kinds of programs will help promote the college attendance of these students. Rather, a political failure prevents us from putting these policies and programs into place and funding them at the levels necessary to support poorer students. In order to return the nation to worldwide leadership in postsecondary education attainment, the nation will have to muster the political will to focus financial aid resources on the most needy students.

Notes

1. For articulation of the economic theory behind private returns to education, see Becker (1993) and Schultz (1963). For information about the social returns, see Bowen (1977).
2. For an overview of this literature through the years, see Baum et al. (2008), Heller (1997), Jackson and Weathersby (1975), Kim (2010), and Leslie and Brinkman (1987).

References

Adelman, C. (2006). *The toolbox revisited: Paths to degree completion from high school through college.* Washington, DC: U.S. Department of Education, Office of Vocational and Adult Education.

Adelman, C., Daniel, B., & Berkovits, I. (2003). *Postsecondary attainment, attendance, curriculum, and performance: Selected results from the NELS:88/2000 Postsecondary Education Transcript Study.* Washington, DC: U.S. Department of Education, National Center for Education Statistics.

Advisory Committee on Student Financial Assistance. (2001). *Access denied: Restoring the nation's commitment to equal educational opportunity.* Washington, DC: Author.

Advisory Committee on Student Financial Assistance. (2002). *Empty promises: The myth of college access in America.* Washington, DC: Author.

Advisory Committee on Student Financial Assistance. (2005). *The student aid gauntlet: Making access to college simple and certain.* Washington, DC: Author.

Advisory Committee on Student Financial Assistance. (2006). *Mortgaging our future: How financial barriers to college undercut America's global competitiveness.* Washington, DC: Author.

Baum, S., Breneman, D.W., Chingos, M.M., Ehrenberg, R.G., Fowler, P., Hayek, J., . . . Whitehurst, G.R. (2012). *Beyond need and merit: Strengthening state grant programs.* Washington, DC: Brown Center on Education Policy at the Brookings Institution.

Baum, S., Ma, J., & Payea, K. (2010). *Education pays 2010: The benefits of higher education for individuals and society.* New York, NY: College Board.

Baum, S., McPherson, M., & Steele, P. (Eds.). (2008). *The effectiveness of student aid policies: What the research tells us.* New York, NY: The College Board.

Becker, G.S. (1993). *Human capital: A theoretical and empirical analysis with special reference to education* (3rd ed.). Chicago, IL: University of Chicago Press.

Bowen, H. (1977). *Investment in learning: The individual and social value of American higher education.* San Francisco, CA: Jossey-Bass Publishers, Inc.

Carnevale, A.P., Rose, S.J., & Cheah, B. (2012). *The college payoff: Education, occupations, lifetime earnings.* Washington, DC: The Georgetown University Center on Education and the Workforce.

Clotfelter, C.T. (1996). *Buying the best: Cost escalation in elite higher education.* Princeton, NJ: Princeton University Press.

College Board. (2011a). *Trends in college pricing, 2011.* Washington, DC: Author.

College Board. (2011b). *Trends in student aid, 2011.* Washington, DC: Author.

Cunningham, A.F., Wellman, J.V., Clinedinst, M.E., & Merisotis, J.P. (2001). *Study of college costs and prices, 1988–89 to 1997–98, Volume 1.* Washington, DC: U.S. Department of Education, National Center for Education Statistics.

Dynarski, S., & Scott-Clayton, J.E. (2008). *Complexity and targeting in federal student aid: A quantitative analysis.* Cambridge, MA: The National Bureau of Economic Research.

Ehrenberg, R.G. (2000). *Tuition rising: Why college costs so much.* Cambridge, MA: Harvard University Press.

Ehrenberg, R.G., Zhang, L., & Levin, J.M. (2005). *Crafting a class: The trade off between merit scholarships and enrolling lower-income students.* Cambridge, MA: National Bureau of Economic Research.

Goldin, C., & Katz, L.F. (2008). *The race between education and technology.* Cambridge, MA: Belknap Press of Harvard University Press.

Heller, D.E. (1997). Student price response in higher education: An update to Leslie and Brinkman. *Journal of Higher Education, 68*(6), 624–659.

Heller, D.E. (1999). The effects of tuition and state financial aid on public college enrollment. *The Review of Higher Education, 23*(1), 65–89.

Heller, D.E. (2001). *Debts and decisions: Student loans and their relationship to career and graduate school choices.* Indianapolis, IN: New Agenda Series, Lumina Foundation for Education.

Heller, D.E. (2004, April). *State funding for higher education: The impact on college access.* Paper presented at the Symposium on Financing Higher Education, Illinois State University, Normal, IL.

Heller, D.E. (2006). Early commitment of financial aid eligibility. *American Behavioral Scientist, 49*(12), 1719–1738.

Heller, D.E. (2011a). The financial aid picture: Realism, surrealism, or cubism? In J.C. Smart & M.B. Paulsen (Eds.), *Higher education: Handbook of theory and research, Volume 26* (pp. 125–160). New York, NY: Springer.

Heller, D.E. (2011b). Trends in the affordability of public colleges and universities: The contradiction of increasing prices and increasing enrollment. In D.E. Heller (Ed.), *The states and public higher education policy: Affordability, access, and accountability* (2nd ed., pp. 13–36). Baltimore, MD: The Johns Hopkins University Press.

Heller, D.E. (2012, May). *The role of finances in postsecondary access and success.* Paper presented at the U.S. Department of Education, Advisory Committee on Student Financial Assistance, East Lansing, MI.

Heller, D.E., & Callender, C. (2010, November). *Institutional grant aid in the United States and England: A comparative analysis.* Paper presented at the annual conference of the Association for the Study of Higher Education, Indianapolis, IN.

Heller, D.E., & Marin, P. (Eds.). (2002). *Who should we help? The negative social consequences of merit scholarships.* Cambridge, MA: The Civil Rights Project at Harvard University.

Heller, D.E., & Marin, P. (Eds.). (2004). *State merit scholarship programs and racial inequality.* Cambridge, MA: The Civil Rights Project at Harvard University.

Higher Education Act of 1965, Pub. L. No. 89–329. (1965).

"I Have a Dream" Foundation. (2012). *About us.* Retrieved from http://www.ihaveadream foundation.org/html/about_us.htm

Jackson, G.A., & Weathersby, G.B. (1975). Individual demand for higher education. *Journal of Higher Education, 46*(6), 623–652.

Kim, J. (2010). The effect of prices on postsecondary access: An update to Heller. *Higher Education in Review,* 7, 23–46.

Leslie, L.L., & Brinkman, P.T. (1987). Student price response in higher education. *Journal of Higher Education, 58*(2), 181–204.

Leslie, L.L., & Brinkman, P.T. (1988). *The economic value of higher education.* New York, NY: American Council on Education/Macmillan Publishing.

Levy, F., & Murnane, R.J. (1992). U.S. earnings levels and earnings inequality: A review of recent trends and proposed explanations. *Journal of Economic Literature, 30,* 1333–1381.

Mumper, M. (2011). The continuing paradox of public college tuition inflation. In D.E. Heller (Ed.), *The states and public higher education policy: Affordability, access, and accountability* (2nd ed., pp. 37–60). Baltimore, MD: The Johns Hopkins University Press.

Murnane, R.J., Willett, J.B., & Levy, F. (1995). The growing importance of cognitive skills in wage determination. *Review of Economics and Statistics, 77*(2), 251–266.

National Association of State Student Grant & Aid Programs. (2012). *NASSGAP 42nd annual survey report on state-sponsored student financial aid 2010–2011 academic year.* Washington, DC: Author.

National Center for Education Statistics. (2005). National Postsecondary Student Aid Study 1995–1996 data analysis system. Retrieved from http://nces.ed.gov/dasol/

National Center for Education Statistics. (2010). National Postsecondary Student Aid Study 2007–2008 data analysis system. Retrieved from http://nces.ed.gov/dasol/

National Center for Education Statistics. (2012). National Educational Longitudinal Study:1988 data analysis system. Retrieved from http://nces.ed.gov/dasol/

Organisation for Economic Co-operation and Development (OECD). (2010). *Education at a Glance 2010.* Paris, France: Author.

Perna, L., Lundy-Wagner, V., Yee, A., Brill, L., & Tadal, T. (2011). Showing them the money: The role of institutional financial aid policies and communication strategies in attracting low-income students. In A. Kezar (Ed.), *Recognizing and serving low-income students in higher education: An examination of institutional policies, practices, and culture* (pp. 72–96). New York, NY: Routledge.

Perna, L.W. (2010). Toward a more complete understanding of the role of financial aid in promoting college enrollment: The importance of context. In J.C. Smart (Ed.), *Higher education: Handbook of theory and research* (pp. 129–179). New York, NY: Springer.

President's Commission on Higher Education. (1947). *Higher education for American democracy.* New York, NY: Harper & Brothers.

Schultz, T.W. (1963). *The economic value of education.* New York, NY: Columbia University Press.

Scott-Clayton, J., & Dynarski, S.M. (2007). *College grants on a postcard: A proposal for simple and predictable federal student aid.* Washington, DC: Brookings Institution.

St. John, E.P. (2004). The impact of financial aid guarantees on enrollment and persistence: Evidence from research on Indiana's Twenty-first Century Scholars and Washington State Achievers Programs. In D.E. Heller & P. Marin (Eds.), *State merit scholarship programs and racial inequality* (pp. 123–140). Cambridge, MA: The Civil Rights Project at Harvard University.

St. John, E.P. (2011). Lessons learned from Indiana's Twenty-first Century Scholars Program: Toward a comprehensive approach to improving college preparation and access for low-income students. In A. Kezar (Ed.), *Recognizing and serving low-income students in higher education: An examination of institutional policies, practices, and culture* (pp. 72–96). New York, NY: Routledge.

St. John, E.P., Musoba, G.D., Simmons, A.B., & Chung, C.G. (2002). *Meeting the access challenge: Indiana's Twenty-first Century Scholars program.* Indianapolis, IN: New Agenda Series, Lumina Foundation for Education.

The Institute for College Access and Success. (2011, March). *Adding it all up: An early look at net price calculators.* Oakland, CA: Author.

U.S. Census Bureau. (2012). *Table F-3: Mean income received by each fifth and top 5 percent of families, all races: 1966 to 2010* [Data file]. Retrieved from http://www.census.gov/hhes/www/income/data/historical/families/2010/F03AR_2010.xls

Wei, C.C., & Horn, L. (2002). *Persistence and attainment of beginning students with Pell grants.* Washington, DC: U.S. Department of Education, National Center for Education Statistics.

7

THE POTENTIAL OF COMMUNITY COLLEGES TO INCREASE BACHELOR'S DEGREE ATTAINMENT RATES

Tatiana Melguizo, Gregory Kienzl, and Holly Kosiewicz

Like the students who attend them, community colleges are complex and multifaceted. They offer a multitude of programs, including vocational training, continuing and adult education, and academic preparation for transfer to a four-year institution (Cohen & Brawer, 1987, 2009). For this reason, some scholars have argued that community colleges serve contradictory functions (Dougherty, 1997; Goldrick-Rab, 2010; Kane & Rouse, 1995), which has fueled a long-standing debate about the role they should serve in higher education as well as their effectiveness (Dougherty, 1997). Both sides of this debate, however, agree that national completion goals, as urged by the Obama administration and several prominent foundations, cannot be achieved without these institutions dramatically ramping up their success efforts, especially among low-income students and racial/ethnic minorities.

Students from low-income and minority backgrounds have been and will continue to start at community colleges (Carnevale & Strohl, 2010), yet between 60% and 70% indicate a desire to earn a bachelor's degree (Kienzl, Wesaw, & Kumar, 2011). Despite these educational expectations, at best only one in four community college students from low-income or minority backgrounds successfully transfer to a four-year institution (Advisory Committee on Student Financial Assistance [ACSFA], 2012; Dougherty & Kienzl, 2006; Melguizo & Dowd, 2009; Kienzl et al., 2011; Lee, Mackie-Lewis, & Marks, 1993; Peter & Forrest-Cataldi, 2005), meaning that most of these students are not achieving their educational goals. Therefore, not only does the definition of educational success need to be expanded, the entire concept of *transfer*—whereby community college students make timely academic progress, transition seamlessly to a four-year institution, and ultimately attain a bachelor's degree—requires rethinking.

Researchers and policymakers need to gain a better understanding of how individual and institutional factors, as well as state- and federal-level policies, can promote transfer and success, particularly for underserved students. In this chapter, we offer a new conceptual framework of transfer that extends Tinto's traditional model[1] focused on the academic and social integration of students (Tinto, 1993). Our new framework includes the following success indicators:

- Community college students' early enrollment behavior and academic habitus;
- Institutions' inclination and provisions to promote and support transfer students; and
- State- and federal-level commitment to more comprehensive articulation policies.

Our chapter reviews several promising programs and policies that have been or are currently being developed to satisfy the above indicators. We conclude this chapter by offering recommendations to federal and state policymakers and community college administrators for streamlining the transfer pathway and increasing baccalaureate degree rates.

A New Way of Explaining Transfer

The new conceptual framework (see Figure 7.1) addresses several limitations of Tinto's (1993) Student Integration Model, which has traditionally been used to understand student persistence and departure. Our Multi-Dimensional Transfer Model identifies three main factors for improving success early in students' collegiate experience and, consequently, increasing the likelihood of transfer: (1) meeting the academic and social demands of college, (2) increasing access to information and financial resources needed for seamless transfer, and (3) better aligning educational and organizational policies. Based on a review of a vast and diverse array of literature that has rigorously tested the relationship between student success and individual, institutional, and policy-level characteristics, our model focuses primarily on studies of the factors that led to greater success among students of color in order to identify steps that institutions and states can take to produce more equitable outcomes (Dowd, 2007).

Meeting the Academic and Social Demands of College

Recognizing, valuing and serving a diverse student body. On the whole, students who attend community college are different from students who enroll directly in four-year universities or colleges. A community college student is more likely to be older, represent an ethnic or racial minority, and come from a low-income family compared to a traditional four-year student (Horn & Neville, 2006). Community college students also tend to lead their lives independently of their parents' support (Horn & Neville, 2006). Consequently, the majority work full time and attend community college on a part-time basis (Horn & Neville, 2006). They also

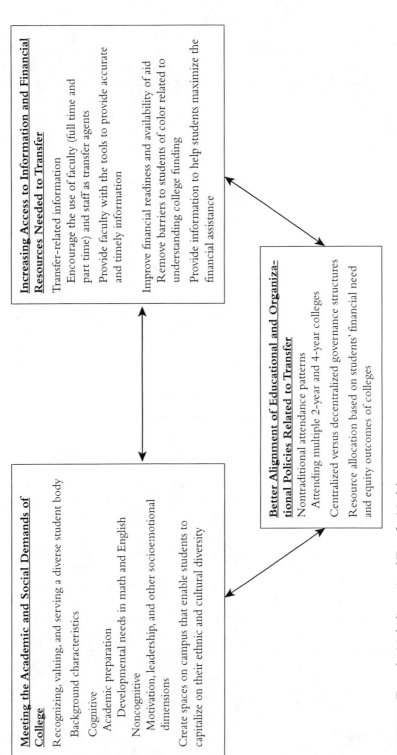

FIGURE 7.1 Toward a Multidimensional Transfer Model

exhibit lower levels of academic preparation than students who attend a four-year institution (Cohen & Brawer, 2009), with recent figures showing that 60% place into developmental education (National Center for Public Policy and Higher Education, 2010).

Evidence has consistently shown the African American and Latino students who enter community college transfer at lower rates than their White and Asian counterparts (Dougherty & Kienzl, 2006; Lee et al., 1993; Wassmer, Moore, & Shulock, 2004). However, Dougherty and Kienzl (2006) found that disparities in transfer rates among Latino, African American, and White students become insignificant after controlling for gender, age, and, especially, socioeconomic status. These results suggest that existing ethnic disparities in transfer rates may be rooted in differences in income, occupations, and rates of employment. Being from a low-income background and living in areas of limited employment options makes paying the cost of attending college more difficult for these students and their families.

Research also suggests that students who are older, have children, work at least part time, and lack U.S. citizenship also have a more difficult time transferring to four-year institutions than students who lack these characteristics (Roksa & Calcagno, 2010; Surette, 2001). Compared with traditional full-time students, Bean and Metzner (1985) suggest that older students have a greater responsibility juggling work and family life with school, which may subtract time from meeting the demands of college. Undocumented students experience other challenges: they are ineligible to receive federal financial aid, and, in the majority of states, state aid as well (Olivas, 2009); undocumented students face significant economic barriers paying for college even though many receive in-state tuition (Abrego, 2006; Olivas, 2009).

In terms of gender differences, recent evidence suggests that females are now as likely to transfer to a four-year institution as males (Dougherty & Kienzl, 2006; Hagedorn, Cypers, & Lester, 2008; Roksa & Calcagno, 2010). Dougherty and Kienzl (2006) suggest that initiatives aimed at narrowing the gender gap in the 1980s and 1990s may have contributed to this temporal shift. Many community college students of both genders enroll in multiple two-year institutions (Andrews, Ling, & Lovenheim, 2012; Goldrick-Rab, 2010), which compounds the barriers they face in terms of familial responsibilities and financial obstacles. There is a need for more research specifically testing the effects of multiple institutional pathways on various educational outcomes, including transfer.

As noted in our introduction, many community college students express a desire to transfer to a four-year institution. Yet a sizable proportion of these students are ill prepared—academically and socially—for the demands of college. What follows is an overview of academic preparation levels among community college students, as well as the postsecondary academic services that foster their success.

Academic preparation of community college students. The chance that community college students will reach their transfer goal depends largely on their course-taking patterns and academic performance in high school (Adelman, 2006; Greene & Forster, 2003; Morgan, 2005; Roderick, Nagaoka, & Coca, 2009). Multiple studies have shown that academically weaker community college students have a lower probability of transferring upward (Adelman, 1999; Calcagno, Crosta, Bailey, & Jenkins, 2007; Dougherty & Kienzl, 2006; Surette, 2001; Wang, 2010). For example, using administrative data from Florida, Roksa and Calcagno (2008) find that, after including individual-level controls, academically under-prepared students were roughly 52% less likely to transfer upward than their academically prepared counterparts.

As other chapters in this volume describe (e.g., Long & Boatman), community colleges make extensive use of developmental education to ensure that students can meet the academic rigors of college. Most studies have found that, for students at the margin, developmental education has a detrimental effect on short- and long-term student success (Bettinger & Long, 2009; Boatman, 2012; Calcagno & Long, 2008; Martorell & McFarlin, 2011; Scott-Clayton & Rodriguez, 2012). On the other hand, in a recent study across seven colleges of the Los Angeles Community College District, Melguizo and colleagues (2012a) found that observed impacts of the complete developmental math sequence (i.e., arithmetic, pre-algebra, elementary algebra, and intermediate algebra) differ by course level and across community colleges.[2] Therefore, a first step in increasing transfer rates involves revising current developmental math sequences, as well as the assessment and placement policies, and providing resources to colleges for training both full- and part-time faculty in program implementation (e.g., acceleration, modularization) and pedagogical strategies (e.g., project-based learning) that have shown promise for improving success in developmental education.

The role of noncognitive and campus climate. Despite the importance of academic preparation, research has consistently shown that variance in college student success is not fully explained by test scores, high school GPA, and other measures of previous academic performance or experience (Breland, 1998; Kuh, Kinzie, Schuh, Whitt, & Associates, 2010; Levin, 2011; Sedlacek, 2004). Recognizing these variations in outcomes, researchers have pointed to noncognitive factors as important determinants of success (Levin, 2011; Sedlacek, 2004). This strand of research attempts to measure the intuitively compelling idea that good problem-solving skills and coping mechanisms may help students meet the academic and social demands of college (Roderick et al., 2009).

Studies in educational psychology have, for example, generally shown that students who are motivated and possess a positive self-concept, high self-efficacy, and developed self-regulation are more likely to succeed in elementary and secondary school (Schunk, 2003). Studies examining college persistence and completion have also found that such noncognitive factors are significant predictors of success (Melguizo, 2010; Wang, 2010). In particular, Tracey and Sedlacek (1987) found that noncognitive factors, but not high school GPA, helped to explain persistence for African American students.

On the whole, very few studies have examined the effects of noncognitive factors on the probability of transfer; however, few available studies have shown small, but positive effects. Using National Education Longitudinal Study of 1988 (NELS) and Postsecondary Education Transcript Study (PETS) data, Wang (2010) found that a one-point increase on a scale measuring self-concept increased the probability of transfer by 2%. Employing individual-level data from the Gates Millennium Scholars program, Melguizo (2010) observed that a one-point increase on a scale measuring leadership skills produced a 2% increase in the likelihood of obtaining a bachelor's degree within six years. Even though the practical significance is markedly low, these results suggest that students who exhibit these characteristics may be more resilient in handling the academic and social demands of college. These findings also suggest that incorporating noncognitive variables into the assessment and placement process as well as the curriculum (i.e., success skills courses) is particularly important for promoting success of students of color.

Case studies of community colleges that exhibit higher than predicted rates of success for students of color show that these schools have created environments that appreciate diverse cultures (Gándara, Alvarado, Driscoll, & Orfield, 2012; Jenkins et al., 2006). In this sense, students who are able to establish a sense of identification and belonging within their community college environments may have a better chance at success than students who do not. Ethnic student organizations, like UMOJA and MECHA (Movimiento Estudiantil Chicano de Aztlán), can serve an important role in improving success by helping students of color develop strong ties with other members of their cultural community in college.

In summary, the literature suggests that academic preparation is one of the main obstacles toward transferring, and that noncognitive factors have the potential to play an important role in the transfer process. Evidence also suggests that students of color transfer at higher rates when they attend institutions that recognize and value the cultural diversity of the populations that they serve. This finding suggests that programs developed to promote transfer should be culturally sensitive to the populations served.

Increasing Access to Information and Financial Resources Needed for Transfer

Providing students with relevant and timely information on planning for transfer, especially the additional financial cost of attending a four-year institution, is another important strategy for increasing transfer rates among community college students. As Adelman (2005) found, a sizable percentage is not taking the necessary steps to transfer in a timely manner. This section identifies ways that community colleges can minimize information barriers that prevent transfer to a four-year institution.

Better use of faculty and administrators. Historically, research suggests that students who have positive and sustained contact with faculty experience an academic advantage in a wide range of educational outcomes over those who do not

(Pascarella & Terenzini, 2005; Strauss & Terenzini, 2007). Other research suggests that administrators, especially those who work in support services, also possess critical practical information that can help students navigate the various challenges higher education presents (Kuh et al., 2010). A number of case studies conducted at selective colleges and universities by Dowd and associates found that frequent interaction with students makes faculty and staff important players in helping students acquire the knowledge needed to transfer (Dowd et al., 2006).

Yet little empirical research focused on the impacts of community college faculty or student support administrators on student persistence and completion (Goldrick-Rab, 2010). The research gap on faculty is particularly worrisome given that part-time instructors, who form the core of community college faculty (Jacoby, 2006), work in conditions that could impair their effectiveness as agents for promoting transfer. A number of studies show that part-time faculty frequently lack access to office space, computers, and professional development opportunities, which undoubtedly limits their time with students and their support of students who wish to transfer (Ellison, 2002; Jacoby, 2006; Wallin, 2004).

Research on four-year colleges suggests that part-time faculty have a negative effect on student success (Bettinger & Long, 2006; Ehrenberg & Zhang, 2005; Jacoby, 2006). Ehrenberg and Zhang (2005) found that a 10% increase in part-time faculty decreases the graduation rate by nearly 3%. Similarly, Bettinger and Long (2006) found that students who attended Ohio four-year public institutions were less likely to persist after the first year of college if most of their instructors were adjuncts. One study focused on two-year colleges revealed that an increase in students' exposure to part-time faculty reduced the likelihood that they would transfer upward, or even obtain an associate's degree (Eagan & Jaeger, 2009). These observed impacts likely result from a combination of factors, including the quality of teaching students receive and limited opportunities for the dissemination of practical information on transfer from faculty (Dowd, 2011).

Ideally interactions with faculty would be only one source of information on how to plan for transfer. College counselors and other support services that exist on many community college campuses should also provide this information. However, the effectiveness of counselors to help with transfer is called into question by the fact that the ratio of counselors to students is low at community colleges (Grubb, 2006).[3] Incorporating some of this crucial information into the curriculum (e.g., first-year study skills courses) may alleviate this problem. This strategy also formalizes the role of the faculty as providers of information.

In addition to the limited availability of counselors, existing scholarship demonstrates little evidence of the role of student support services in promoting upward transfer for community college students. Jacobs, Cutright, Niebling, Simon, and Marling (2010) identified best practices in promoting transfer among community college students enrolled at Texas higher education institutions. Some of the most innovative student services approaches included offering community college students privileges at four-year institutions, such as access to the library and events, as well as specific advisement to new students about the importance of placement and course selection.

For the most part, higher education scholars have not evaluated the effectiveness of academic advising, counseling, or transfer centers in disseminating the kinds of information students need to transfer, including the types of courses required for transfer, details of articulation agreements between two-year and four-year colleges, and the financial costs associated with transfer (Melguizo, Hagedorn, & Cypers, 2008). To date, only one known study has rigorously evaluated the impact of student support services. A 2010 study by the U.S. Department of Education found that federally and state-funded student support service programs had been successful in helping students persist after the first year of college, but unsuccessful in encouraging students to transfer to a four-year institution (U.S. Department of Education, 2010). Incorporating transfer-related information in support service programs would certainly pay dividends.

Improving financial readiness and availability of aid. Many students choose community colleges over four-year institutions because the cost to attend is lower. The College Board's 2011 *Trends in College Pricing* reports that the average tuition and fees at public two-year institutions was $2,963 per year compared with $6,604 at public baccalaureate degree-granting institutions. Tuition and fees were highest at private doctoral universities, averaging approximately $35,000 (College Board, 2011). For many students, attending a four-year institution is not perceived as a financially viable option.

However, some research shows that many of these perceptions are based on incomplete information about college pricing and financial aid (Grodsky & Jones, 2004; Perna, 2004). Lack of awareness about paying for college is particularly acute for students of color and their families (Gloria & Segura-Herrera, 2004; Grodsky & Jones, 2004; Horn, Chen, & Chapman, 2003). Zarate and Pachon (2006) found that the majority of college-age Latino students whom they surveyed overestimated the cost of attending college at the University of California and California State University systems. They also found that just over half of college-age Latinos who did not attend college were unfamiliar with Cal Grants—California's state grant program for higher education—compared with 85% of their college-going counterparts. Providing adequate information on different types of aid to finance college for different student groups may produce higher transfer rates. H&R Block's program to help low-income families complete the Free Application for Federal Student Aid (FAFSA) shows potential in improving transfer rates (Bettinger, Long, Oreopolous, & Sanbonmatsu, 2009) because it highlights the student aid resources available to defray the higher cost of four-year colleges.

Students who are particularly debt averse may also perceive starting at a community college as an effective way to minimize the cost of obtaining a four-year degree. Even though the federal government has taken an active role in offering subsidized and unsubsidized loans to students whose institutions cannot cover their cost of attendance, some evidence suggests that this type of aid may not be the most effective mechanism in broadening higher education access to and increasing retention of nontraditional students. Perna (2000) found that financial aid in the form of loans deters African American students from enrolling in a four-year institution. Similarly, Kim, DesJardins, and McCall (2009) found that African Americans are less likely to enroll in college than any other racial group regardless of the aid package they receive. These authors conjecture that the amount of aid deemed adequate for White students may be inadequate for students of color because they are likely to have greater financial need.

Studies examining the association of financial aid on persistence and success in college show variations by type of aid and race of student. Using a variety of datasets, several studies have shown that grants have a large and positive association with persistence for African American and Latino students (Chen & DesJardins, 2010; Hu & St. John, 2001; St. John, Paulsen, & Carter, 2005). This positive association may be explained by the fact that students do not have to repay a grant. Chen and DesJardins (2010) observed that students are less likely to drop out when awarded higher Pell grants. Other research has found that subsidized loans also have a positive effect on retention (Chen & DesJardins, 2010; Singell, 2004). Since students are more price sensitive at the start of college, DesJardins, Ahlburg, and McCall (2006) suggest that frontloading financial aid may be an effective way to keep students in college. Focusing on community colleges, Dowd and Coury (2006) found that loans were unrelated to attainment of an associate's degree, but negatively related to persistence.

In summary, current scholarship suggests that faculty and staff are critical sources of information related to the transfer process, especially if information about four-year college costs and potential scholarships comes early in enrollment. It is, therefore, worrisome that the role of counselors is disappearing, in part due to high personnel costs and hard economic times. Regarding the role of financial aid assistance in persistence and degree attainment, consensus points to students of color being more receptive only to specific types of financial aid such as grants.

Better Aligning Educational and Organizational Policies Related to Transfer

Overcoming academic and financial barriers to transfer may be negatively offset by the institutional and policy environment in which students study and live. In this section, we identify these environmental factors that ought to be taken into account when devising policies and strategies to improve transfer rates.

Governance and funding structures. Little research on student success examines the effects of state governance and finance structures. This omission from research is perplexing given that states are the greatest providers of higher education funding and, thus, have a significant amount of leverage to incentivize community colleges to increase transfer rates. Since the 1990s, states have used performance measures to ensure that universities and colleges met their intended goals (Burke,

1998). For example, McGuiness (2003) identified 19 different structures used to govern higher education institutions. While some two-year institutions are regulated by the same governing body as the state's four-year university system, other community colleges are governed by local boards.

Literature within the field of public policy lends some perspective on the effectiveness of accountability frameworks for improving the delivery of public services. Heckman, Heinrich, and Smith (2011) found that frameworks that benchmark performance of U.S. workforce training programs failed to produce long-term gains for participants as a result of evidence that suggests accountability measures may influence agency employees to alter conditions to show improved institutional performance. Therefore, the design of accountability frameworks should take into account factors outside the control of agents and effectively balance competing principle interests (Courty, Henrich, & Marschke, 2005). Indeed, Wong (1994) found that efforts to allocate education resources more equitably are constrained by fragmentation in governance. From his analysis, Wong (1994) suggests that equity polices at the local, state, and federal levels work against each other and have, in turn, largely failed to narrow the resource gap between rich and poor districts.

To the best of our knowledge, only one study to date has foregrounded governance within the context of transfer. Wellman (2002) finds that the only difference between states with high versus low grades for retention and completion (according to the state report card produced by the National Center for Public Policy and Higher Education, *Measuring Up 2000*) was their governance structure. Specifically, Wellman (2002) found that high-grade states governed their postsecondary institutions through a centralized system while low-grade states governed their postsecondary institutions through local boards. This result suggests that states may be able to govern institutions in a way that improves their performance through incentives (Wellman, 2001), but what these incentive structures look like was not identified.

Transfer and articulation agreements. Research examining the effects of state-level factors on transfer has centered on articulation agreements (Anderson, Alfonso, & Sun, 2008; Anderson, Sun, & Alfonso, 2006; Banks, 1994; Goldhaber, Gross, & DeBurgomaster, 2008; Roksa & Keith, 2008; Wellman, 2002), which facilitate the transfer of credit acquired in community college to four-year institutions. How articulation agreements reduce the risk of losing credit in this transfer process varies. As of 2010, the most common approach was a transfer associate's degree; 31 states reported this kind of policy. The least common approach was common course numbering; only 7 states reported this policy (Hezel Associates & WICHE, 2010). Other types of articulation policies and practices include block credit transfer, statewide major articulation, and general education transfer (Hezel Associates & WICHE, 2010). In many states, these policies overlap (Roksa, 2009).

Policymakers and researchers commonly assume that articulation policies enable two-year students to transfer to four-year institutions (Wellman, 2002); however, results from empirical studies question the validity of this assumption. On the one hand, Banks (1994) finds, using institutional-level data from UCLA's Transfer Assembly Project, that states with formalized articulation policies produce higher transfer rates than states that lack such policies. Using the same data, Higgins and Katsinas (1999) find similar evidence when they restrict the sample to rural community colleges. On the other hand, various researchers find that articulation policies are unrelated to upward transfer. Using individual-level data from the Beginning Postsecondary Student Survey (BPS:89), Anderson et al. (2006) find community college students in states without articulation agreements as likely to transfer as students in states with articulation agreements, even when restricting samples to students who aspire to a bachelor's degree. The inconsistency of these findings may be due to differences in definitions of transfer, samples, and methods (Roksa & Keith, 2008).

Setting these problems aside, several researchers question whether articulation agreements are devised to help students transfer to four-year institutions. After reviewing articulation agreements for all 50 states, Roksa and Keith (2008) find that articulation agreements are meant to prevent loss of credit for community college students already intending to transfer, not for the general student population. Anderson et al. (2008) attribute the growth of statewide articulation agreements to the increasing need to manage growing student populations. Seen in this light, it is not surprising that several researchers find a nonexistent relationship between articulation agreements and transfer rates.

In summary, the few available studies suggest that governance and accountability structures are an important and understudied dimension in explaining transfer. We urge researchers and policymakers to devote more attention to understanding the effects of these structures. In the next section, our focus shifts from indicators to action; specifically, we describe promising programs and policies that have been developed nationwide to support student success and that are related to some of the factors identified in the multidimensional transfer model.

Programs and Policies to Increase Transfer Rates

A number of programs and policies have been designed to increase the percentage of community college students eligible for transfer. This section delves deeper into specific promising programs and policies that address some of the factors of the multidimensional transfer model. The first factor focuses on programs related to *academic preparation*, the second on *information*, and the third on policies that can lead to *systemic reform and cooperation* (see Figure 7.2). Each of the three factors targets a specific goal with examples of programs and interventions to reach them:

Factor 1: Meeting the Academic and Social Demands of College

- Goal 1: Enhance academic preparation through programs designed to enhance students' academic success before and during college.

	Meeting the Academic and Social Demands of College ---------->					Raising Awareness of the Steps and Financial Resources Needed to Transfer ---------->				Social, Institutional, and Policy Environments					
	Preparation ---------->					Information ---------->				Systemic Reform and Cooperation ---------->					
	Programs									Policies					
Program or policy type	Summer bridge programs	Student success courses	Supplemental instruction	Accelerated courses	Learning communities	Early assessment	Structured mentoring	Transfer orientation	Financial aid counseling	Common core	Common course numbering	Statewide articulation	Cooperative agreements	Joint admission	Incentives and rewards
Primary level of intervention	K-12 & 2-year	2-year	2-year	2-year	2-year	K-12 & 2-year	2- & 4-year	2- & 4-year	2- & 4-year	2- & 4-year	2- & 4-year	2- & 4-year	2- & 4-year	2- & 4-year	2- & 4-year
Description and objective	Designed for incoming students who may have difficulty adapting to college life and demands, these programs typically include residential living, summer college orientation, and credit coursetaking	Course(s) that: teach students how to write notes, take tests, manage their time, and encourage students to develop plans for college and careers	An academic support program that provides regularly scheduled, peer-led study sessions for traditionally difficult courses in order to improve students' academic success	Shorter in length (6 to 8 weeks) and often taking place in the evenings/ weekends or online, these programs allow students to move more quickly through their studies	Enabling a cohort of students to register for two or more courses together to share knowledge around a larger theme and enrich the learning experience	An effort to bring together a diverse group of educational sectors to address the (misalignment) of K-12 educational standards with the requirements of postsecondary education in order to reduce the need for remediation	Face-to-face mentoring that provides students with the most current information, such as online course catalogs and handbooks with admissions applications, to ensure a smooth transition to four-year universities and colleges	Students are required to meet with their academic advisor to discuss major requirements (and any special major-related admissions requirements) before transferring and registering at the four-year institution	Learn about the cost of attendance (including tuition, housing, and books), scholarship opportunities, campus reciprocity agreements, and campus jobs at both the current and future postsecondary institution	A common core streamlines the articulation process by colleges and four-year universities eliminating the confusion that can arise when separate institutions require different core courses to fulfill graduation requirements	If course numbers at community colleges and four-year universities are identical, the possibility of a student taking non-transferable credits is greatly reduced	State legislatures and higher education systems adopt articulation policies to simplify transfer process	Cooperative agreements between postsecondary institutions or departments within such institutions that allow articulation in situations where no state or system policy exists	Guaranteed admission at certain four-year institutions for community college students who have completed a designated transfer program, with or without an associates degree	To encourage transfer between two- and four-year colleges, some states provide extra incentive by offering financial aid, guaranteed transfer, or priority admission
Evidence	Early results from random-assignment study in Texas reveal a significant decrease in developmental coursework for students who participated in the summer bridge program	Students who enrolled in student success courses were 8 percent more likely to earn a degree than those who did not enroll. The effect was slightly stronger for students who did not need remediation	When support is linked to the learning environment, students are more likely to persist in key first-year courses	When adults self-select into an accelerated program, they learn material as satisfactorily as they would in conventional coursework	The learning communities program initially did not have a meaningful impact on students' academic college success, but over time the program had positive impacts on some educational outcome	An evaluation of California's Early Assessment Program (EAP) found that participation in the EAP reduces the probability of students taking remediation in college by 6.2 percent in English and by 4.3, percent in math	Successful transition to a four-year institution requires students to have strong institutional information, to develop strong relationships at four-year institutions, and adjust academic expectations to increase success	Typically smaller than freshman orientation sessions and, if structured properly, can effectively cover a number of issues unique to transfer students	The high counselor-student ratio prevents financial aid counselors from adequately meeting student demand for financial aid advising	Common core credits will follow students to any participating institution and students will not need to satisfy additional general education requirements, thus saving time and money	Common course numbers help to define core competencies and curricular content, as well as ensure that courses taken by community college students are accepted at four-year institutions	Little empirical evidence showing that statewide articulation agreements improve two- to four-year transfer	No empirical evidence showing that cooperative agreements improve two- to four-year transfer	Joint admission can help to bridge information gaps on what courses will count toward general and major-specific degree requirements	No empirical evidence showing that incentives and rewards improve two- and four-year transfer

FIGURE 7.2 Existing Programs and Policies Designed to Increase Community College Transfer and Bachelor's Degree Attainment

Limitation(s)												
Difficulty finding suitable mentors and tutors, loose connection to typical first semester courses, and summer courses were composed of students of varying readiness for college	Courses not designed to improve transfer but to indirectly improve the odds of transferring by improving student persistence	Not universally utilized and financial support varies	Often targets adult learners, who may not be seeking additional education beyond an associate's degree	Findings may not be generalizable to other community colleges who may differ in terms of their student composition and faculty enthusiasm for the learning communities model	The reduction in the remediation rate may be due to the professional development component of EAP and not the direct result of the "early warning" component		Traditional orientation model may not be sufficient and address the needs of transfer students	Counseling may be successful, but it cannot change federal financial aid definitions whereby students are no longer financially dependent on their parents but do not automatically qualify as independent students	Lack of adoption at the national levels means that students can only benefit if they transfer to a four-year institution in the same state or state system	Not comprehensive enough, in terms of the breadth of courses covered by the agreement and the number of institutions that engaged in such agreements	Even though a statewide agreement exists, institutions still engage in institution-to-institution and program-to-program agreements, which can lead to confusion	
Reference												
Wathington, 2010	Zeidenberg, Jenkins, & Calcagno, 2007	Bowles & Jones, 2003	Wlodkowski, 2003	Weiss, Visher, & Wathington, 2010	Howell, Kurlaender, & Grodsky, 2010	Flaga, 2006	Handel, 2011	McKinney & Roberts, 2012	Boswell, 2006	Boswell, 2006	Anderson, Sun, & Alfonso, 2006	Townsend, 2008

FIGURE 7.2 (*Continued*)

Factor 2: Increasing Access to Information and Financial Resources Needed to Transfer

- Goal 2: Expand awareness about transfer-related information through programs that equip students attitudinally and financially for transfer.

Factor 3: Aligning Organizational and Educational Policies Related to Transfer

- Goal 3: Embrace systemic reform and cooperation through polices that facilitate a seamless transition from two- and four-year institutions and provide four-year institutions the financial and regulatory support they need to ensure success for transfer students.

In short, the three stated goals aim to both expand the pool of transfer students and ensure their success at both two- and four-year institutions.

Enhancing Academic Preparation

A student's chance of success in college stems in part from his or her academic preparation and performance in elementary and secondary education. Although not typically viewed as a "transfer" problem, failure to reach credit-bearing coursework due to developmental education can have a deleterious effect on efforts to improve transfer rates. Programs that help community college students persist to the second year also fit this description. In short, adequate preparation for the demands of college—not just for transition to a four-year institution—is a vital first step to achieve transfer success.

Examples of programs that seek to prepare students for early success in postsecondary education are student success courses, supplemental instruction, summer bridge programs, accelerated courses, and learning communities (Bowles & Jones, 2003; Wathington, 2010; Weiss, Visher, & Wathington, 2010; Wlodkowski, 2003; Zeidenberg, Jenkins, & Calcagno, 2007). The long-term effectiveness of some of these programs is uncertain. For example, a recent rigorous evaluation of eight developmental summer bridge programs offered in Texas found a positive effect in terms of passing rates on a first college-level course in math and writing, but not in reading. The evaluation also found no impact on persistence or the average number of credits attempted or earned (Barnett et al., 2012).

Despite the growing use of learning communities, the findings of descriptive and rigorous studies have been mixed (Bloom & Sommo, 2008; Minkler, 2002; Weisman et al., 2012). An early review of learning communities suggested that they promote student persistence and student satisfaction with classes, and improve student success and intellectual development (Minkler, 2002). In a comparative longitudinal study of learning communities across three institutions, Tinto and Love (1995) reported that students in learning communities demonstrated higher academic achievement and lower dropout rates, as well as deeper social, emotional, and academic involvement than students who took stand-alone courses. As Stephen DesJardins and Allyson Flaster explain in their chapter, students who participate in learning communities may be different from those who do not participate, and these differences must be taken into account when measuring the effects of learning communities.

A recent report of the Opening Doors demonstration in Kingsborough Community College in Brooklyn, New York, found positive long-term impacts for students who participated in a one-semester learning community program. Specifically, the study found that after six years, more students in the learning communities program earned a degree (35.9%) than students in the control group (31.3%), a difference of 4.6 percentage points. They also reported that even though the impact was larger for students placed in college-level English, the program also improved outcomes of students with the greatest developmental needs (Sommo, Mayer, Rud, Cullinan, & Fresques, 2012). More recently, results from the Learning Communities Demonstration project that tested the effectiveness of learning communities in six community colleges across the United States concluded that, on average, these programs produced no impact on persistence. However, students who participated in learning communities earned a half credit more in the targeted subject (English or mathematics), no more credits outside that subject, and a half credit more in total credits (Weisman et al., 2012).

In summary, the impact of learning communities remains inconclusive at best. The benefits of learning communities on community college students only appear to persist as long as the program does. With one exception, there are no substantial or long-lasting effects of learning communities on promoting persistence or credit accumulation, which suggests that learning communities are labor intensive and not readily scalable.

Yet another strategy to enhance academic preparation is acceleration, for example, combining courses of math sequences and creating modules so that students can advance at their own pace. The high proportion of students placed in developmental math coupled with relatively low success rates in very long sequences has led to an acceleration movement, and colleges are experimenting with approaches. For the past several years, the Carnegie Foundation for the Advancement of Teaching has been working with faculty at a number of community colleges in the country to test the effectiveness of reforms in the delivery of developmental math (Bryk & Treisman, 2010; Carnegie Foundation for the Advancement of Teaching, n.d.). Basically, these reforms assume that having a long sequence of remedial math courses will structurally guarantee attrition. They argue that students need to enroll in courses that address their deficiencies and focus on the algebraic concepts required to master and succeed in college-level math courses. To carry out such reforms, faculty must tailor the curriculum so that students can identify and work on specific conceptual and reasoning deficiencies needed to succeed in college-level math. Despite widespread experimentation, however, no rigorous evaluation has determined whether acceleration increases students' academic preparation or prospects for transfer.

These bold initiatives—financially supported and coordinated by large philanthropic organizations—illustrate that developmental education still exhibits a potential to prepare students for collegiate-level coursework. However, in response
to pressure from different constituencies, state policymakers may feel that they
need to provide quick and simple solutions to a very complex problem. As Long
and Boatman note in their chapter, some state leaders and policymakers (e.g.,
Complete College America initiative) have proposed defunding developmental
education and, in the case of Connecticut, banning developmental education altogether. It is worrisome that political pressure to solve the problem quickly may
result in states defaulting on serving the most needy populations.

An alternative avenue for the federal government to pursue reform by increasing accountability is to condition receipt of federal student aid funds on
transfer-related outcomes. The federal student aid funds—in the form of grant,
loan, and work-study programs authorized under the Higher Education Act of
1965 (HEA)—constitute a substantial resource to postsecondary institutions.
These programs have generally focused on providing accessibility and affordability for students, but rarely have accountability measures been incorporated
into individual program eligibility. However, recent amendments to the HEA
and Obama administration policies have sought to increase programmatic accountability measures (U.S. Department of Education, 2011). The new gainful
employment regulations strive to hold most programs at for-profit colleges, and
certificate and vocational programs at nonprofit institutions, to a new federal
standard on student debt and employability. The state of California also recently
passed regulation preventing students at for-profit colleges and universities from
receiving financial aid from the state's Cal grant program.

The federal and state governments could also create incentives for minimum
goals in terms of increasing transfers from community colleges to four-year institutions. Yet conditioning access to financial aid on outcomes may bring unintended consequences as institutions may be encouraged to pursue policies that
hamper students' progress toward a bachelor's degree. For example, colleges may
respond to such policies by redirecting students from Science, Technology, Engineering, and Math (STEM) major fields of study toward liberal arts majors so
that students take less time to transfer. States may reduce this type of unintended
consequence by developing or revising a master plan for higher education that
creates mechanisms to make both community colleges and four-year colleges accountable for transferring and graduating students.

Expanding Awareness about Transfer-Related Information

The next critical step in the transfer process involves the acquisition and transmission of information on costs of and expectations for success. Information may
take the form of in-person counseling and/or resources available on a website.
Regardless of how information is conveyed, sharing crucial information early in

students' academic lives is ideal (Perna, 2007; Zarate & Gallimore, 2005). Certain educational trajectories pose particular challenges for students, such as changing majors, which can delay the transfer decision and have substantial cost implications, because new courses may need to be taken and completed courses may no longer satisfy general education requirements. Understanding these implications can save time, effort, and money.

Examples of formal programs designed to transmit information are early assessment, structured mentoring, transfer orientation, and financial aid counseling (Bettinger et al., 2009; Flaga, 2006; Handel, 2011; Howell, Kurlaender, & Grodsky, 2010). To the best of our knowledge, there are no rigorous evaluations of structured mentoring or transfer orientation programs. As mentioned in other chapters in this volume (Conley; Long & Boatman), California's Early Assessment Program (EAP) is designed to provide information to high school students about their academic readiness in English and math, and give them tools to overcome their deficiencies while in high school. A recent evaluation provides evidence that participation in EAP reduces the probability of needing remediation in both English and mathematics in the CSU colleges (Howell et al., 2010). However, it is important to note that students should be receiving the information earlier in the summer so they have time to change their course schedule and enroll in the courses that they need to strengthen their academic preparation. Finally, as mentioned previously, there is preliminary evidence that H&R Block's program to help low-income families complete the FAFSA may improve transfer rates by providing info about the net cost of attending different types of colleges and universities (Bettinger et al., 2009).

Technology and social media may also be effective mechanisms for providing accurate and timely information. Games and texting are examples of technology that may provide accurate and timely information related to the application process. Collegeology Games have recently been designed to help students master the knowledge necessary to gain college admission (Corwin, Tierney, Swensen, Bouchard, & Fullerton, 2012). And the federal government has also funded a program that uses text messaging to reach out to high school students during the year that they prepare applications for college (Chin, Phillips, & Reber, n.d.). More research is needed to fully understand the effects of these and other uses of technology in facilitating the transfer process.

The EAP and H&R Block programs are examples of interventions that can be implemented at the state level and that have the potential to generate higher success and transfer rates for underserved student populations. Unlike institution-level programs, those implemented at the state or federal levels reach a much wider population and have the potential to have a larger impact. Even though these programs still need more thorough evaluation, they represent examples of broad interventions that have the potential to provide crucial academic and financial information to students and institutions.

One final recommendation related to improving the timing and quality of information is to require institutions receiving Title IV funds to provide information to students related to the transfer process and the associated costs. As part of the agreement to participate in the federal student aid programs, colleges and universities are required to have net price calculators on their websites (as discussed in chapters by Laura Perna and Elizabeth Kurban, as well as Don Heller). Along those lines, institutions could be required to include transfer calculators, which should include information related to transferable courses and illustrate the most effective way for students to use both federal and state funding to minimize student debt.

Embrace Systemic Reforms That Encourage Cooperation

As interest in transfer grows, so do the number of programs and policies aimed to ease the transition from a two- to a four-year institution. Systemic reform and cooperation focus on the importance of enrollment momentum because transfer means not only attending another institution, but continuing at an intensity to graduate in a timely manner. As described earlier in this chapter, to minimize or eliminate any loss of credit, many states have implemented policies that designate a common core of courses and common course numbering throughout their higher education systems (Boswell, 2006). About 31 states in the country currently offer associate degrees for transfer such as the AAT, or associate of arts, in teaching. This type of degree has the potential to streamline the transfer process and increase degree attainment rates. However, to accomplish this goal there must be clear coordination and agreement between the two-year and four-year sectors; if the students who attain the degrees do not have a guaranteed space in a four-year college, the purpose of the policy is defeated. For example, California recently passed regulation to facilitate transfer by offering associate degrees with guaranteed admission to some colleges of the California State University (CSU). While colleges wait for students to obtain this new degree, the number of transfer students to the CSUs has been reduced by 30% in only one year, due to factors relative to the recent economic downturn. To the best of our knowledge, none of the transfer policies designed to induce intersectoral coordination of efforts have been formally evaluated (Kienzl et al., 2011). Determining whether these popular policies are effective beyond rhetoric is needed before recommending them further.

Conclusion

Presenting a multidimensional transfer model illustrates transfer as a complex process affected by a number of interrelated factors and influenced by social, organizational, and economic forces. This complexity suggests that any effort to increase transfer rates requires major reforms and that isolated institution-level programs are likely insufficient. The goal of this chapter is to highlight this complexity and review current institutional-, state-, and federal-level programs. Institutional-level programs should be rigorously evaluated to test whether they can be brought to scale. State-level policies should build on successful efforts such as the common core initiative, define college readiness, align academic content throughout K–20, and provide colleges the logistic and financial support necessary to redesign their master plans. Finally, at the state and federal levels there is a need to change current funding mechanisms, so that institutions are more accountable for producing equity outcomes and provide the support necessary to help vulnerable populations attain degrees and reach middle-class status. The goals of the Obama administration cannot be attained without coupling enough financial support with substantial reform at the institutional, state, and federal levels.

Notes

1. For more background on Tinto's Student Integration Model and its application to persistence and retention, please see the discussion by Hossler, Dundar, and Shapiro in Chapter 8 of this volume.
2. The authors conclude that studies using regression discontinuity design models should avoid making broad generalizations about the impact of developmental education. Given that results vary by course level and by college, they only apply to students at the margin. Along with Robinson (2011), the authors caution that negative coefficients might not be indicative of a negative impact of the program but, rather, the need to adjust the cut-scores in the assessment and placement exams (Melguizo, Kosiewicz, Prather, & Bos, 2012b).
3. Treating full-time and part-time students equally, Grubb (2006) finds that the student-counselor ratio likely exceeds 1:1000.

References

Abrego, L.J. (2006). "I can't go to college because I don't have papers": Incorporation patterns of Latino undocumented youth. *Latino Studies, 4*, 212–231.

Adelman, C. (1999). *Answers in the toolbox: Academic intensity, attendance patterns, and bachelor's degree attainment.* Washington, DC: Office of Educational Research and Improvement, U.S. Department of Education.

Adelman, C. (2005). *Moving into town—and moving on: The community college in the lives of traditional-age students.* Washington, DC: U.S. Department of Education.

Adelman, C. (2006). *The toolbox revisited: Paths to degree completion from high school through college.* Washington, DC: U.S. Department of Education.

Advisory Committee on Student Financial Assistance (ACSFA). (2012). *Access matters: How financial barriers will undermine bachelor's degree completion in America.* Washington, DC: Author.

Anderson, G., Alfonso, M., & Sun, J. (2008). Rethinking cooling out at public community colleges: An examination of fiscal and demographic trends in higher education and the rise of statewide articulation agreements. *Teacher's College Record, 108*(3), 422–451.

Anderson, G., Sun, J., & Alfonso, M. (2006). Effectiveness of statewide articulation agreements on the probability of transfer. *Review of Higher Education, 29*(3), 261–291.

Andrews, R.J., Ling, J., & Lovenheim, M.F. (2012). *Heterogeneous paths through college: Detailed patterns and relationships with graduation and earnings.* Manuscript submitted for publication. Retrieved from http://www.human.cornell.edu/pam/people/upload/College_Path-2.pdf

Banks, D.L. (1994). Effects of environmental conditions on student-transfer activity. *Community College Journal of Research and Practice, 18*(4), 245–259.

Barnett, E.A., Bork, R.H., Mayer, A.K., Pretlow, J., Wathington, H.D., & Weiss, M.J. (2012). *Bridging the gap: An impact study of eight developmental summer bridge programs in Texas.* New York, NY: The National Center for Postsecondary Research.

Bean, J.P., & Metzner, B. (1985). A conceptual model of nontraditional undergraduate student attrition. *Review of Educational Research, 55,* 485–540.

Bettinger, E.P., & Long, B.T. (2006). The increasing use of adjunct instructors at public institutions: Are we hurting students?" In Ronald Ehrenberg (Ed.), *What's happening to public higher education* (pp. 51–70). Westport, CT: Greenwood Press.

Bettinger, E.P., & Long, B.T. (2009). Addressing the needs of underprepared students in higher education: Does college remediation work? *Journal of Human Resources, 44*(3), 736–771.

Bettinger, E.P., Long, B., Oreopoulos, P., & Sanbonmatsu, L. (2009). *The role of simplification and information in college decisions: Results from the H&R Block FAFSA experiment.* (NBER Working Paper No. 15361). Cambridge, MA: National Bureau of Economic Research.

Bloom, D., & Sommo, C. (2008). *Building learning communities: Early results from the opening doors demonstration at Kingsborough Community College.* New York, NY: MDRC.

Boatman, A. (2012, March). *Examining the causal effects of instruction and delivery in postsecondary remedial and developmental courses: Evidence from the Tennessee Developmental Course Redesign Initiative.* Paper presented at the 2012 annual conference of The Association for Education Finance and Policy, Boston, MA.

Boswell, K. (2006). Bridges or barriers? Public policy and the community college transfer function. *Change, 36*(6), 22–29.

Bowles, T., & Jones, J. (2003). The effect of supplemental instruction on retention: A bivariate probit model. *College Student Retention: Research, Theory, and Practice, 5,* 431–439.

Breland, H.M. (1998). *National trends in the use of test scores in college admissions.* Princeton, NJ: Educational Testing Service.

Bryk, S., & Treisman, U. (2010, April 18). Make math a gateway, not a gatekeeper. *The Chronicle of Higher Education.* Retrieved from http://chronicle.com/article//65056

Burke, J.C. (1998). Performance funding: Present status and future prospects. *New Directions for Institutional Research, 97,* 5–13.

Calcagno, J.C., Crosta, P., Bailey, T., & Jenkins, D. (2007). Stepping stones to a degree: The impact of enrollment pathways and milestones on community college student outcomes. *Research in Higher Education, 48*(7), 775–801.

Calcagno, J.C., & Long, B.T. (2008). *The impact of remediation using a regression discontinuity approach: Addressing endogenous sorting and noncompliance* (Working Paper No. 14194). Cambridge, MA: National Bureau of Economic Research.

Carnegie Foundation for the Advancement of Teaching. (n.d.). *Developmental Math.* http://www.carnegiefoundation.org/developmental-math

Carnevale, A.P., & Strohl, J. (2010). How increasing college access is increasing inequality and what to do about it. In R. Kahlenberg (Ed.), *Rewarding strivers* (pp. 71–201). Washington, DC: The Century Foundation.

Chen, R., & DesJardins, S. (2010). Investigating the impact of financial aid on student dropout risks: Racial and ethnic differences. *The Journal of Higher Education, 81*(2), 179–208.

Chin, T., Phillips, M., & Reber, S. (n.d.). *Promoting college enrollment among disadvantaged students: A randomized controlled evaluation of two low-cost interventions.* Los Angeles, CA: UCLA. Retrieved from http://l1.ccpr.ucla.edu/papers/VSOURCE-Milestones-Project Description.pdf

Cohen, A., & Brawer, F.B. (1987). *The collegiate function of community colleges: Fostering higher learning through curriculum and student transfer.* San Francisco, CA: Jossey-Bass.

Cohen, A.M., & Brawer, F.B. (2009). *The American community college* (5th ed.). San Francisco, CA: Jossey-Bass.

College Board. (2011). *Trends in college pricing.* Washington, DC: Author.

Corwin, Z.B., Tierney, W.G., Swensen, E., Bouchard, S., & Fullerton, T. (2012). *Gaming the system: Fostering college knowledge through play.* Los Angeles: Pullias Center for Higher Education, Game Innovation Lab, University of Southern California.

Courty, P., Henrich, C., & Marschke, G. (2005). Setting the standard in performance measurement systems. *International Public Management Journal, 8*(3), 1–27.

DesJardins, S.J., Ahlburg, D., & McCall, B.P. (2006). An integrated model of application, admission, enrollment, and financial aid. *The Journal of Higher Education, 77*(3), 381–429.

Dougherty, K. (1997). *The contradictory college: The conflict origins, impacts, and futures of the community college.* Albany, NY: The State University of New York.

Dougherty, K.J., & Kienzl, G.S. (2006). It's not enough to get through the open door: Inequalities by social background in transfer from community colleges to four-year colleges. *Teachers College Record, 108*(3), 452–487.

Dowd, A. (2007). Community colleges as gateways and gatekeepers: Moving beyond the access "saga" toward outcome equity. *Harvard Educational Review, 77*(4), 407–419.

Dowd, A. (2011). Improving transfer access for low-income community college students. In A. Kezar (Ed.), *Recognizing and serving low-income students in higher education: An examination of institutional policies, practices, and culture* (pp. 217–231). New York, NY: Routledge.

Dowd, A.C., Bensimon, E.M., Gabbard, G., Singleton, S., Macias, E., Dee, J.R., ... Giles, D. (2006). *Transfer access to elite colleges and universities in the United States: Threading the needle of the American dream.* Washington, DC: Jack Kent Cooke Foundation.

Dowd, A.C., & Coury, T. (2006). The effect of loans on the persistence and attainment of community college students. *Research in Higher Education, 47*(1), 33–62.

Eagan, M.K., & Jaeger, A.J. (2009). Effects of exposure to part-time faculty on community college transfer. *Research in Higher Education, 50*, 168–188.

Ehrenberg, R.G., & Zhang, L. (2005). Do tenured and tenure-track faculty matter? *Journal of Human Resources, 40*(3), 647–659.

Ellison, A.B. (2002). *The accidental faculty: Adjunct instructors in community colleges.* Tampa: University of South Florida.

Flaga, C. (2006). The process of transition for community college transfer students. *Community College Journal of Research and Practice, 30*(1), 3–19.

Gándara, P., Alvarado, E., Driscoll, A., & Orfield, G. (2012). *Building pathways to transfer: Community colleges that break the chain of failure for students of color.* Los Angeles, CA: The Civil Rights Project/El Proyecto Derechos Civiles.

Gloria, A.M., & Segura-Herrera, T.M. (2004). Ambrocia and Omar go to college: A psychosociocultural examination of Chicanos and Chicanas in higher education. In R.J. Velasquez, B. McNeill, & L. Arellano (Eds.), *Handbook of Chicana and Chicano psychology* (pp. 401–425). Mahwah, NJ: Lawrence Erlbaum.

Goldhaber, D., Gross, B., & DeBurgomaster, S. (2008). *Community colleges and higher education: How do state transfer and articulation policies impact student pathways?* Seattle: University of Washington.

Goldrick-Rab, S. (2010). Challenges and opportunities for improving community college student success. *Review of Educational Research, 80*, 437–469.

Greene, J.P., & Forster, G. (2003). *Public high school graduation and college readiness rates in the United States* (Education Working Paper No. 3). New York, NY: The Manhattan Institute.

Grodsky, E., & Jones, M. (2004). Real and imagined barriers to college entry: Perceptions of cost. Retrieved from http://escholarship.org/uc/item/7v87v3j0

Grubb, W.N. (2006). "Like, what do I do now?": The dilemmas of guidance counseling. In T. Bailey and V. Morest (Eds.), *Defending the community college equity agenda* (pp. 195–222). Baltimore, MD: Johns Hopkins University Press.

Hagedorn, L.S., Cypers, S., & Lester, J. (2008). Looking in the review mirror: Factors affecting transfer for urban community college students. *Community College Journal of Research and Practice, 32*(9), 643–664.

Handel, S. (2011). *Improving student transfer from community colleges to four-year institutions: The perspective of leaders from baccalaureate-granting institutions*. New York, NY: College Board.

Heckman, J. J, Heinrich, C.J., & Smith, J. (2011). Performance standards and the potential to improve government performance. In J.J. Heckman, C.J. Heinrich, P. Courty, G. Marschke, and J. Smith (Eds.), *The performance of performance standards* (pp. 1–14). Kalamazoo, MI: W.E. Upjohn Institute for Employment Research.

Hezel Associates & Western Interstate Commission for Higher Education (WICHE). (2010). *Promising practices in statewide articulation and transfer systems*. Boulder, CO: Western Interstate Commission for Higher Education.

Higgins, C.S., & Katsinas, S. (1999). The relationship between environmental conditions and transfer rates of selected rural community colleges: A pilot study. *Community College Review, 27*(2), 1–25.

Horn, L., Chen, X., & Chapman, C. (2003). *Getting ready to pay for college: What students and their parents know about the cost of college tuition and what they are doing to find out*. Washington, DC: National Center for Educational Statistics and MPR Associates.

Horn, L., & Neville, S. (2006). *Profile of undergraduates in U.S. postsecondary education institutions: 2003–04: With a special analysis of community college students* (Report No. NCES 2006–184). Washington, DC: National Center for Education Statistics, U.S. Department of Education.

Howell, J., Kurlaender, M., & Grodsky, E. (2010). Postsecondary preparation and remediation: Examining the effect of the Early Assessment Program at California State University. *Journal of Policy Analysis and Management, 29*(4), 726–748.

Hu, S., & St. John, E.P. (2001). Student persistence in a public higher education system: Understanding racial and ethnic differences. *The Journal of Higher Education, 72*(3) 265–286.

Jacobs, B.C., Cutright, M., Niebling, G.F., Simon, J.F., & Marling, J.L. (2010). *Exploring promising practices in transfer student services: A Texas initiative*. Denton: University of North Texas, National Institute for the Study of Transfer Students.

Jacoby, D. (2006). Effects of part-time faculty employment on community college graduation rates. *The Journal of Higher Education, 77*(6), 1081–1103.

Jenkins, D., Bailey, T.R., Leinbach, T., Marshall, J., Soonachan, A., & Van Noy, M. (2006). *What community college policies and practices are effective in promoting student success? A study of high- and low-impact institutions*. New York, NY: Community College Research Center, Columbia University.

Kane, T.J., & Rouse, C.E. (1995). Labor-market returns to two- and four-year college. *The American Economic Review, 85*(3), 600–614.

Kienzl, G.S., Wesaw, A.J., & Kumar, A. (2011). *Understanding the transfer process*. Washington, DC: The Institute of Higher Education Policy.

Kim, J., DesJardins, S., & McCall, B. (2009). Exploring the effects of student expectations about financial aid on postsecondary choice: A focus on income and racial/ethnic differences. *Research in Higher Education, 50*, 741–774.

Kuh, G., Kinzie, J., Schuh, J.H., Whitt, E.J., & Associates. (2010). *Student success in college: Creating conditions that matter.* New York, NY: Jossey-Bass.

Lee, V.E., Mackie-Lewis, C., & Marks, H.M. (1993). Persistence to the baccalaureate degree for students who transfer from community college. *American Journal of Education, 102*(1), 80–114.

Levin, H. (2011). The utility and need for incorporating noncognitive skills into large-scale educational assessments. In M. von Davier, E. Gonzalez, I. Kirsch, and K. Yamamoto (Eds.), *The role of international large-scale assessments: Perspectives from technology, economy, and educational research* (pp. 67–86). New York, NY: Springer.

Martorell, P., & McFarlin, I. (2011). Help or hindrance? The effects of college remediation on academic and labor market outcomes. *The Review of Economics and Statistics, 93*(2), 436–454.

McGuiness, A.C. (2003). *Models of postsecondary education coordination and governance in the states.* Denver, CO: Education Commission of the States.

McKinney, L., & Roberts, T. (2012). The role of community college financial aid counselors in helping students understand and utilize financial aid. *Community College Journal of Research and Practice, 36*(10), 761–774.

Melguizo, T. (2010). Are students of color more likely to graduate from college if they attend more selective institutions? Evidence from a cohort of recipients and non-recipients of the Gates Millennium Scholarship Program. *Educational Evaluation and Policy Analysis, 32*(2), 230–248.

Melguizo, T., & Dowd, A. (2009). Baccalaureate success of transfers and rising four-year college juniors. *Teachers College Record, 111*(1), 55–89.

Melguizo, T., Hagedorn, L.S., & Cypers, S. (2008). The need for remedial/developmental education and the cost of community college transfer: Calculations from a sample of California community college transfers. *The Review of Higher Education, 31*(4), 401–431.

Melguizo, T., Kim, B., Bos, J., & Prather, G. (2012a, April). *Evaluation of the basic skills math sequence in California: Evidence from Los Angeles.* Paper presented at the annual conference of the American Educational Research Association, Vancouver, Canada.

Melguizo, T., Kosiewicz, H., Prather G., & Bos, J. (2012b, April). *Grounding our understanding of college remedial education in reality: Implications for further research.* Paper presented at the American Educational Research Association, Vancouver, CA.

Minkler, J. (2002). ERIC review: Learning communities at the community college. *Community College Review, 30*(3), 46–62.

Morgan, S.L. (2005). *On the edge of commitment: Educational attainment and race in the United States.* Stanford, CA: Stanford University Press.

National Center for Public Policy and Higher Education & Southern Regional Education Board. (2010). *Beyond the rhetoric: Improving college readiness through coherent state policy.* Washington, DC: Author.

Olivas, M.A. (2009). Undocumented college students, taxation, and financial aid: A technical note. *Review of Higher Education, 32*(3), 407–416.

Pascarella, E.T., & Terenzini, P.T. (2005). *How college affects students: A third decade of research.* San Francisco, CA: Jossey-Bass.

Perna, L.W. (2000). Differences in the decision to attend college among African-Americans, Hispanics, and Whites. *The Journal of Higher Education, 71*(2), 117–141.

Perna, L.W. (2004). *Impact of student aid program design, operations, and marketing on the formation of family college-going plans and resulting college-going behaviors of potential students.* Boston, MA: The Education Resources Institute.

Perna, L.W. (2007). Studying college access and choice: A proposed conceptual model. In J.C. Smart (Ed.), *Higher education handbook of theory and research: Vol. 11* (pp. 99–157). Netherlands: Springer.

Peter, K., & Forrest-Cataldi, E. (2005). *The road less traveled? Students who enroll in multiple institutions* (Report No. NCES 2005–157). Washington, DC: U.S. Department of Education, National Center of Education Statistics.

Robinson, J.P. (2011). Evaluating criteria for English learner reclassification: A causal-effects approach using a binding score regression discontinuity design with instrumental variables. *Educational Evaluation and Policy Analysis, 33*(3), 267–292.

Roderick, M., Nagaoka, J., & Coca, V. (2009). College readiness for all: The challenge for urban high schools. *The Future of Children, 19*(1), 185–210.

Roksa, J. (2009). Building bridges for student success: Are transfer policies effective? *Teachers College Record, 111*(10), 2444–2478.

Roksa, J., & Calcagno, J.C. (2008). *Making the transition to four-year institutions: Academic preparation and transfer* (CCRC Working Paper No. 13). New York, NY: Community College Research Center, Teachers College, Columbia University.

Roksa, J., & Calcagno, J.C. (2010). Catching up in community colleges: Academic preparation and transfer to four-year institutions. *Teacher's College Record, 112*(1), 260–288.

Roksa, J., & Keith, B. (2008). Credits, time, and attainment. Articulation policies and success after transfer. *Educational Evaluation and Policy Analysis, 30*(2), 236–254.

Schunk, D. (2003). Learning theories: An educational perspective (4th ed.). Upper Saddle River, NJ: Pearson.

Scott-Clayton, J., & Rodriguez, O. (2012, March). *Development, diversion, or discouragement? A new framework and new evidence on the effects of college remediation.* Paper presented at annual conference of the Association for Education Finance and Policy, Boston, MA.

Sedlacek, W.E. (2004). *Beyond the big test: Noncognitive assessment in higher education.* San Francisco, CA: Jossey-Bass.

Singell, L.D. (2004). Come and stay a while: Does financial aid effect retention conditioned on enrollment at a large public university? *Economics of Education, 23*, 459–471.

Sommo, C., Mayer, A.K., Rudd, T., Cullinan, D., & Fresques, H. (2012). Commencement day: Six-year effects of a freshman learning community program at Kingsborough community college. Retrieved from http://www.mdrc.org/publications/642/overview.html

St. John, E.P., Paulsen, M.B., & Carter, D.F. (2005). Diversity, college costs, and postsecondary opportunity: An examination of the financial nexus between college choice and persistence for African Americans and Whites. *The Journal of Higher Education, 76*(5) 545–569.

Strauss, L.C., & Terenzini, P.T. (2007). The effects of students in- and out-of-class experiences on their analytical and group skills: A study of engineering education. *Research in Higher Education, 48*(8), 967–992.

Surette, B.J. (2001). Transfer from two-year to four-year college: An analysis of gender differences. *Economics of Education Review, 20*, 151–163.

Tinto, V. (1993). *Leaving college: Rethinking the causes and cures of student attrition.* Chicago, IL: University of Chicago Press.

Tinto, V., & Love, A.G. (1995). A longitudinal study of learning communities at LaGuardia Community Colleges. University Park, PA: National Center on Postsecondary Teaching, Learning, and Assessments.

Townsend, B.K. (2008). "Feeling like a freshman again": The transfer student transition. *New Directions in Higher Education, 144*, 69–77.

Tracey, T.J., & Sedlacek, W.E. (1987). Comparison of White and Black student academic success using noncognitive variables: A LISREL analysis. *Research in Higher Education, 27*(4), 333–348.

U.S. Department of Education. (2010). National evaluation of student support services: Examination of student outcomes after six years. Washington, DC: Author.

U.S. Department of Education. (2011). Obama administration announces steps to protect students from ineffective career college programs. Retrieved from http://www.ed.gov/news/press-releases/gainful-employment-regulations

Wallin, D.L. (2004). Valuing professional colleagues: Adjunct faculty in community and technical colleges. *Community College Journal of Research and Practice, 28*(4), 373–391.

Wang, X. (2010). Factors contributing to the upward transfer of baccalaureate aspirants beginning at community colleges (WISCAPE Working Paper). Madison: University of Wisconsin.

Wassmer, R., Moore, C., & Shulock, N. (2004). Effects of racial/ethnic composition on transfer rates in community colleges: Implications for policy and practice. *Research in Higher Education, 45*(6), 651–672.

Wathington, H. (2010). *Developmental summer bridge programs: Implementation and early evidence from a random assignment study*. New York, NY: National Center for Postsecondary Research, Columbia University.

Weisman, E., Cullinan, D., Cerna, O., Safran, S., Richman, P., & Grossman, A. (2012). *Learning communities for students in developmental English: Impact studies at Merced College and the community college of Baltimore County*. New York, NY: The National Center for Postsecondary Research, Columbia University.

Weiss, M., Visher, M., & Wathington, H. (2010). *Learning communities for students in developmental reading: An impact study at Hillsborough community college*. New York, NY: National Center for Postsecondary Research.

Wellman, J.V. (2001). Assessing state accountability systems. *Change, 33*(2), 46–52.

Wellman, J.V. (2002). State policy and community college—baccalaureate transfer. Washington, DC: The Institute for Higher Education Policy.

Wlodkowski, R. (2003). Accelerated learning in colleges and universities. *New Directions for Adult and Continuing Education, 97*, 5–16.

Wong, K. (1994). Governance structure, resource allocation, and equity policy. *Review of Research in Education, 20*, 257–289.

Zarate, M.E., & Gallimore, R. (2005). Gender differences in factors leading to college enrollment: A longitudinal analysis of Latina and Latino students. *Harvard Educational Review, 75*(4), 383–349.

Zarate, M.E., & Pachon, H.P. (2006). Perceptions of college financial aid among California Latino Youth (Policy Brief). Los Angeles, CA: The Tomás Rivera Policy Institute.

Zeidenberg, M., Jenkins, D., & Calcagno, J.C. (2007). *Do student success courses actually help community college students succeed?* New York, NY: Community College Research Center.

8

LONGITUDINAL PATHWAYS TO COLLEGE PERSISTENCE AND COMPLETION

Student, Institutional, and Public Policy Perspectives

Donald Hossler, Afet Dundar, and Douglas T. Shapiro

Applied research in the field of higher education is often driven by concerns pressing to postsecondary institutions and of interest to public policymakers. One such issue is the retention and graduation of students enrolled in postsecondary education. Research shows that increased enrollments in the last few decades have not been followed by similar increases in college completion (Bound, Lovenheim, & Turner, 2010; Reason, 2009). Large disparities remain in college completion rates among ethnic groups as well as between traditional and nontraditional students (Radford, Berkner, Wheeless, & Shepherd, 2010). Postsecondary institutions have clear incentives to focus on student retention, as every student retained is one less student to be recruited in successive classes. In addition, with the rise of college rankings publications, student retention and graduation rates have become important indicators of institutional quality.

Many states have also created public institution funding formulas for which incentives are determined by campus-based retention and/or graduation rates (Harnisch, 2011). Although performance funding incentives vary across states, Harnisch (2011) reports that Ohio, Tennessee, Louisiana, Pennsylvania, and Indiana, for example, have all seen some positive results either in college completion rates or in the number of students earning degrees as a result of these funding incentives. At the federal level, President Obama has made college completion a centerpiece of his postsecondary educational policy (Bland, 2010). The president's first budget proposal included a five-year, $2.5 billion Access and Completion Incentive Fund to support state efforts to help low-income students complete a college education (U.S. Department of Education, 2012). Referring to efforts to increase college graduation rates, U.S. Secretary of Education Arne Duncan stated, "Obama is trying to kick-start a measurement that has 'flat-lined' for decades" (Bland, 2010). However, the president has relatively few policy levers to use in conjunction with this goal.

This chapter focuses on student retention and persistence, but we differentiate between those terms. Following Adelman's (2006) lead, we define *retention* as students who remain enrolled at the same institution at which they began. Most extant studies of student retention may be described as presenting a single institutional perspective. Yet, because students are increasingly attending multiple institutions—both sequentially and even concurrently—serious limitations arise when analyzing a student's enrollment at only a single institution. *Persistence*, on the other hand, expands the notion of retention to include students who leave their original institution and transfer to another; in other words, students who continue their enrollment anywhere within postsecondary education. Because it requires tracking student information across institutions, persistence is more appropriately considered a student measure than an institutional one.

Research on retention in postsecondary education as defined above (retention from matriculation through graduation at the institution of origin) has garnered a great deal of attention from academic researchers and public policymakers since the 1970s (Tinto, 2005). Working with Tinto's original model of student integration (1975, 1993), derived from Durkheim's sociological theory of suicide, and, later, with Bean's Job-Turnover Model of Student Attrition (1980), a spate of studies examine how student background characteristics interact with the attributes of institutions and social and academic experiences postmatriculation. Much of the research that empirically tested the Tinto model was undertaken by Pascarella and Terenzini (e.g., Pascarella, 1980; Pascarella & Terenzini, 1979, 1980, 1983), while Bean undertook much of the original research to validate the model he developed (e.g., Bean, 1980, 1982). Nevertheless, as Tatiana Melguizo, Gregory Kienzl, and Holly Kosiewicz also observe in their chapter in this volume, notable shortcomings in our understanding of student retention and persistence remain.

Our review and analysis of retention and persistence is organized into the following four sections. Our initial section provides a brief review of student retention, in two parts. The first describes theories, models, and empirical research on the impact of student characteristics, institutional attributes, and student experience on retention at the institution of origin. The second examines recent studies on the effects of institutional programs and policies intended to enhance student retention at particular campuses. A full review of student retention and persistence literature is beyond the scope of this chapter. Instead, we offer here a high-level overview of key findings, with implications for institutional and public policymakers discussed in subsequent sections of this chapter.

In our second section we describe persistence pathways, considering transfer students who attend multiple postsecondary institutions and analyzing the ability of public policy to enable or inhibit such pathways from the institution of origin through graduation anywhere within the higher education system. Our third section examines methodological approaches and types of research data needed to enable tracking of individual student persistence through graduation across sectors and state lines. In a concluding section, we offer recommendations for public and institutional policymakers.

Review of Research on Retention: Existing Theory and Institutional Practice

The rich body of research on this topic typically draws on sociological models of student retention advanced by Tinto (1975) and Bean (1980, 1982, 1985). Tinto's Student Integration Model draws on the notion of college as a social system, in which students achieve varying levels of integration with the institutional culture in social and academic domains. Tinto's model suggests that peer and faculty interactions are important factors in developing and maintaining a student's commitment to staying in the institution (*retention*), and that attrition, in turn, can be viewed as a failure of the student to form meaningful interactions or to engage with institutional culture.

Bean's Student Attrition Model, in contrast, focuses on the notion of college as a transaction, in which students invest varying amounts of time, money, and effort in exchange for such benefits as intellectual development and employability. Students' implicit cost-benefit analysis of factors such as efforts required, grades received, tuition paid, and external job markets conditions their commitment to completing a degree. Bean's model theoretically applies to the outcome of degree completion anywhere (*persistence*); however, the bulk of the research conducted in its service is limited to single institution datasets and, hence, measurements and analyses of student retention.

Refinements or derivatives of these early models have been developed over the years. Cabrera, Nora, and Castenada (1993) demonstrate that the theories by Tinto and Bean overlap significantly and place greater emphasis on college environmental factors. Braxton (2000) and Braxton, Hirschy, and McClendon (2004) enrich the models of student departure by addressing different institutional contexts, such as commuter colleges and universities, thereby extending extant theories beyond the early research that focused on traditional campus environments. Cabrera, Burkum, and LaNasa (2005) focus on student socioeconomic status as a conditioning factor in retention, while Rendón, Jalomo, and Nora (2000) and others add new theoretical considerations for applying the models to minority students.

An additional empirical model of student retention is the nexus model advanced by St. John, Paulsen, and Starkey (1996). This model asserts an interaction among the factors that enter into a student's initial college choice process (including both the decision to attend and the selection of a particular college), and the subsequent choice to stay in college. Social and academic reasons for choosing a college (such as peer or family influences) condition future social and academic integration to the institution (retention) while financial reasons for choosing a college, such as cost or financial aid, condition the way students respond to market forces (persistence). Again, data availability largely governs the use of the nexus model, so that most research using it focuses on the institution-level impact of financial aid on student retention (e.g., St. John & Paulsen, 2002).

Key Theoretical Constructs: Academic and Social Integration

Two key constructs from the Tinto model have become important theoretical concepts in our understanding of student retention: academic and social integration. Tinto (1975, 1987) presents academic and social integration as complementary but independent constructs that define how students adjust to and move through the postsecondary educational experience. These two constructs have influenced the thinking of many scholars who have focused on student retention, persistence, and success. For example, Kuh, Kinzie, Buckley, Bridges, and Hayek (2007) define the two as follows:

> Academic integration represents both satisfactory compliance with explicit norms, such as earning passing grades, and the normative academic values of the institution, such as an engineering school that values the physical sciences over the arts. Social integration represents the extent to which a student finds the institution's social environment to be congenial with his or her preferences, which are shaped by the student's background, values, and aspirations. Social integration is often measured as a composite of peer-to-peer interactions and faculty–student interactions, while academic integration reflects satisfaction with academic progress and choice of major (Kuh et al., 1994). Thus, student persistence is a function of dynamic relationships between the individual and other actors within the college and their home community. (p. 11)

Kuh's conclusion is his most important point: retention is a function of dynamic relationships between the individual student and other actors within the college and the student's home community. Tinto also posits that stronger educational goals and institutional commitment, when aligned with institutional mission, lead to higher retention (Tinto, 1993).

As we will see from the following overview of student characteristics, experiences, and finances, theory and research suggest that academic and social integration are critical to an understanding of retention. Students whose experiences in college are incongruent with their expectations, formed from academic preparation, family influences, and precollege peer influences, are less able to adjust to challenges and persist (Kuh et al., 2007). In terms of academic integration, interaction with faculty, including out-of-class social interactions, mentoring, and other related activities, is almost universally associated with retention and success (Pascarella & Terenzini, 1991). Social integration that focuses on interaction with other students—discussing coursework, group projects, tutoring, intramural sports, social organizations, and clubs—is also positively associated with retention (Pascarella & Terenzini, 1991).

Student Demographic and Background Characteristics

Research has established that a number of student characteristics are associated, positively and negatively, with retention at the institution of origin. Student academic ability and preparation are the strongest predictors of college retention and are associated with the intensity of high school curriculum, particularly the highest level of mathematics achieved (Adelman, 2006; Kuh et al., 2007; Lotkowksi, Robbins, & Noeth, 2004; Pascarella & Terenzini, 1983). Student degree aspirations and parental encouragement play important roles in college access, but not all scholars agree on the role of student aspirations in retention. Parental encouragement exerts a strong influence on aspirations (Hossler, Schmit, &Vesper, 1999). Several scholars suggest that student aspirations play a direct and positive role in postsecondary matriculation (Kuh et al., 2007; Pascarella &Terenzini, 1991; Perna & Titus, 2005;Tinto, 1993), whereas Adelman (2006) finds them unrelated to attrition once enrolled. Kuh et al. (2007) notes that the findings are mixed, but that most research suggests that student educational aspirations are positively related to student retention.

In terms of other characteristics that affect retention, we know, for example, that White and Asian students are more likely to be retained, while African American and Latino students are less likely to be retained (Adelman, 2006;Astin, 1997; Kuh et al., 2007; Swail, Redd, & Perna, 2003;Tross, Harper, Osher, & Kneidinger, 2000). However, these relationships can be largely attributed to other characteristics that are associated with race, particularly income, parental education, and academic preparation (Adelman, 2006). Parental education, particularly mother's education, as well as parental income, are also positively associated with student retention. First-generation students are more likely to engage in behaviors that increase risk of attrition, such as delayed enrollment, part-time attendance, and working full time (Adelman, 2006; Choy, 2001; Ishtani, 2006; Kuh et al., 2007; Pascarella & Terenzini, 1983, 1991).

Student Educational Experiences

Almost 30 years of research on student retention concur that six educational experiences in particular are positively related to retention at the institution of origin. Four of these are more related to social integration and two others are more closely related to academic integration.The four student experiences related to social integration that promote retention include

- Living on campus (Choy, 2001; Kuh et al., 2007; Pascarella & Terenzini, 1991);
- Transition experiences including orientation, university 101 programs, freshmen interest groups, and learning communities (Kuh et al., 2007; Muraskin & Lee, 2004; Pascarella & Terenzini, 1991);
- Engagement, determined by student behaviors and institutional practices and measured by academic challenge, interaction with faculty, active and collaborative learning, extracurricular activities, and interaction with diverse peers (Kuh et al., 2007); and
- Enrollment characteristics including enrolling in college immediately after high school graduation, enrolling full time, and maintaining continuous enrollment (Adelman, 2006; Goldrick-Rab, 2006; Goldrick-Rab & Pfeffer, 2009).

The two experiences related to academic integration are

- Academic support including tutoring, advising, and academic skill development (Kuh et al., 2007; Tinto, 2004); and
- Curricular choices, including successful completion of gateway and college-level math courses and earning at least 20 credits in the first year (Adelman, 2006).

Finances

Although the Bean model (1980, 1982) posits that financial concerns can influence student retention, most early research on student retention did not consider the role of finances. Over time, however, scholars have focused on student ability to pay and the role of institutional, state, and federal financial aid in retention. As a result, sociologic and economic frameworks have been advanced to study the role of finances in student retention. As already noted, St. John et al.'s (1996) nexus model provides a solid framework for examining the effects of ability to pay and financial aid on student retention.

There is no doubt that ability to pay is positively related to student retention. Studies consistently demonstrate the positive effects of ability to pay, where ability to pay is determined by the income level of students' parents or, if financially independent, the students themselves, also incorporating institutional, state, and federal financial aid (Astin, 1975; Leslie & Brinkman, 1988; St. John, 2000). The amount and types of financial aid (grants and scholarships versus loans) are also related to student retention. Not surprisingly, grants and scholarships are positively related to student retention (Hossler, Ziskin, Gross, Kim, & Cekic, 2009; St. John, 2000; Swail, Redd, & Perna, 2003). In a thorough review of research, Hossler et al. (2009) conclude that the Federal Stafford loan program either has had no effect, or at best a very modest impact, on retention; however, increasing levels of debt are negatively related to student retention. Finally, several studies have found that work-study and on-campus employment are positively associated with retention, whereas off-campus employment (particularly full-time) is associated with attrition (Astin, 1975; Hossler et al., 2009; St. John, 2000; Swail et al., 2003).

In sum, research on student characteristics, educational experiences, and finances has led to conceptual and empirical leads on what institutions can do to increase retention of matriculated students. Indeed, this line of research suggests a number of good practices for institutions to improve retention and graduation rates. For example, Swail et al. (2003) recommend a campus-wide retention plan that integrates financial aid, recruitment, academic and student services, curriculum, and instruction. Kuh et al. (2007) recommend early intervention and persistent effort to assist students at risk of attrition, including learning support networks and classroom communities, as well as ongoing focused assessment of interventions. Berger (2001, 2002) provides a thorough review of empirically derived suggestions for campus programs and policies to enhance student retention.

Effects of Institutional Policies and Practices on Retention

Despite the widespread use of the good practices described above, over more than three decades at colleges and universities across the country, only recently have scholars and institutional researchers started to more carefully examine the effects of campus programs and policies on student retention. This is a nuanced area of inquiry. If we know from efforts to test the Tinto Model of Student Retention that participation in orientation programs is positively associated with student retention, can we assume that if a community college without an orientation program adds one, it will likely retain those students who participate? If tests of Bean's Causal Model of Student Attrition (1980) reveal that students who participate in academic support programs are more likely to be retained, does this mean that a college or university instituting a policy requiring students with GPAs of C or lower to participate in an academic support program will be likely to retain those students? The efforts to test causal models of student retention have led to many empirical insights into student retention, but do these empirical leads readily translate into programmatic initiatives that will unquestionably improve campus retention rates?

Until recently there has been a dearth of research on topics such as these. Therefore, in this section, we examine the following questions:

1. To what extent do institutions organize themselves to enhance student persistence, and what do we know about the efficacy of these efforts?
2. Do program evaluation studies show that students who participate in campus programs such as orientation, structured academic support programs, university 101 courses, or career planning workshops are more likely to be retained?

Two main strands of inquiry inform research on the effects of institutional policies and practices. The first are straightforward program evaluation efforts. The second is a multiple-institution studies approach to assess the global effects of policies and practices implemented to enhance retention on campuses. By policies and practices, we refer to a range of formal and informal rules, actions, activities, and traditions that institutions enact or enhance to support student retention and graduation. Examples of such policies include formal early warning systems that focus on students who show signs of academic difficulty, a requirement that students meet with their academic advisor every semester, or transition programs as part of new student orientation. Examples of institutional practices that enhance retention and graduation could include long-standing traditions of including student government leaders on senior campus policy committees or the board of trustees, or campus norms that emphasize high levels of faculty contact with students outside of class (these might even be reflected in promotion and tenure criteria).

With regard to program evaluation efforts, it is often difficult to establish cause and effect relationships between a programmatic intervention and retention and/ or persistence-related outcomes. Long (2006) urges researchers "to consider the implications of their work and spend time giving more prescriptive recommendations, which involves predicting what steps and actions could remedy a problem that has been documented" (p. 7). However, researchers find prescriptive recommendations challenging because program evaluation studies are difficult to undertake. Patton, Morelon, Whitehead, and Hossler (2006) examined research published in refereed journals between 1990 and 2005 to determine whether the policies and practices that are asserted to improve student retention were confirmed through rigorous methods and program evaluation. The authors concluded that prior research shows moderate support for counseling and mentoring services, and positive support for developing campus-based initiatives that facilitate student-faculty interaction, as well as support for orientation and other transition efforts (Patton et al., 2006).

Braxton, McKinney, and Reynolds (2006) requested all institutions in Indiana to submit documents on evaluations and studies of programs on their campuses. Only one-third of the institutions responded to this request. Most of the studies were descriptive; only five institutions provided results of rigorous evaluation efforts that focused on one or more programs designed to retain students at their institution. Among the five, one institution found a positive impact as a result of learning communities and first-year residence hall living. Another institution reported positive effects of student mentoring on retention.

As Stephen DesJardins and Allyson Flaster describe in their chapter in this volume, conducting rigorous evaluations of programs or interventions in educational settings is usually difficult because of the challenges associated with having control groups and making random assignments. These methodological obstacles often do not allow researchers to be more prescriptive in their recommendations. However, education researchers are increasingly using quasi-experimental designs such as regression discontinuity, propensity score matching, and others to overcome these challenges. The use of these methods may lead to more methodologically rigorous studies that enable postsecondary education researchers to offer concrete solutions to issues.

The second line of research studies examines relationships among different institutional policies and practices and student outcomes. Grounded in theory and research on the influence of factors on student retention, Braxton and McClendon (2001) developed recommendations that cover eight domains of practice for institutions: academic advising, administrative policies and practices, enrollment management, faculty development, faculty reward system, student orientation programs, residential life, and student affairs programming. Among other findings, the authors recommended that academic advisors encourage students to establish memberships in social communities, that rules and regulations be effectively communicated to students, that cooperative/collaborative learning become the focus of faculty development events, and that retention programs enable first-year students to socially interact with their peers.

Two studies conducted by the Pell Institute (Engle & O'Brien, 2007; Muraskin & Lee, 2004) examined institutional practices associated with student graduation at institutions with higher- and lower-than-expected rates. Expected graduation rates were estimated based on the characteristics of the institutions' incoming student population. Using information collected from the institutions, the authors analyzed retention policies and practices at small public and private institutions with high percentages of low-income students in the first study, and at large public colleges and universities with high percentages of low-income students in the second study. Engle and O'Brien (2007) concluded that what higher-performing institutions "do in terms of policies and programs, not just who they are in terms of their student and institutional characteristics, contributes to the success of their students" (p. 3). They provided recommendations based on common practices and policies at higher-performing institutions, such as offering individualized services and support in special programs, creating a sense of shared community by promoting student involvement in campus activities and events, and ensuring campus-wide coordination and collaboration in retention programs.

Extending investigations by the Pell Institute, Dadashova, Ziskin, and Hossler (2010) examined how institutions organize themselves to improve student retention and whether the policies and practices prevalent in student retention are positively associated with institutional outcomes related to student persistence. Conducting regression analyses of data collected from surveys of 441 four-year institutions, Dadashova and colleagues found that such institutional practices as availability of a formal written retention plan, availability of academic support programs, and flagging courses with high percentages of Ds, Fs, or withdrawals were not associated with a higher-than-predicted retention rate. The analyses did show a modest positive relationship between the retention coordinator's authority to implement new initiatives without seeking approval from other administrators on campus and the institution having a with a higher-than-predicted retention rate, as well as a strong positive relationship between support for retention of students of color and with a higher-than-predicted retention rate.

In sum, we still know relatively little about what institutional policies and practices really make a difference in student retention efforts. Although research suggests some positive support for the efficacy of a few campus-based initiatives and practices for improving student retention (e.g., orientation/transition programs, support of faculty-student interaction), the modest amount of available evidence suggests that many policies and practices believed to improve student retention either have very limited impact or have not been examined empirically. The good news is that this situation creates many opportunities for researchers interested in student retention and graduation, and encourages study of this phenomenon in new ways.

Persistence in Contrast to Retention: Institutional and Public Policy Imperatives

Providing new insights requires a paradigm shift from considering students enrolled at a single institution to a perspective that includes student enrollments beyond the institution of origin. In addition, such new thinking requires the consideration of measures associated with state public policies, including retention and persistence measures embedded in state funding formulas, transfer and articulation policies, and financial aid policies. A recent study published by the National Student Clearinghouse Research Center demonstrates the shortcomings of student success measures that focus on retention and completion solely at the institution of origin. In *National Postsecondary Enrollment Trends: Before, During, and After the Great Recession*, Dundar et al. (2011) report that national persistence rates are between 10 and 18 percentage points higher across the various sectors of postsecondary educational institutions than the institutional retention rates reported by IPEDS.

Studies like this illuminate the need for new benchmarking reports that public and institutional policymakers can use to measure student success to degree completion at any institution. Many current benchmarking measures understate student persistence and graduation rates because they rely on retention and graduation rates at the institution of origin only. For example, Adelman (2006) and Reason (2009) have called for greater focus on persistence rates as a broad measure of students' continued enrollment within higher education as well as a better understanding of factors that influence persistence to graduation. As Adelman (2006) noted:

> We falsely believe that beginning students drop out of higher education in appalling numbers by the end of their scheduled first academic year of attendance. In fact, about 90% of traditional-age beginning students turn up somewhere during the academic year (which we measure as July 1 through June 30) (maybe not at the first school attended) and at some time (maybe not in the fall term) during the subsequent academic year. (p. 21)

Although numerous studies have analyzed students who persist while attending multiple institutions (e.g., Adelman, 2006; Cabrera, Burkum, & LaNasa, 2005; Calcagno, Crosta, Bailey, & Jenkins, 2006; Ewell, Schild, & Paulson, 2003; Goldrick-Rab, 2006; Goldrick-Rab & Pfeffer, 2009; Hagedorn, Cabrera, & Prather, 2010; Long & Kurlaender, 2009; National Center for Higher Education and Public Policy, 2011; Peter & Carroll, 2005; Reynolds, 2012), most research continues to focus on student retention at the institution of origin. As we have noted, this is a complex area of research. In particular, we call attention to the large body of policy-oriented research examining the relationship between community college matriculation and completion of a baccalaureate degree. Several earlier studies concluded that starting at a community college reduces the odds of a student earning a four-year degree (e.g., Bernstein, 1986; Brint & Karabel, 1989; Dougherty, 1992), but many of these early empirical studies did not control for issues of student self-selection. In our summary of research on student persistence, we call special attention to more recent findings that control for self-selection (e.g., Long & Kurlaender, 2009; Reynolds, 2012) in order to understand the multifaceted nature of research on this topic.

Although the need for studies of persistence (as opposed to retention) has become more widely acknowledged by researchers, a large gap remains in our understanding of how student characteristics and aspirations interact with educational experiences at multiple institutions, and the role state policies play in persistence and graduation. We also have limited knowledge, for example, on how the timing of transfers and the type of institution transferred from affect educational outcomes. In this section we examine what is known about the predictors of student persistence.

An Overview of Extant Research

Student Background Characteristics

Many of the student-level predictors of persistence are similar to those that predict retention at the institution of origin. Student background characteristics positively related to persistence include being female, and Caucasian or Asian; having higher levels of parental education and income; having friends planning on attending or enrolled; and being younger. Factors that are negatively related include coming from a single parent family and being African American or Hispanic (Adelman, 2006; Anderson, Sun, & Alfonso, 2006; Bailey, Calcagno, Jenkins, Kienzl, & Leinbach, 2005; Blose, Porter, & Kokkelenberg, 2006; Cabrera et al., 2005; Dougherty & Kienzel, 2006; Eddy, Christie, & Rao, 2006; Goldrick-Rab, 2006; Goldrick-Rab & Pfeffer, 2009; Grubb, 1991; Vélez & Javalgi, 1987).

Student Educational Experiences

A number of educational behaviors are positively related to persistence, and, undoubtedly, some of these are associated with student background characteristics.

However, not all studies we reviewed had good measures of a student's educational plans. Researchers were not always certain if students who started at a community college planned to earn a baccalaureate degree, two-year degree, or vocational certificate (Cohen & Brawer, 2008); thus, these findings need to be considered with some caution. However, behaviors associated with retention or persistence anywhere include earning a higher grade point average in high school and/or in college, being enrolled in more demanding high school and postsecondary curricula, not delaying enrollment into postsecondary education after high school, having high levels of enrollment intensity, starting postsecondary enrollment at a four-year institution (particularly a private four-year college or university), attending fewer institutions, and stopping-out fewer times (Bailey et al., 2005; Goldrick-Rab, 2006; Goldrick-Rab & Pfeffer, 2009).

Institutional Characteristics

In terms of institutional characteristics, persistence rates are higher at four-year than two-year institutions, institutions with higher levels of selectivity, private rather than public institutions, and community colleges with high levels of funding per student, as well as institutions with higher percentages of full-time students, full-time faculty, and women students; higher levels of expenditures on instruction, academic support programs, student services, and administrative services; higher average family income of enrolled students; and higher levels of tuition (Bailey et al., 2005; Goldrick-Rab, 2006; Goldrick-Rab & Pfeffer, 2009).

State Policies

Several scholars have examined the effects of state transfer and articulation policies on student transfer behaviors. Until recently, most of these studies have used a dichotomous outcome variable—did the student transfer from a two-year to a four-year college, yes or no (Bender, 1990; Hungar & Lieberman, 2001; Knoell, 1990; Wellman, 2002). Hagedorn, Maxwell, Cypers, Moon, and Lester (2007) and Roksa and Keith (2008), among others, have called for more nuanced outcome measures. Hagedorn et al. (2010), for example, report that only 50% of the students enrolled at one community college system who indicated they plan to transfer to a four-year institution actually transferred. Roksa and Keith (2008) provide a solid overview of research on the efficacy of transfer and articulation agreements, concluding that these agreements have little or no impact on transfer rates. While citing some studies that find a positive impact (e.g., Banks, 1994; Higgins & Katsinas, 1999), Roksa and Keith offer a strong critique of the representativeness of the data used and the reliance on aggregate data rather than data that track the transfer of individual students. They recommend that future analyses consider all forms of transfer and additional outcome measures including the number of credits accumulated after transferring, the number of credits counted toward graduation at the receiving institution, and the number of successive semesters post-transfer that students remain enrolled at the transfer institution. In their own analyses, Roksa and Keith examined a more robust set of outcome measures and found no relationship between state transfer and articulation policies and student transfer behaviors.

In addition, little is known about the effects of state financial aid policies on student transfer behaviors, although many studies examine the effects of state financial aid on persistence using data from the National Postsecondary Student Aid Study (NPSAS) or the Education Longitudinal Study of 2002 (ELS). While these data allow researchers to examine persistence among students who have transferred one or more times, most authors do not focus on multiple transfers. As noted by Dowd and Coury (2006) and Hossler et al. (2009), most studies that use these datasets focus on students who attend just one college or university (retention) or aggregate students who remain enrolled in a single institution with those who have attended more than one college or university. Goldrick-Rab et al. (2009) call for state financial aid policies that encourage and support student transfer and persistence anywhere, but to date few studies of these policies have been undertaken.

Federal Financial Aid Policies

Federal financial aid policies may also influence persistence, but no known studies have been undertaken examining the effects of federal or state financial aid on persistence and graduation for students who attend more than one institution. Thus, we are unable to make any definitive statements about the effects of federal or state financial aid on students who attend multiple institutions.

Moving Forward: Data, Methods, and Future Studies

To enhance our understanding of student retention, persistence, and college completion, this chapter posits two goals that should frame future efforts of researchers and policymakers: the first, to increase understanding of the efficacy of campus-based retention efforts; and the second, to improve knowledge regarding student mobility, which involves understanding the role that student characteristics, institutional factors, and state and federal policies play in determining the educational outcomes of students who attend multiple postsecondary institutions. We begin this discussion by first focusing on mobile students and then move to an examination of the impact of campus-based policies and practices on student retention and graduation.

Studying Student Mobility

Data Requirements

The lack of available data to study mobile students is the most pressing limitation from a public and institutional policy perspective as no public databases exist that permit annual benchmarking of retention, persistence, and graduation rates for all enrolled students. Both public and institutional policymakers use annual benchmarking reports to gauge their progress on retention and graduation efforts. Benchmarking reports are also used to inform state funding formulas; assess the quality of individual institutions; and, increasingly, to compare the educational progress of nations. However, because databases to study persistence and graduation across multiple institutions are unavailable, many policymakers are simply unaware of the diverse set of enrollment paths of transfer students, who comprise approximately one-third of all first-time college students (Hossler et al., 2012). Although many states are in the process of building state longitudinal data systems (SLDS), state database interoperability issues and the ability to analyze student enrollment patterns across multiple institutions and state lines continue to be a challenge. Making data available to study students who attend multiple institutions will only become more important as more states encourage students to start at a community college and transfer to a four-year college (Indiana Commission for Higher Education [ICHE], 2008).

Student-level longitudinal data are available through U.S. Institute for Education Sciences studies, such as NPSAS, ELS, and Beginning Postsecondary Students (BPS), all of which can be used to track students across institutions nationally. However, because these databases consist of limited student samples, they are not broadly representative of students at the institution or state levels and, thus, do not permit examination of the effects of state and institutional policies and practices (e.g., financial aid, retention programs, policies at individual institutions, diverse types of public and private institutions within a state, etc.) while accounting for student-level characteristics at multiple levels.

State data systems are generally not sample based, but, instead, cover all students within a state. As states build and link their K–12 and postsecondary SLDS, it becomes possible to follow students across many institutions longitudinally. These enhanced SLDS make it possible to study mobile students, who are students who move within and between the two- and four-year public sectors within states. Some states, such as Florida and Ohio, are making their databases available to researchers, thus enabling studies of persistence among multiple transfer students (e.g., Bettinger & Long, 2010; Hu, 2008). These databases may be adequate for some researchers' needs, particularly for large states with relatively low levels of student out-migration (e.g., Texas, California, Florida). However, SLDS in neighboring states likely use different data structures and definitions, inhibiting their usefulness for national research or for states with high levels of out-migration (e.g., New Jersey, Massachusetts). Many SLDS do not include information on students who begin college out of state, transfer across state borders, or enroll in private nonprofit colleges and universities or for-profit institutions.

With support from the federal government, hopefully all states will build state longitudinal databases containing cross-sector educational data as well as workforce data. Many policymakers and policy analysts hope that these databases will be readily shared across stakeholders and enable policymakers and academic researchers to track a student's postsecondary educational progress to eventual degree completion (Data Quality Campaign, 2009a). However, progress toward this goal remains uncertain. Even the most optimistic assessments (e.g., Data Quality Campaign, 2009b) report that states are in the process of working toward the goal of interoperability, but that these goals have not been achieved. Multiple players are interested in building interoperability among state data systems and promoting the usage of common data definitions (e.g., Postsecondary Electronic Standards Council [PESC] and Common Education Data Standards [CEDS]), but to date most of the interoperability work has focused on K–12 data, not postsecondary data. State stakeholders have frequently expressed doubts about the movement toward interoperability because standards are not yet finalized and/or were developed and released after many states were already far along in the development of their databases. These same stakeholders express additional concerns about available funding and legislative process issues. A spate of legal questions as to whether states can, or will, enact the necessary regulations to enable data sharing are yet to be resolved (Reidenberg et al., 2009).

One promising approach that has emerged is to combine state and institutional datasets with data from the National Student Clearinghouse (NSC). The NSC was established in 1993 to enable institutions to easily share enrollment information among themselves and student loan servicers in order to alleviate loan defaults arising when students changed institutions faster than registrars and lenders could keep track. Over time, the NSC evolved to provide additional services based on enrollment data that it maintains on behalf of colleges and universities. These services have encouraged a majority of institutions to participate on a voluntary basis and at no cost to the institution. Consequently, the NSC is a repository for student-level enrollment data covering roughly 94% of students attending U.S. Title IV degree-granting institutions as of fall 2011. Enrollment data coverage rates relative to IPEDS fall 2011 enrollment reports vary somewhat by institutional sector: public four-year institutions are best represented at 99.5%, followed closely by public two-year institutions at 97.4%, and private, nonprofit, four-year institutions at 93.9%. The lowest coverage rates are among private for-profit four-year institutions: 68.0% of students in this sector in the fall 2011 were enrolled in institutions sending data to the NSC. All categories of institutions provide monthly files throughout the academic year listing each student's dates of enrollment, enrollment status, and degree or certificate completion status during the term enrolled. Most of the participating institutions send detailed degree data to the NSC as well, including award level, title, discipline, and CIP (Classification of Instructional Programs) code.

Currently, the NSC Research Center offers valuable research opportunities not only to institutions that want to follow up on the enrollments of admitted students, stop-outs, and graduates, but also to other educational organizations, particularly high schools and college access organizations that want to gauge their graduates' entrance and success in higher education. Academic researchers and states interested in students' postsecondary pathways longitudinally and nationally will also find the data useful.[1] Institutional researchers at NSC-member institutions can examine the extent to which institutional programs contribute to the educational progress of students who subsequently transfer and graduate from other institutions. Similarly, state longitudinal data systems can create studies that allow examinations of the contributions of programs throughout the P–16 pipeline to the educational progress of students, even when that progress takes students along pathways involving postsecondary institutions in different states and sectors.

Methods

Assuming that academic researchers and policy analysts can gain access to the requisite databases, future research on mobile students also requires more complex analytic plans. We suggest that researchers use analytic techniques that capture causal relationships longitudinally over time and simultaneously account for student background characteristics and educational experiences, institutional characteristics, and policy contexts, as well as student self-selection. Having acknowledged the limitations of studying the complex phenomena associated with persistence and multiple transfers, there are analytic techniques that more readily lend themselves to studying various patterns associated with student persistence (see the chapter by DesJardins & Flaster in this volume for further discussion of related issues and approaches). We briefly highlight some of these techniques and data requirements:

1. Multilevel Modeling—Conceptualizing student postsecondary outcomes such as transfer or persistence as multilevel phenomena and using multilevel models allows researchers to examine the relationship of the institutional and/or state context to student outcomes while taking student-level characteristics into account. Reflecting data availability, two-level models are commonly used in educational research with the students being nested within institutions. However, if the data are available, three-level multilevel models can be employed with the students (at level one), nested in institutions (at level two), and nested within varying state policies associated with funding or transfers (at level three). Cross-classified multilevel models will allow researchers to nest students at two different types of institutions, for example, high schools and postsecondary institutions or four-year and two-year institutions, as relevant to the research question.

2. Panel data enable scholars to observe multiple outcomes over multiple time periods for students or institutions. In other words, panel data allow for longitudinal analyses of student transfer and persistence. A combination of multilevel modeling and longitudinal research methods, such as multilevel hazard models, enable researchers to examine not only the effects of variables at more than one level but also the effects of time-varying variables, such as financial aid or students' college GPA, on student outcomes at different points in their enrollment.

Recommendations for Policy, Practice, and Research

In this chapter we have provided an overview of what is known about the relationship among student characteristics, institutional attributes, and college experience variables on student retention at institution of origin; the effects of institutional programs and policies intended to enhance student retention at the institution of origin; and persistence among students who transfer to different institutions one or more times. An additional important consideration is that, to date, most public policy accountability metrics and reports focus only on retention at the institution of origin, a focus that makes mobile students look like failures and institutions that serve large numbers of mobile students appear inferior. Against this backdrop we offer recommendations for institutional and public policymakers, as well as future research.

Recommendations for Policy and Practice

In this section we focus on actionable items for federal, state, and institutional policymakers. For example, stating that more affluent students are more to likely be retained at the institution of origin or persist anywhere and eventually graduate is not particularly actionable; other than attempting to recruit or admit more affluent students, there is relatively little that policymakers can do with this information. However, it is potentially actionable to say that institutional funding per student exerts a positive influence on the odds of persisting until graduation.

We also developed these recommendations based on a synthesis of findings from research on the factors that influence student retention as well as student persistence. In many instances both lines of research report similar findings, but in some cases we relied more heavily on one line of research rather than research on both topics. For example, considerably more research considers the effects of grants and loans on student retention than on student persistence.

Student Enrollment Behaviors and Educational Experiences

Two important limitations frame our recommendations pertaining to student enrollment behaviors and educational experiences. First, public and institutional policymakers are not always certain of students' educational goals. For example, many students who enroll in not-for-profit and for-profit institutions choose curricula that are focused on two-year or less than two-year certificate programs, not degrees. These students are simply seeking a few courses for work-related reasons or personal enrichment of their skills and knowledge, so policy suggestions to increase their persistence to a degree are out of place. In addition, the extent to which information and encouragement from educators or state policymakers can truly influence student enrollment behaviors and educational goals is an open question. With these caveats, we offer the following recommendations.

Our review of available research suggests the utility of several policies and practices. Encouraging high school students to enroll in a demanding curriculum in high school (and then while in college) is likely to promote persistence until graduation. Students should also be encouraged not to delay postsecondary enrollment after graduating from high school and to enroll full time rather than part time. Although the evidence is mixed, more recent studies using advanced econometric techniques suggest that students who are committed to earning a four-year degree would see modest improvements in the odds that they would reach their goal if they began enrollment at a four-year institution, rather than a two-year institution. Similarly, the accumulated evidence across several studies suggests that students should be encouraged to minimize the number of times they transfer or stop-out en route to a degree (Bailey et al., 2005; Goldrick-Rab, 2006; Goldrick-Rab & Pfeffer, 2009). Policymakers should encourage students to develop realistic plans that account for and recognize the implications of different enrollment choices and pathways for the likelihood of degree completion.

Institutional Characteristics, Programs, and Policies

Students are more likely to be retained or continue to persist until graduation at colleges and universities that have higher levels of tuition; not surprisingly, those are the institutions that provide higher levels of financial support for instruction, academic support, and so forth. Students are also more likely to persist at institutions that hire more full-time faculty as opposed to institutions that depend more heavily on part-time faculty. Students who attend institutions with higher proportions of full-time students are also more likely to persist and be retained. Finally, our review of the literature suggests that institutions most likely to retain and assist students toward degree completion have a strong commitment to student success as evidenced by the following: strong orientation and transition programs, strong academic support programs, administrators with the authority to enact new retention initiatives, encouragement of student involvement, and a special focus on providing support for students of color (Bailey et al., 2005; Goldrick-Rab, 2006; Goldrick-Rab & Pfeffer, 2009).

State and Federal Policies

First and foremost, policymakers should develop policies consistent with research findings on encouraging student persistence and college completion. There is clear evidence that institutions that spend more per student enrolled (after controlling for student background characteristics) are more likely to retain and graduate larger percentages of their students (Hagedorn et al., 2007; Roksa & Keith, 2008). Thus, for public institutions, this would entail either providing higher levels of state subsidy per student enrolled, or permitting public institutions to increase tuition to enable higher levels of funding per student enrolled. Also, because student financial assistance in the form of grants has a positive impact on retention, and loans have little or no impact (Alon, 2007; DesJardins, Ahlburg, & McCall, 2002; Perna 1998; Singell, 2004; St. John, 1989), it is axiomatic that more generous state grant programs would enhance the odds of student persistence and graduation.

A recurring theme in this chapter is the need for institutional leaders and state and federal policymakers to develop more complex benchmarks for student progress toward degree completion. We need to be able to track student enrollments across multiple institutions, and Adelman (2007) has proffered a new approach to tracking mobile students and attributing contributions to such students' education. Adelman's approach may or may not be the best formula; nevertheless, benchmarking formulas create incentive structures that, in turn, drive behaviors on the part of institutions, states, and the federal government. We need new metrics that provide better measures of progress toward degree, persistence anywhere, and college completion if we hope to better measure student progress and encourage institutions to improve student success and college completion.

Recommendations for Research

Regarding retention at the institution of origin, our review suggests relatively little new to be learned by employing variables derived from such widely used models as Tinto (1975, 1993), Bean (1980, 1982), Cabrera and colleagues (1993), St. John (1996), or Braxton and colleagues (2000) unless they are applied to students in new types of institutions like for-profit institutions. However, new theoretically derived models may be advanced to shed new light on this outcome. For example, Bean's (1980) original model considered financial concerns that set the stage for research on the effects of financial aid on retention. Bean, along with Metzner (Bean & Metzner, 1985), provided conceptual leads for studying retention among adult students. St. John's nexus model (St. John, Paulsen, & Starkey, 1996) further invigorated research on the effects of financial aid. More recently, models have been developed for Latino and Asian students (e.g., Flowers, 2006; Nora, 1987; St. John & Paulsen, 2005; Torres, 2006) that may lead to new insights on success outcomes of these particular groups of students.

Developing new metrics is an especially important undertaking for states and public institutions. Many states are enacting state funding formulas intended to create incentives for postsecondary institutions to retain and graduate more students. For example, Harnisch (2011) reports that Tennessee's emphasis on increasing graduation rates has resulted in change that led campuses to bring in extra student advisors, increase tutoring and remedial classes, fast-track majors, and develop extra courses between semesters. At the moment, however, states only have simple metrics such as the proportion or total number of first-time first-year students who persist at the institution of origin or percentage or total number of students who graduate. If states had outcome measures that capture the complexity of student enrollment behaviors and some of the incentives created by state transfer and articulation policies, they might see more desirable results.

Therefore, more program evaluation research is needed to identify the impact of initiatives such as university 101 programs, learning communities, and remedial education programs. Researchers should make the best use of quasi-experimental research methods, such as regression discontinuity and propensity score matching, to avoid biases introduced by the absence of control groups and random assignment, and to isolate the effects of these programs with more confidence (see the chapter in this volume by DesJardins and Flaster for a comprehensive discussion on using such methods for research on college access, persistence, and completion). More research is also needed on the intensity and efficacy of overall institutional efforts. It may not be possible to fully tease out the causal effects of total campus efforts, but one study (Dadashova et al., 2010) found that the retention coordinator's authority to implement new initiatives without seeking prior approval and support for the retention of students of color both were significantly and positively related to the institution having a higher-than-predicted retention rate. Engle and O'Brien (2007) and Muraskin and Lee (2004) also reported a number of policies and practices that institutions with higher-than-expected graduation rates had in place, such as campus-wide coordination and collaboration in retention programs and offering individualized services and support in special programs among others. However, more research is needed to understand how institutions organize themselves to enhance student retention and the impact of campus policies and practices on student retention and graduation. Such research should focus on both two- and four-year institutions, as well as for-profit and not-for-profit institutions.

Finally, this chapter demonstrates the pressing need for more research on students who attend more than one institution and students who persist at any institution, and on the intersection of student characteristics, institutional characteristics, and public policy to encourage or constrain student persistence and degree completion anywhere. We have already outlined the databases and analytical techniques needed for such research. The U.S. Department of Education's recent *Action Plan for Improving Measures of Postsecondary Student Success* (2012) also emphasizes the need to develop better definitions and measures for various types of student enrollment patterns and to collect more data so policymakers can benchmark a broad variety of enrollment patterns. Currently, due to limitations of IPEDS, efforts to benchmark improvements in college completion rates are limited to four-year and six-year graduation rates.

Until additional research is conducted and metrics developed, evaluating progress toward degree completion will remain limited to measures of retention at the institution of origin. The growing emphasis on student success and college completion creates a sense of urgency to perform these studies. The complex web of state, federal, and institutional policies, combined with student characteristics and enrollment patterns, remains the most pressing area for a greater understanding of student persistence and retention among public policymakers.

Note

1. Academic researchers and policy analysts can arrange (with appropriate permissions from relevant agencies) to secure NSC data for studies; however, because NSC does not receive federal or state funding to maintain the data it holds, the NSC charges users for securing and/or matching NSC data with extant datasets for the purposes of research.

References

Adelman, C. (2006). *The toolbox revisited: Paths to degree completion from high school through college.* Washington, DC: U.S. Department of Education.

Adelman, C. (2007, March 12). Making graduation rates matter. *Inside Higher Education.* Retrieved from http://www.insidehighered.com/views/2007/03/12/adelman

Alon, S. (2007). The influence of financial aid in leveling group differences in graduating from elite institutions. *Economics of Education Review, 26,* 296–311.

Anderson, G., Sun, J.C., & Alfonso, M. (2006). Effectiveness of statewide articulation agreements on the probability of transfer: A preliminary policy analysis. *Review of Higher Education, 29*(3), 261–291.

Astin, A.W. (1975). *Preventing students from dropping out.* San Francisco, CA: Jossey-Bass.

Astin, A.W. (1997). How "good" is your institution's retention rate? *Research in Higher Education, 38*(6), 647–658.

Bailey, T., Calgano, J.C., Jenkins, D., Kienzl, G., & Leinbach, T. (2005). *The effects of institutional factors on the success of community college students.* New York, NY: Community College Research Center, Teachers College, Columbia University.

Banks, D.L. (1994). Effects of environmental conditions on student-transfer activity. *Community College Journal of Research and Practice, 18,* 245–259.

Bean, J. (1980). Dropouts and turnover: The synthesis and test of a causal model of student attrition. *Research in Higher Education, 12*(2), 155–187.

Bean, J. (1982). Conceptual models of student attrition: How theory can help the institutional researcher. *New Directions for Institutional Research: Studying Student Attrition, 1982*(36), 17–33.

Bean, J.P., & Metzner, B. (1985). Conceptual model of nontraditional undergraduate student attrition. *Review of Educational Research, 55*(4), 485–540.

Bender, L.W. (Ed.). (1990). *Spotlight on the transfer function: A national study of state policies and practices.* Washington, DC: American Association of Community Colleges.

Berger, J.B. (2001). Understanding the organizational nature of student persistence: Recommendations for practice. *Journal of College Student Retention: Research, Theory & Practice, 3,* 3–22.

Berger, J.B. (2002). The influence of the organizational structures of colleges and universities on college student learning. *Peabody Journal of Education, 77,* 40–59.

Bernstein, A. (1986). The devaluation of transfer: Current explanations and possible causes. *New Directions for Community Colleges, 54,* 31–40.

Bettinger, E.P. & Long, B.T. (2010). Does cheaper mean better? The impact of using adjunct instructors on student outcomes. *The Review of Economics and Statistics, 92*(3), 598–613.

Bland, S. (2010, August 9). Obama aims to lift college graduation rates, but his tools are few. *Christian Science Monitor.* Retrieved from http://www.csmonitor.com/USA/Education/2010/0809/Obama-aims-to-lift-college-graduation-rates-but-his-tools-are-few

Blose, G.L., Porter, J.D., & Kokkelenberg, E. (2006). The effect of institutional funding cuts on baccalaureate graduation rates in public higher education. In R.G. Ehrenberg (Ed.), *What's happening to public higher education?* (pp. 71–82). Westport, CT: Praeger.

Bound, J., Lovenheim, M., & Turner, S. (2010). Why have college completion rates declined? An analysis of changing student preparation and collegiate resources. *American Economic Journal: Applied Economics, 2*(3), 129–157.

Braxton, J.M. (Ed.). (2000). *Reworking the student departure puzzle.* Nashville, TN: Vanderbilt University Press.

Braxton, J.M., Hirschy, A.S., & McClendon, S.A. (2004). *Understanding and reducing college student departure* (ASHE-ERIC Higher Education Report Series, Vol. 30, No. 3). San Francisco, CA: Jossey-Bass..

Braxton, J.M., & McClendon, S.A. (2001–2002). The fostering of social integration and retention through institutional practice. *Journal of College Student Retention, 3*(1), 57–71.

Braxton, J.M., McKinney, J.S., & Reynolds, P. (2006). Cataloguing institutional efforts to understand and reduce college student departure. *New Directions for Institutional Research, 130,* 25–32.

Brint, S., & Karabel, J. (1989). The diverted dream. New York, NY: Oxford University Press.

Cabrera, A.F., Burkum, K.R., & LaNasa, S.M. (2005). Pathways to a four-year degree: Determinants of transfer and degree completion. In Alan Seidman (Ed.), *College student retention: A formula for success* (pp. 155–214). Westport, CT: ACE/Praeger Series on Higher Education.

Cabrera, A.F., Nora, A., & Castenada, M.B. (1993). College persistence: Structural equation modeling test of an integrated model of student retention. *Journal of Higher Education, 64*(2), 123–139.

Calcagno, J.C., Crosta, P., Bailey, T., & Jenkins, D. (2006). *Stepping stones to a degree: The impact of enrollment pathways and milestones on older community college student outcomes* (CCRC Working Paper No. 4). New York, NY: Community College Research Center. Retrieved from http://www.inpathways.net/SteppingStonestoaDegree.pdf

Choy, S.P. (2001). *Students whose parents did not go to college: Postsecondary access, persistence and attainment* (Report No. NCES 2001–126). Washington, DC: National Center for Education Statistics, U.S. Department of Education.

Cohen, A.M., & Brawer, F.B. (2008). *The American community college.* San Franscisco, CA: Jossey-Bass.

Dadashova, A., Ziskin, M., & Hossler, D. (2010, November). *An examination of institutional practices surrounding student retention.* Paper presented at the annual conference of the Association for the Study of Higher Education, Indianapolis, IN.

Data Quality Campaign. (2009a). Common data standards [June 19 Webinar]. Retrieved from http://www.dataqualitycampaign.org/files/CDS_Webinar_Presentation_2009–06–19-PUBLIC_2_.pdf

Data Quality Campaign. (2009b). *Annual progress report on state data systems.* Washington DC: Author. Retrieved from http://www.dataqualitycampaign.org/files/DQC_11–19.pdf

DesJardins, S.L., Ahlburg, D.A., & McCall, B.P. (2002). Simulating the longitudinal effects of changes in financial aid on student departure from college. *Journal of Human Resources, 37*(3), 653–679.

Dougherty, K.J. (1992). Community colleges and baccalaureate attainment. *The Journal of Higher Education, 63*(2), 188–214.

Dougherty, K.J., & Kienzel, G.S. (2006). It's not enough to get through the open door: Inequalities by social background in transfer from community colleges to four-year colleges. *Teachers College Record, 108*(3), 452–487.

Dowd, A.C., & Coury, T. (2006). The effect of loans on the persistence and attainment of community college students. *Research in Higher Education, 42*(1), 33–62.

Dundar, A., Hossler, D., Shapiro, D., Chen, J., Martin, S., Torres, V., . . . Ziskin, M., (2011). *National postsecondary enrollment trends: Before, during and after the great recession.* Herndon, VA: National Student Clearinghouse Research Center.

Eddy, P., Christie, R., & Rao, M. (2006). Factors affecting transfer of "traditional" community college students. *Community College Enterprise, 12*(1), 73–92.

Engle, J., & O'Brien, C. (2007). *Demography is not destiny: Increasing the graduation rates of low-income college students at large public universities.* Washington, DC: The Pell Institute for the Study of Opportunity in Higher Education.

Ewell, P.T., Schild, P.R., & Paulson, K. (2003). *Following the mobile student: Can we develop the capacity for a comprehensive database to assess student progression?* Indianapolis, IN: Lumina Foundation for Education.

Flowers, L.A. (2006). Effects of attending a 2-year institution on African American males' academic and social integration in the first year of college. *Teachers College Record, 108*(2), 267–286.

Goldrick-Rab, S. (2006). Their every move: An investigation of social-class differences in college pathways. *Sociology of Education, 79*(1), 61–79.

Goldrick-Rab, S., & Pfeffer, F.T. (2009). Beyond access: Explaining socioeconomic differences in college transfer. *Sociology of Education, 82*(2), 101–125.

Grubb, W.N. (1991). The decline of community college transfer rates: Evidence from national longitudinal surveys. *Journal of Higher Education, 62*(2), 194–222.

Hagedorn, L., Cabrera, A., & Prather, G. (2010). The community college transfer calculator: Identifying the course-taking patterns that predict transfer to a four-year institution. *Journal of College Student Retention: Research, Theory and Practice, 12*(1), 105–130.

Hagedorn, L.S., Maxwell, W.E., Cypers, S., Moon, H.S., & Lester, J. (2007). Course shopping in urban community colleges: An analysis of student drop and add activities. *Journal of Higher Education, 78*(4), 464–485.

Harnisch. T.L. (2011). *Performance-based funding: A re-emerging strategy in public higher education financing.* Washington, DC: American Association of State Colleges and Universities. Retrieved from http://www.congressweb.com/aascu/docfiles/Performance_Funding_AASCU_June2011.pdf

Higgins, C.S., & Katsinas, S.G. (1999). The relationship between environmental conditions and transfer rates of selected rural community colleges: A pilot study. *Community College Review, 27*(2), 1–23.

Hossler, D., Schmit, J., & Vesper, N. (1999). Going to college: How social, economic, and educational factors influence the decisions students make. Baltimore, MD: Johns Hopkins University Press.

Hossler, D., Shapiro, D., Dundar, A., Ziskin, M., Chen, J., Zerquera, D., & Torres, V. (2012). *Transfer and mobility: A national view of pre-degree student movement in postsecondary institutions.* Herndon, VA: National Student Clearinghouse Research Center.

Hossler, D., Ziskin. M.B., Gross, J.P.K., Kim, S., & Cekic, O. (2009). Student aid and its role in encouraging persistence. *Higher Education: Handbook of Theory and Research, 24,* 389–425.

Hu, S. (2008, May). *Merit-based financial aid and student enrollment in baccalaureate degree programs in science and engineering: What can Florida's Bright Futures Program tell us?* Paper presented at the annual forum of the Association for Institutional Research, Seattle, WA. Retrieved from http://www3.airweb.org/webrecordings/forum2008/743%20-%20Merit-Based%20Financial%20Aid%20and%20Student%20Enrollment.pdf

Hungar, J.Y., & Lieberman, J. (2001). *The road to equality: Report on transfer for the Ford Foundation.* New York, NY: LaGuardia Community College.

Indiana Commission for Higher Education. (2008). *Reaching higher with Ivy Tech Community College of Indiana: Focusing on the role of community colleges.* Indianapolis, IN: Author. Retrieved from http://www.che.state.in.us

Ishtani, T. (2006). Studying attrition and degree completion behavior among first-generation college students. *The Journal of Higher Education, 77*(5), 861–885.

Knoell, D. (1990). *Transfer, articulation, and collaboration: Twenty-five years later.* Washington, DC: American Association of Community and Junior Colleges.

Kuh, G.D., Kinzie, J., Buckley, J.A., Bridges, B.K., & Hayek, J.C. (2007). *Piecing together the student success puzzle: Research, propositions and recommendations* (ASHE-ERIC Higher Education Report Series, Vol. 32, No. 5). San Francisco, CA: Jossey-Bass.

Leslie, L.L., & Brinkman, P.T. (1988). *The economic value of higher education.* Old Tappan, NJ: Macmillan.

Long, B.T. (2006). *Using research to improve student success: What more could be done?* Washington, DC: National Center for Education Statistics. Retrieved from http://nces.ed.gov/npec/pdf/resp_Long.pdf

Long, B.T., & Kurlaender, M. (2009). Do community colleges provide a viable pathway to a baccalaureate degree? *Educational Evaluation and Policy Analysis, 31,* 30–53.

Lotkowksi, V.A., Robbins, S.A., & Noeth, R.J. (2004). *The role of academic and non-academic factors in improving college retention: ACT policy report.* Iowa City, IA: ACT, Inc.

Muraskin, L., & Lee, J. (2004). *Raising the graduation rates of low-income college students.* Washington, DC: The Pell Institute for the Study of Opportunity in Higher Education.

National Center for Higher Education and Public Policy. (2011). *Affordability and transfer: Critical to increasing baccalaureate degree completion.* San Jose, CA: Author. Retrieved from http://inpathways.net/PolicyAlert_06–2011.pdf

Nora, A. (1987). Determinants of retention among Chicano college students: A structural model. *Research in Higher Education, 26,* 31–59.

Pascarella, E.T. (1980). Student-faculty informal contact and college outcomes. *Review of Educational Research, 50,* 545–595.

Pascarella, E.T., & Terenzini, P.T. (1979). Interaction effects in Spady's and Tinto's conceptual models of college dropout. *Sociology of Education, 61,* 197–210.

Pascarella, E.T., & Terenzini, P.T. (1980). Predicting freshman persistence and voluntary dropout decisions from a theoretical model. *Journal of Higher Education, 51,* 60–75.

Pascarella, E.T., & Terenzini, P.T. (1983). Predicting voluntary freshman year persistence/withdrawal behavior in a residential university: A path analytic validation of Tinto's model. *Journal of Educational Psychology, 75*(2), 215–226.

Pascarella, E.T., & Terenzini, P.T. (1991). *How college affects students: A third decade of research.* San Francisco, CA: Jossey-Bass.

Patton, L.D., Morelon, C., Whitehead, D.M., & Hossler, D. (2006). Campus-based retention initiatives: Does the emperor have clothes? In E.P. St. John & M. Wilkerson (Eds.), *Reframing persistence research to improve academic success* [Special Issue]. *New Directions for Institutional Research, 2006*(130), 9–24. San Francisco, CA: Jossey-Bass.

Perna, L.W. (1998). The contribution of financial aid to undergraduate persistence. *Journal of Student Financial Aid, 28*(3), 25–40.

Perna, L.W., & Titus, M.A. (2005). The relationship between parental involvement as social capital and college enrollment: An examination of racial/ethnic group differences. *Journal of Higher Education, 76*(5), 485–518.

Peter, K., & Carroll, C.D. (2005). *The road less traveled? Students who enroll in multiple institutions.* Washington, DC: National Center for Educational Statistics. Retrieved from http://inpathways.net/road-less-traveled.pdf

Radford, A.W., Berkner, L., Wheeless, S.C., & Shepherd, B. (2010). *Persistence and attainment of 2003–04 beginning postsecondary students: After 6 years.* Washington, DC: National Center for Education Statistics.

Reason, R.D. (2009) An examination of persistence research through the lens of a comprehensive conceptual framework. *Journal of College Student Development, 50*(6), 659–682.

Reidenberg, J., Debelak, J., Gross, A., Mayberry, L.A., Simms, J., & Woodard, E. (2009). *Children's educational records and privacy: A study of elementary and secondary school state reporting systems* (Fordham Law Legal Studies Research Paper No. 1495743). Retrieved from http://papers.ssrn.com/sol3/papers.cfm?abstract_id=1495743

Rendón, L.I., Jalomo, R., Jr., & Nora, A. (2000). Theoretical considerations in the study of minority student retention in higher education. In J.M. Braxton (Ed.), *Reworking the student departure puzzle* (pp. 127–156). Nashville, TN: Vanderbilt University Press.

Reynolds, C.L. (2012). Where to attend? Estimating the effects of beginning college at a two-year institution. *Economics of Education Review, 31*(4), 345–362.

Roksa, J., & Keith, B. (2008). Credits, time, and attainment: Articulation policies and success after transfer. *Educational Evaluation and Policy Analysis, 30*(3), 236–254.

Singell, L. (2004). Come and stay a while: Does financial aid effect enrollment and retention at a large public university? *Economics of Education Review, 23*, 459–472.

St. John, E.P. (1989). The influence of student aid on persistence. *Journal of Student Financial Aid, 19*(3), 52–68.

St. John, E. (2000). The impact of student aid on recruitment and retention: What the research indicates. *New Directions for Student Services, 89*, 61–75.

St. John, E.P., & Paulsen, M.B. (2002). Social class and college costs: Examining the financial nexus between college choice and persistence. *Journal of Higher Education, 73*(2), 189–236.

St. John, E.P., & Paulsen, M.B. (2005). Diversity, college costs, and postsecondary opportunity: An examination of the financial nexus between college choice and persistence for African Americans and whites. *Journal of Higher Education, 76*(5), 545–569.

St. John, E., Paulsen, M., & Starkey, J. (1996). The nexus between college choice and persistence. Research in Higher Education, 37(2), 175–220.

Swail, W.S., Redd, K.E., & Perna, L.W. (2003). *Retaining minority students in higher education: A framework for success* (ASHE-ERIC Higher Education Report Series, Vol. 30, No. 2). San Francisco, CA: Jossey-Bass.

Tinto, V. (1975). Dropout from higher education: A theoretical synthesis of recent research. *Review of Educational Research, 45*, 89–125.

Tinto, V. (1987). *Leaving college.* Chicago, IL: University of Chicago Press.

Tinto, V. (1993). *Leaving college: Rethinking the causes and cures of student attrition* (2nd ed.). Chicago, IL: University of Chicago Press.

Tinto, V. (2004). *Student retention and graduation: Facing the truth, living with the consequences* (Occasional Paper No. 1). Washington, DC: The Pell Institute for the Study of Opportunity in Higher Education.

Tinto, V. (2005). *Student retention: What next?* Washington, DC: The Pell Institute for the Study of Opportunity in Higher Education. Retrieved from http://faculty.soe.syr.edu/vtinto/Files/Student%20Retention-What%20Next_.pdf

Torres, V. (2006). A mixed method study testing data-model fit of a retention model for Latino/a students at urban universities. *Journal of College Student Development, 47*(3), 99–318.

Tross, S.A., Harper, J.P., Osher, L.W., & Kneidinger, L.M. (2000). Not the usual cast of characteristics: Using personality to predict college performance and retention. *Journal of College Student Development, 4*(3), 323–334.

U.S. Department of Education. (2012, April). *Action plan for improving measures of postsecondary student success.* Washington, DC: Author. Retrieved from http://www.ed.gov/edblogs/ous/initiatives

Vélez, W., & Javalgi, R.G. (1987). Two-year college to four-year college: The likelihood of transfer. *American Journal of Education, 96*(1), 81–93.

Wellman, J. (2002). *State policy and community college—baccalaureate transfer* (National Center Report No. 02–6). San Jose, CA: The National Center for Public Policy and Higher Education and the Institute for Higher Education Policy. Retrieved from http://www.csn.edu/PDFFiles/Counseling%20and%20Transfer/NACADA%202009/Higher%20Education%20Transfer%20Report.pdf

9

ACCESS, PERSISTENCE, AND COMPLETION IN THE STATE CONTEXT

James C. Hearn, Anthony P. Jones, and Elizabeth R. Kurban

Success in entering, continuing, and completing postsecondary education in the United States varies dramatically across income, age, gender, and race/ethnicity groups (Advisory Committee on Student Financial Assistance [ACSFA], 2010; College Board, 2010; and both the Heller and Perna & Kurban chapters in this volume). Unquestionably, a critical factor in these patterns is affordability, constrained in recent years by rising tuition levels (spurred by tightening state budgets) and slowed growth in need-based student aid. Clearly, lower-income families have been jolted by these developments, but many middle-income families are also feeling "squeezed out" of higher education (Clawson & Leiblum, 2008; Quinterno, 2012; Rowan-Kenyon, Bell, & Perna, 2008). As a result, policymakers and the public understandably seek improvements in the efficiency and effectiveness of policies promoting postsecondary attendance, but this drive for increased accountability comes in a context of aspirations for improving the quality of education and producing a well-trained, globally competitive workforce for the 21st century. Therein lies the emerging dilemma: as state funding for higher education has come under increasing pressure, educational systems are asked not only to do more with less, but to ensure that their improved performance is adequately reported and defended for external stakeholders, who are increasingly setting performance metrics.

At center stage in this drama stand the states. State legislatures have long been the principal governmental decision arenas for higher education, because of the decentralized nature of educational policymaking in the United States (McLendon, Mokher, & Flores, 2011). Yet for a period in the 1960s and 1970s, the federal government assumed a more assertive role (e.g., the Higher Education Act of 1965 brought increased federal funding of institutions; its reauthorization in 1972 brought robust funding levels for students, notably through need-based grant programs; and its reauthorization in 1978 greatly expanded loan coverage and subsidization). It began to appear that expanding enrollment opportunities would become an ongoing national focus. Subsequently, however, national attention waned as federal funding priorities shifted from grants to loans, and loans themselves became less generously subsidized. Once again, states assumed a primary role in funding postsecondary attendance and completion. Arguably, over the past 20–30 years, we have seen a retreat by the federal government from a central role in conceptualizing and funding a postsecondary equity agenda. Significant amounts of public funding are devoted to higher education, but national leaders less frequently address postsecondary affordability in any systematic way. Instead, many now take, primarily, a "bully pulpit" role focused on quality and efficiency. From the *Nation at Risk* report commissioned by the Reagan administration in the early 1980s to the Spellings Commission and similar federal efforts of recent years, national policy initiatives have become more hortatory, less robustly funded, and less actively incentivizing (Hearn, 2001). At the same time, many states have ramped up attention to access and completion, as indicated by numerous task forces and policy statements from national organizations, including the National Governors Association (NGA, 2012), the National Center for Higher Education Management Systems (NCHEMS, n.d.), and the State Higher Education Executive Officers (SHEEO, 2008).

As states once again become the central players in postsecondary enrollment policy,[1] there is wide variety in their policy activities. Three initiatives merit special attention, however: affordability, readiness and alignment, and accountability. Affordability is clearly one of the primary issues affecting access and completion for low-, moderate-, and middle-income families as they face college cost increases that are outpacing increases in income and savings as well as student financial assistance programs (see the chapters in this volume by Perna & Kurban and Heller for additional insight on affordability issues). Readiness and alignment initiatives influence access and completion because they aim to ensure there is adequate academic preparation at the primary and secondary education levels for what is expected at the postsecondary level to ensure success in college and careers (see the chapters by Perna & Kurban, Conley, and Long & Boatman for further perspective on readiness aspects). And, accountability issues address the extent to which states are able to encourage institutions to achieve statewide goals and priorities around educational attainment. Accountability measures also shape goals for institutional quality of academic programs as well as the nature and extent of information provided to students and families to promote informed choices about academic programs and institutions. These three policy domains will be discussed, in turn, with particular attention to their connection to broad national goals.

Affordability Initiatives

Affordability is at the heart of opportunity for postsecondary access, persistence, and completion. While postsecondary pricing and student aid are complex and evolving, some truths are constant and worth repeating. In choosing whether or where to enroll, each student faces a total outlay[2] consisting of tuition, fees, books and supplies, and associated costs of living. These costs vary by institutional sector, course load, residency considerations, and other factors. State appropriations to public colleges and universities are a general subsidy benefiting all students who attend. Such appropriations, as well as private sources of funding to institutions, affect how the level of tuition and other costs are established. For students and families, however, the primary offset to these costs is the various forms of grant aid awarded by state and federal governments, the institution, and private parties, based on student level of financial need, academic merit, or other considerations. The difference between the total cost and total grants constitutes the student's "net price" (Higher Education Opportunity Act, 2008; The Institute for College Access and Success [TICAS], 2011) for that choice. Students and their families must meet that net price through out-of-pocket (current or future) means such as parental and student contributions (e.g., funds from checking, savings, investments, gifts of cash, etc.), employment, or loans (ACSFA, 2011a).

In this context, states create or constrain opportunity and affordability through a series of policy choices affecting support for student attendance. Such policies include regulation of the tuition and fees charged or direct appropriations as subsidy to the institutions. Direct appropriations generally result in a low tuition model that is often accompanied by a "low aid" approach as well. Policies or strategies that effectively establish higher prices require a tandem policymaking decision: whether to offset prices with a substantial commitment to need-based student aid, including targeting need-based aid using merit factors (Ness & Noland, 2007). Making a commitment to "high tuition/high aid" represents a targeted, albeit more complicated, approach to providing postsecondary opportunity. Both the low tuition/low aid approach and the high tuition/high aid approach provide lower net prices for students in need of funding for postsecondary attendance (Hearn & Longanecker, 1985).

Strikingly, however, during the last two decades a third path has emerged in the United States: high tuition paired with low aid. Facing taxpayer resistance and financial constraints, many states have restrained need-based aid or avoided such commitments altogether, while allowing tuition levels to rise at public institutions. The result has been greater percentage growth in tuition and fees at public institutions in recent years, and slowed or stalled growth in state need-based aid (College Board, 2012).[3] In this context, states have recognized the political appeal of efforts to make college attendance affordable and provide attractive vehicles for savings. Growing numbers of states have adopted three alternative policy instruments: merit-aid programs, prepaid tuition plans, and college savings plans. Each addresses some measure of affordability, and each may increase opportunity, although not equally, by providing state support for attendance. Nevertheless, none of the three serves as a sufficiently effective or efficient effort to expand educational opportunity, even when combined with federal efforts.

State Merit-Aid Programs

Since the early 1990s, the development and proliferation of merit-based programs for college students represents a remarkable policy shift for the states (Doyle, 2006; Ness, 2008). Merit programs began when Georgia initiated the Helping Outstanding Pupils Educationally (HOPE) scholarship as a broad-based aid program providing funds to high-achieving high school graduates attending college.[4] Awards were based solely on student academic accomplishment and would be discontinued if a student's grade point average fell below a certain standard. In the years that followed, numerous other states followed Georgia's lead in initiating merit programs, and most followed Georgia's financing model, relying on lottery revenues to fund scholarships. Those that did not use lottery funding relied instead on video gambling tax revenues, tobacco lawsuit settlement funds, state income and sales taxes, and revenue from land leases and sales (Cornwell, Misztal, & Mustard, 2009). Most adopting states also followed Georgia's lead in focusing primarily or entirely on academic achievement, although some, such as Tennessee, adopted a mixed program with need-based elements (Heller, 2002a; Ness & Noland, 2007).

While there is no irrefutable evidence that states have supported merit aid at the expense of need-based aid (Cornwell et al., 2009; Doyle, 2010; Longanecker, 2002), the suspicion remains. It is at least clear that states with large merit programs are not generous in providing other forms of student aid. For example, states with merit-aid programs have been found to spend three times as much on merit aid as compared to need-based aid (Heller, 2002b). As Ness and Tucker (2008) suggest, growth in non-need-based aid far outpaced need-based aid during the 1990s and early 2000s, and that trend continues (NASSGAP, 2011, 2012), albeit at a slower rate.

From an equity perspective, merit-aid policies and programs raise numerous concerns. When merit-aid program designs focus solely on academic qualifications, the correlations among income levels, racial and ethnic characteristics, and certain academic indicators can lead such programs toward favoring middle- and sometimes upper-income students, as well as White students (Binder & Ganderton, 2002, 2004; Heller & Rasmussen, 2002; Ness & Tucker, 2008). Several studies (ACSFA, 2010; Cornwell & Mustard, 2002; Dynarski, 2002; Heller, 2006) find that gaps in college access "by income and ethnic/racial strata persist and, indeed, may be increasing" (Ness & Tucker, 2008, p. 571).

The literature regarding merit-aid programs suggests that these programs have some redeeming features, including the potential to expand awareness and knowledge of postsecondary opportunities, widen student institutional choice sets, and stanch state "brain drain"[5] (Dynarski, 2004; Zhang & Ness, 2010). In addition, most merit-aid states fund their efforts through state lotteries; thus, these programs have an added political advantage of not requiring tax dollars, even though they have been found to be regressive. Some have seen an operational advantage as well, in that merit programs tend to be beneficiaries of state lottery sales, a more stable revenue source than "vulnerable and vacillating" state general funds (Ness & Tucker, 2008, p. 582). However, that advantage is increasingly suspect: the economic difficulties of the past few years have shaken the lottery-funded base of several state programs and prompted retrenchment and eligibility restrictions, thus raising academic achievement requirements, in Georgia's HOPE program, the most visible of the merit-aid programs (University System of Georgia, 2011).

Notably, some states combine need-based criteria with merit-based criteria, and the results may lead to less deleterious outcomes than those in other states with merit-aid programs. For example, Ness and Tucker (2008) state that

> considering the broad eligibility criteria of the Tennessee Education Lottery Scholarship program, under-represented students are eligible for these merit-aid awards in much greater proportions than in other states with similar programs. One could argue this has the effect of 'targeting' merit aid to under-represented students by making the awards nearly universal for college bound students. (p. 581)

In this way, states can create targeting strategies that parallel those of pure need-based aid, with the added advantage of being less regressive than Georgia-style programs. That is, in pure merit-based programs, the largely lower- and middle-income lottery-purchasing population subsidizes the awards of the largely middle- and upper-income scholarship-winning population (Clotfelter & Cook, 1991; Cornwell & Mustard, 2002; Dynarski, 2002; Heller, 2002b). In blended programs like that in Tennessee, however, this regressivity can be muted. Although states generally develop merit-based programs to serve purposes other than the expansion of opportunity to lower-income students, encouraging such targeting may hold promise for maintaining states' higher education policy focus toward need-based factors (see chapters in this volume by Perna & Kurban; Bragg; Heller; Melguizo, Kienzl, & Kosiewicz; and Hossler, Dundar, & Shapiro for further discussion on the clear benefits of need-based aid to college enrollment).

Prepaid Tuition Programs and College Savings Plans

Unlike state scholarship programs, two additional state program types aim to build student and family resources for meeting college expenses *prior* to enrollment, by providing families methods of saving for college attendance (Baird, 2006a, 2006b; McLendon, Heller, & Lee, 2009; Olivas, 2003). When the dependent becomes old enough to enroll in a postsecondary institution, the accumulated savings may be drawn down to pay eligible college-related expenses. These programs work through provisions in federal and state taxation systems to provide incentives to use these methods. Specifically, prepaid tuition plans and savings plans are covered under Section 529 of the U.S. Internal Revenue Code,[6] which allows parents and guardians to make investments not subject to federal taxes on capital gains, interest, and dividends. By providing substantial tax benefits for those putting aside money early for college expenses, states and the federal government hope to raise savings rates and thus reduce financial burdens on governments seeking to improve college access and choice, even though there is evidence that these plans are used disproportionately by middle- and upper-income families (Olivas, 2003; Roth, 2001).

State prepaid tuition plans, the first of the two precollege affordability approaches of interest, guarantee coverage of tuition expenses at state-affiliated public institutions, regardless of growth in tuition rates between initial investments and actual college attendance. Prepaid tuition plans are financially secure options for families who expect their children to attend an in-state public institution. The plans tend to be financially conservative investments, however, and usually cover only tuition and fees, not the full cost of attendance. What is more, should family plans and expectations change, there are clear downsides: the costs of nonpublic institutions are rarely covered, and there are usually strong penalties for early withdrawal of funds.

College savings programs, the second of the precollege affordability approaches, provide tax advantages to families who set aside funds to pay for their dependents' eventual college educations. While state prepaid tuition plans are tied contractually to tuition rates at in-state public institutions, college savings plans have no assured connection to changes in tuition rates. As college costs change, families may find their savings unequal to the amount needed for college attendance. On the other hand, participants can invest as they wish, and can use their savings for attendance at any eligible postsecondary institution.

College savings plans have several politically attractive features, in that they represent a helpful government program that provides advantageous tax treatment for a plan's contributors and beneficiaries. Because these programs are funded with foregone taxes and are, in most cases, administratively self-supporting, they offer the potential benefit to the state of being "off-budget." Further, when considering the range of college costs that can be paid, such savings plans provide greater participant control and flexibility than prepaid tuition plans. Because some states have encountered fiscal problems with prepaid tuition plans, the college savings plans have grown more in dollar terms than the prepaid tuition plans and have been offered somewhat more frequently by the states (Roth, 2001). Currently, all states offer either the prepaid tuition or college savings plan, and 16 states offer both (Kantrowitz, 2012b).

Similar to merit-aid programs, both prepaid tuition plans and state savings plans have been affected by the economic challenges of recent years. In each case, families' participation has been constrained by reduced discretionary income. This difficulty is compounded by the weak performance of investment vehicles over the past few years: with interest rates at historic lows and stock market performance modest relative to previous years, returns on investment have not been at the levels anticipated by the initial policy implementation. Finally, in the case of prepaid tuition plans, several states have scaled back or suspended programs in the face of unanticipated rises in tuition level and other costs (Blankinship, 2012; Carey, 2009).

Both prepaid tuition programs and college savings plans represent a shift in state policy since the early to mid-1990s toward individualism rather than governmental responsibility for college affordability. That is, by retreating from assurances of ongoing low tuition levels through direct appropriations to institutions, states are in essence withdrawing blanket support of attendance and moving instead toward asking families to take greater responsibility through advance planning (Doyle, McLendon, & Hearn, 2010). To the extent that knowledge about college options is limited by parental educational background (Cabrera & LaNasa, 2000; Flint, 1992; Perna & Titus, 2005), and funds for college attendance are limited by family income levels (ACSFA, 2010; Bettinger, Long, Oreopoulos, & Sanbonmatsu, 2012; Dynarski, 2000), such plans are not equitable in their support of prospective students across socioeconomic groups (Dynarski, 2004; Long & Bettinger, 2011).

Despite recent attempts to regulate tuition costs or protect against fluctuations in state appropriations in a few states (e.g., Maryland, see Perna, Finney, & Callan, 2012), the dominant state affordability initiatives of the last 20 years, from merit aid to prepaid tuition to college savings plans, have uniformly tended to be popular with, and to most clearly serve the needs of, the middle class. As McLendon et al. (2009), have noted, "Although the financial burden posed by soaring tuition increases has fallen disproportionately on families from lower-income backgrounds, it is the concern of middle-class Americans that provided much of the impetus for a variety of new postsecondary financing programs in the states" (p. 389). With increases in college costs outpacing increases in need-based grant aid (College Board, 2012), those with the fewest resources continue to face the greatest obstacles in meeting rising net prices (ACSFA, 2010, 2011a; Cornwell & Mustard, 2004; Heller, 2006). In historical perspective, this is not surprising: even passage of the groundbreaking Higher Education Act of 1965, often hailed as a paragon of public attention to the educational needs of disadvantaged students, relied critically for its passage on attention to middle-class values and interests (Gladieux & Wolanin, 1976; Hearn, 1993).

Readiness and Alignment Initiatives

National initiatives for college readiness and curricular alignment, such as P–16 councils[7] and the Common Core State Standards, strive to integrate and substantially link the K–12 and higher education systems, which historically have operated largely independently of one another in the states (Pipho, 2001). As the value of postsecondary education in the United States continues to increase, both for individual student achievement and international competitiveness, it is imperative to ensure smooth, successful transitions for students from preschool through college. As David Conley discusses in his chapter in this volume, existing college readiness indicators, such as admission test scores, high school grade point averages, and exit exams, may not accurately predict performance in college or reflect appropriate preparation for future achievement. This misalignment in readiness can cause a gap in education between K–12 and higher education, which, in the transition from high school to college, can contribute to "diminished student access, impaired student performance and achievement, and increased cost as a result of duplication, waste, and inefficiency" (McLendon et al., 2009, p. 398).

The notion of linking education from preschool through the senior year of college takes into account the importance of early childhood learning and academic cohesion, and the necessity of closing gaps throughout the teaching and learning process. Such a system, integrated and aligned through multiple levels, would be student-focused and comprehensive, far superior to current, atomized approaches (Krueger, 2002). Many states have sought to implement a truly integrated P–16 system in order to shape and guide children's educational careers from age five through grade school and college, and into the workplace, providing at each level high-quality, timely, and appropriately targeted learning activities. The goal for each level is to feature forward-looking emphases on rich, challenging academic curricula, individualized learning plans, and integrated development of critical thinking skills necessary for each subsequent level. From this perspective, the high school years should be geared toward forging pathways to college or the workplace, utilizing these years to prepare students with a strong, comprehensive curriculum that lays a strong foundation for any career aspiration. Similarly, along with individualized learning plans to suit the needs and pace of each student, assessment instruments should guide the plans and accountability to meet standards and goals more efficiently (Krueger, 2002).

Alignment Issues and Degree Completion

Initiatives such as P–16 councils were developed not only to enhance the quality and outcomes of the current education system, but also to align primary and secondary preparation with expectations of postsecondary education and improve opportunities for access and success. Although ability to pay costs is a critical factor to enrolling and persisting to completion, without sufficient knowledge about college as well as adequate readiness and academic preparation, high school students are unlikely to complete, persist, or even enroll in college (Kirst & Bracco, 2004; also see related discussions by Bragg; Conley; Melguizo, Kienzl, & Kosiewicz; and Perna & Kurban in their chapters in this volume).

State policies play a critical role in this process. As other chapter authors in this volume argue (e.g., Perna & Kurban and Conley), states pursuing improved postsecondary outcomes must craft policies that strengthen alignments to facilitate academic readiness, must smooth high school-to-college transitions, and must provide adequate financial support for both college entry and college completion. Such efforts also help reduce the need for remediation during postsecondary education (see further discussion on this topic in the chapters in this volume by Long & Boatman and Melguizo, Kienzl, & Kosiewicz). In order to address the gap between K–12 education and what is expected at the college level, initiatives such as P–16 alignment connect K–12 and postsecondary curriculum and standards in an incremental approach, more closely connecting high school graduation requirements and college admission requirements.

Common Core Standards Initiative

Approximately 30 states have adopted some form of a P–16 alignment system (Krueger, 2006). Some have implemented P–16 efforts over a period of time, easing the transition by gauging success along the way. Others have pursued more comprehensive, and more immediate P–16 reform, "addressing governance, finance, standards, assessments, admissions and program changes at all levels" (Krueger, 2002, p. 3). A state's likelihood of adopting such policies is dependent on current state programs and on the stance and relative power of the governor and legislators of a state. Clearly, investment in a P–16 system requires an adequate budget, support from legislative leaders of both parties, and support from state citizens, and obtaining all three is no easy matter (Kirst & Venezia, 2004; Venezia, Callan, Finney, Kirst, & Usdan, 2005). Furthermore, attributes of successfully implemented P–16 systems include commitment to long-term reform, representation from key stakeholder groups, coordinated initiatives, and integrated reform efforts (Krueger, 2006).

Implementation of P–16 initiatives facilitates college readiness by aligning K–12 preparation with the academic expectations of colleges and universities. With that logic in mind, the National Governors Association (NGA) and the Council of Chief State School Officers (CCSSO) launched the Common Core State Standards Initiative[8] in 2010 to establish a set of consistent secondary educational standards across states to improve the quality and success of the U.S. education system and help teachers and students better understand the skills and knowledge needed to succeed in college and the workforce (NGA & CCSSO, n.d.). The standards were developed in collaboration with teachers and administrators, policy experts, and other leaders, and included feedback from the general public. The standards encourage a "common core of knowledge" required of all citizens and define the "knowledge and skills students should have within their K–12 education careers so that they will graduate high school able to succeed in entry-level, credit-bearing academic college courses and in workforce training programs" (NGA & CCSSO, n.d.). This, in turn, should help diminish the need for remediation and increase persistence (Kirst & Bracco, 2004). National standards give states the advantage of knowledge developed elsewhere as they design and implement strategies to meet their own goals.

Alignment and Data Collection Challenges

Bridging state-level readiness/alignment issues and accountability measures are state longitudinal data systems, also known as student unit-record (SUR) systems. Over the last decade, policymakers and researchers have sought to utilize and strengthen a state's ability to match several years of student-level data from key databases (e.g., those containing data on demographic information, enrollment, test results, etc.) in order to measure academic growth and preparation for college and the workforce, as well as identify areas of need (Data Quality Campaign, 2009). SUR systems "permit the tracking of an individual student's progress over time—from entry into elementary school to exit from college and eventually into the labor market," which are critical data for informing issues of educational effectiveness (Vernez, Krop, Vuollo, & Hansen, 2008, p. xi) and can inform not only academic preparation issues and needs, but also patterns of enrollment and completion. As noted by Hossler, Dundar, and Shapiro in their chapter in this volume, students are enrolling increasingly in multiple institutions, often among different sectors, and data systems that record student enrollment only at institution of origin no longer capture a true picture of persistence and completion. Clearly, there is value in having a single source of data that allows policymakers and researchers to understand not only the number and characteristics of students in a state or region, but also the students' progress and deficiencies in relation to a state's broader educational, social, and civic goals, and workforce needs.

At their best, adequately designed and appropriately used SURs can effectively address a state's formative and summative policy evaluation needs related to student success. By providing evidence regarding the transitions and outcomes of students throughout educational levels and systems, SURs not only contribute to policy review but can also play a significant role in identifying problems with existing policies and targeting solutions. At the same time, however, SURs raise a familiar specter: the potential corruption of a developmental tool when it is used as an evaluative tool. That is, to the extent systems (and people) are evaluated on the outcomes highlighted by such new data-analytic capabilities, those systems' openness to neutral, thorough data gathering, data use, and review can be compromised. To the extent efforts to address readiness and alignment can conflict with efforts to improve accountability, progress will be slowed. Further, high stakes decisions, such as basing distribution of state support to institutions or financial aid to students on market-based assessments of educational programs, could be problematic at best.

Accountability Initiatives

While higher education institutions have always carried a measure of accountability for performance, recent years have brought heightened scrutiny and expectations. Many state governments have adopted performance-based funding and budgeting systems and, increasingly, states require that institutions provide more comprehensive, more detailed, and more frequent performance reporting and consumer disclosures than in the past. In terms of access and completion, accountability measures may shape the quality and types of educational programs offered within the state, as well as enhance consumer information, awareness, and choice. Ultimately, students' educational success can and should benefit from well-designed accountability efforts.

Performance *funding* links state funding for public colleges and universities to measures of performance (Burke & Minassians, 2003; Harnisch, 2011). Thus, it represents an incentive-based system that allocates some portion of a state institution's budget based on the institution meeting or exceeding an established threshold of performance, rather than allocating funds through a traditional funding formula tied closely to enrollment levels. Examples of performance measures include graduation rates, retention rates, time to degree completion, and job placements (Dougherty & Natow, 2009; Hearn & Holdsworth, 2002). First adopted by Tennessee in 1979, performance-based funding policies were developed with the purpose of improving overall performance within constrained budgets, while strengthening the link between accountability and higher education funding (McLendon, Hearn, & Deaton, 2006).

A somewhat less direct approach, performance *budgeting* allows governors, legislators, and state board officials consideration of "campus achievement on performance indicators as one factor in determining allocations for public campuses" (Burke & Minassians, 2003, p. 3). Under performance budgeting, specific funding levels are based on performance, but appropriators have some discretion over the proportion of the entire appropriation that is based on performance (Burke, Rosen, Minassians, & Lessard, 2000).

Efficacy of Incentive Structures

Performance funding and budgeting approaches are designed to create incentives for improving institutional performance through fiscal reward, and often have goals of improving the connection and communication among administrators, policymakers, and overall institutional efficacy. As incentives, these approaches hold higher education institutions accountable for supporting students throughout college, improving undergraduate education and student learning, and encouraging college access and completion at the state and institutional levels (Hearn & Holdsworth, 2002). Expectations for improvements in performance may be geared toward: targeted increases in access and success (e.g., by demonstrating improvements in enrollment and completion for select groups of students), improvements in responding to needs of the state and local economies (e.g., by producing graduates in degree or certificate programs identified as critical to the state or its localities), and lower overall operating costs (Doughtery & Natow, 2009). Nonetheless, the evidence is slim regarding the validity of these expectations.

A study by Sanford and Hunter (2011) raised doubts regarding the benefits of performance-based funding policies, suggesting that performance funding has no relationship to retention and graduation rates. In fact, although Tennessee was the original state to implement performance-based funding practices, Sanford and Hunter's results suggest a lack of responsiveness from public institutions in Tennessee to monetary incentives: even though institutions were directly incentivized to improve retention or graduation rates, the rates did not demonstrably change.

Other analyses are more sanguine. Research by Zhang (2009) suggests a positive relationship between state funding and college graduation rates. Specifically, Zhang found a 10% increase in per-student state appropriations was associated with just over a half-percentage point increase in graduation rates. But the causal mechanisms for such patterns remain unclear, as do the particular policy approaches most likely to bolster such relationships. While some analysts have explored the motivations and social, economic, and political conditions favoring the adoption of performance regimes (e.g., see Dougherty & Natow, 2009; McLendon et al., 2006), the connections among these policies' contexts, characteristics, and outcomes are, at best, poorly understood.

What is clear is the contrast between the lofty motivating ideals of these systems and the difficulty states have encountered in successfully implementing them. Cuts to higher education funding, a lack of support from key stakeholders (such as legislators, state governing boards, and the business community), inflexibility toward institutional differences, and the instability of establishing performance funding in the context of inevitable state revenue cycles, can contribute to the breakdown of these systems, as evidenced in states such as Florida, Illinois, and Washington (Doughtery & Natow, 2009; Miao, 2012). Policies in those three states were hampered by a lack of support from higher education institutions as well as defections by key supporters (Doughtery & Natow, 2009). In Florida and Illinois, declines in higher education funding and weak support from the business community created further stress on the states' commitments to performance initiatives.

Performance Funding 2.0

States slowed in their rates of adopting performance funding and budgeting systems in the late 1990s, but there has been a resurgence in recent years. Often termed "performance funding 2.0," the new state interest reflects the heightened importance of accountability in higher education today (Albright, n.d.). With the recent negative economic climate and a renewed focus on improving institutional performance in areas of perceived shortcomings, states are designing and adopting newer forms of performance-based funding. Pennsylvania's new performance-funding system allocates $36 million to incentivize colleges and universities to meet performance standards (Miao, 2012). Ohio and Tennessee have addressed failures in past performance funding policies and implemented new systems.

Ohio's new performance funding model accounts for diverse institutional types and student body composition, and expands upon nuances of "completion" (Miao, 2012). Tennessee, having implemented "the most aggressive performance-based funding model," recently allocated 80 percent of the total state budget based on performance, incorporating refined indicators of "student retention, degree attainment, and completion of remedial courses" (Miao, 2012, p. 5).

While state policymakers are aware of past problems with performance-based funding and adopting newer strategies in state funding systems, intrinsic problems with this approach may continue to limit its effectiveness. Notably, while states are moving away from the simplistically uniform approaches of some earlier systems, it is increasingly evident that tailoring systems to individual institutions' distinctive missions and contexts can impose daunting costs for designing individualized metrics, monitoring performance along these disparate metrics, and refining institutional metrics as necessary. Just as important is the ongoing tension between risk and reward in such systems. Consider college completion as perhaps the most prominent and popular indicator in performance systems: increasing graduation *rates* can compel tighter admissions standards, at the expense of students who are barely qualified academically, while increasing graduating *numbers* can compel lesser quality control, all else equal. No conceivable amount of individualizing can totally remove these trade-offs. Completion is a proxy for neither access nor quality, and focusing on completion single-mindedly can actually work against both goals.

Accountability Measures

All performance-based funding initiatives seek to increase accountability among higher education institutions with a hope of increasing quality, choice, and awareness; the focal indicators and measures vary from state to state, however. Although performance-based funding usually is not entirely based on enrollment data, the most commonly used measures are graduation rates and degrees awarded (Carey & Aldeman, 2008; Community College League of California, 1999; Harnisch, 2011). Clearly, policymakers are assuming that completion rates are an adequate proxy for "quality." Unfortunately, focusing performance standards on the production of graduates has the potential to, unintentionally, sacrifice rigor and quality (Community College League of California, 1999). An additional concern is that by encouraging states to focus on completion goals and agendas, institutions could compromise on equity and opportunity goals and missions. That is, there is danger that a focus on completion favors traditional over nontraditional students and campuses, and can serve to diminish campus diversity (Community College League of California, 1999). Completion-driven systems can make admission of large numbers of at-risk students less attractive to institutions, thus potentially creating another barrier to college access for the students most at risk, including low- and moderate-income students, who may be less likely to complete in comparison to their more privileged peers (Kantrowitz, 2012a).

Many states are becoming aware of the potential risks of performance-based funding models. Ideally, state policies will focus on the need "to reward progress over completion, to recognize the differences that exist between community colleges and universities, and to partition off larger percentages of base funding in order to incentivize transformative change" (Miao, 2012, p. 2). Accountability measures also require significant review and assessment by the state, which can create tensions and pressures among institutions. Because of the complexities associated with assessment instruments and measures, it is difficult to design a performance-based funding system that can account for all limitations.

Reporting and Disclosure

The other accountability instrument potentially affecting college enrollment is the reporting and disclosure of consumer information available for students, families, and the general public. Such requirements direct institutions to release information and data on a range of measures of institutional performance, academic offerings, and campus climate and culture. This disclosure may promote college enrollment and choice by improving the availability of relevant information for students, families, and other decision makers (see further discussions on the role of information in the chapters in this volume by Bragg; Conley; Heller; Long & Boatman; Melguizo, Kienzl, & Kosiewicz; and Perna & Kurban). Noting that enrollment is primarily driven by consumer choice, Carey and Kelly (2011) point out policymakers' desire for greater accountability but reluctance toward regulating college behavior directly. As such, relations between postsecondary institutions and federal and state governments have moved toward an uneasy truce, "[i]n recent years, a familiar compromise between regulation and autonomy has emerged: require colleges to provide more information" (Carey & Kelly, 2011, p. 1).

Although reporting data to federal, state, and other entities has long been a measure of accountability and consumer information, increases in the volume and scope in reporting and consumer disclosures have been noted (ACSFA, 2011b). As part of the agreement to participate in the federal student financial aid programs, institutions must agree to disclose and make publicly available significant information and data on costs of attendance, graduation rates, job placement rates, enrollment rates, campus crime, and numerous other data related to college operations and outcomes (O'Donnell & Hattan, 2009). State agencies also collect similar data as a condition of institutions receiving state student financial aid dollars. Students, families, institutional employees, researchers, and policymakers rely upon such information to make decisions relative to their roles and interests, but the information can be difficult to locate, compare, and use (National Postsecondary Education Cooperative, 2009).

Although important for consumer information and accountability purposes, the processes of data collection, data analysis, reporting, disclosure, and dissemination can be time consuming, costly, and duplicative. Campus officials reported in a recent survey (ACSFA, 2011b) that

> [F]ederal reporting and disclosure requirements often overlap and duplicate similar requirements from state agencies and non-government organizations.... [A]dditions to and modifications of these requirements over the years have led to an unwieldy volume and expansive scope of reports and disclosures, with some requirements considered irrelevant [to participation in student financial aid programs]. (p. 37)

Respondents to the ACSFA survey also suggested that the volume and scope of information required tends to be overwhelming for both students and families, contributing to "confusion rather than awareness" (ACSFA, 2011b, p. 37). If students and families are unable to make informed decisions because they are overwhelmed or confused by the information, and if institutional resources that could be productively employed elsewhere are expended in the pursuit and preparation of reporting of doubtful utility, the cost effectiveness of providing such information is undermined.

Recommendations

Numerous aspects of state-level policy relating to postsecondary access, persistence, and completion extend beyond what can be covered in this chapter. Early information and awareness initiatives, dual-enrollment policies, integrated student success initiatives, transfer and articulation policies, and remedial/developmental education strategies are covered in detail elsewhere in this volume (e.g., see chapters by Bragg; Long & Boatman; Melguizo, Kienzl, & Kosiewicz; and Perna & Kurban). Also, beyond the scope here is the ongoing blurring of mission differentiation in many states, as community colleges are increasingly allowed to offer baccalaureate degrees and online programs cross over traditional mission and degree demarcations. Further, the growth of online programs and expansion of the for-profit sector are clearly influencing access and completion in the states, and merit extensive policy discussion.

There is plenty in this chapter, however, to prompt thoughts about how best to move forward at the state level in pursuit of student postsecondary access and success. Following are some recommendations based on our review of this arena.

Fully Consider Context in Any Reform Initiative

Every state reform needs to be thoughtfully developed with an eye to not only what has worked elsewhere, but also to what might work in that particular state. That is, context is critical. States constitute, in effect, at least 50 different ecosystems for policy development, and each is different in terms of resources, histories, and cultures. For example, states with centralized governance systems, low tuition rates, heavy reliance on community colleges, and a small private sector constitute remarkably different environments for students' college decision making from states featuring decentralized governance, high-priced four-year institutions, and large private sectors. What works in one may well not work in another. The diffusion of good ideas from state to state, and even the national imposition of certain reforms, can be beneficial, but successful innovations must always be astutely contextualized.

Nourish the Natural Roots of Reform While Maintaining Measures of Accountability and Consumer Protections

As an extension of the consideration of context in reform, policymakers need to recognize that "one size fits all" mandates are unlikely to succeed, or to be well received, given the extraordinary variation across states, and across institutions within states. Indeed, recent experience with federal initiatives in student unit-record systems provides ample evidence of the advisability of more indirect approaches. Capably designed, incentive-centered policies to enlist states in federal efforts that widen access and ensure persistence and completion hold great promise, because evidence-based information is critical to policy decisions. Reciprocal communication among students, counselors, practitioners, educational leaders, policymakers at the federal and state levels, researchers, business leaders, and other stakeholders is a goal to be sought in and of itself, independent of particular issues in student success. Sorely lacking in policymaking and individual decision making regarding access, persistence, and completion is a visible, stable information and communication infrastructure to ensure both knowledge dissemination and ongoing dialogue among actors in this arena. Regulatory control of academic quality has been vested far more at the state level than at the federal level. And at the state level, there is wide variation in institutional quality and in the role states play in monitoring that variation. Although current political will tends toward deregulation and marketization in education, as well as in other policy domains, it is important that regulatory regimes not be compromised or abandoned. As larger socioeconomic and technological conditions change, fiscal and social progress and integrity require restraint as well as freedom. Incentives for greater efficiency or increased degree production should never come at the expense of program quality, institutional quality, and access.

Ensure Policy Development Includes Critical Evaluation of the Entire Spectrum of Access and Completion

The myriad demands on higher education need to be clear, as does the understanding of the evolving diversity of the student population and the way by which education is delivered. Policymakers need to undertake more detailed consideration of the definitions of acceptable levels of access, persistence, and completion. Over recent years, we have increasingly lost clarity on, and need rigorous research to inform, such questions as "What is a student?," "What is enrollment?," "What constitutes persistence?," "What constitutes completion?," and "What degrees and certificates comprise goals for completion?" These are not merely rhetorical questions—there are real equity considerations at stake. We have long known that higher education enrollments and degree outcomes look more and more equitable as we extend the definition of enrollment from traditional images of college to encompass part-time attendance as well as full-time attendance; two-year institutions, vocational-technical institutions, for-profit institutions as well as non-profit four-year institutions; certificates as well as degrees, online degrees as well as traditional degrees; and so forth. In an era in which even the most elite institutions are offering increasing numbers of MOOCs (massively open online courses), and thus, further widening the doors to postsecondary participation, it is critical to ask, "How much is enough?" That is, what is the point at which one draws the line, stating this constitutes access and this does not, and for whom? As we dilute core indicators, we, in turn, increase the difficulty of the task, and in that process we may dilute as well the prospects for achieving true equity of opportunity.

Adopt Performance Funding With Careful Consideration and Realistic Expectations

Performance funding, despite its limitations, maintains strong appeal to many stakeholders, including state legislators and governors, so it is important for policymakers at the institutional, state, and national levels to be aware of best practices and opportunities to provide incentives that will demonstrably improve performance. In developing any such system, it is essential for all involved to thoroughly consider the most critical state- and institution-specific goals to be incorporated into funding, consider the relative importance of various stakeholders in the prospective system, scan available resources to learn what is known about the most effective funding mechanisms for pursuing key goals, remain sensitive in funding approaches to the needs of individual colleges, reward progress in meeting these goals (Miao, 2012), plan from the start to accommodate the fiscal and planning uncertainty that can plague colleges under such systems, and develop knowledge about who will be implementing the system in institutions.

Resurrect and Strengthen the Notions of Federal-State Partnership and Cross-Sector Partnership

One of the valuable aspects of the relative comity around postsecondary policy issues in the 1970s was the ongoing sense among various actors that they shared a common goal of expanding educational opportunity. Obviously, no era is ever as harmonious as it might appear in retrospect, and the 1970s were no exception (see Hearn, 1993), but there is little doubt that tension across levels and sectors rose as the seeds of political and economic atomization grew in the following decades. Too often, suspicions, cynicism, and redress of past grievances have driven polarized stances. Now, the time seems ripe for shared thinking and compromise. Many of the programs in the Higher Education Act arose out of implicit and explicit partnership between federal and state governments to establish and carry out policies for postsecondary access, with further partnership with institutions for persistence and completion. The strength of these partnerships is necessary to ensure local, state, and national educational goals are met, especially in the critical domains of postsecondary access, persistence, and completion.

Refocus Efforts to Reduce Financial Barriers

Regardless of the philosophy adopted toward public funding of education, states' continuing de facto commitment to a high tuition/low aid model must be assiduously reconsidered and ameliorated. Students with the least financial resources need to have opportunities to pursue the postsecondary education for which they have prepared and to which they aspire. The current stance of high tuition/low aid is pricing out growing numbers of students who seek to enroll and complete postsecondary education. Institutions must do their part in keeping costs down as well, as all stakeholders need to put in place models that effectively minimize financial barriers. As efforts to improve academic preparation advance, it is important not to let financial barriers negate that progress.

Conclusion

Despite the recent recession and subsequent economic turmoil, access, persistence, and completion are as important now as they were at the time the Higher Education Act was enacted in 1965, nearly a half-century ago. Indeed, these goals may very well be more important, as the U.S. faces global economic challenges while progressively losing its historic pre-eminence in postsecondary education. In the current context, it would be entirely unrealistic to rely on the federal government to play as critical a role in educational opportunity as it played in the 1960s and 1970s—as a central, primary policy champion, creator, and funder in this arena. States will continue to have critical policy roles in ensuring college affordability, standards for and alignment among the stages of education, and accountability for outcomes. In pursuing those goals, they ultimately play major *national* roles in ensuring access, persistence, and completion.

Notes

1. Although private foundations are taking increasingly prominent roles in national postsecondary education policy (Clotfelter, 2012; Hall & Thomas, 2012; Lumina

Foundation, 2011), this chapter focuses on efforts at the state level, including those state initiatives or policies that were scaled nationally by representative associations.

2. We distinguish "total outlay" from "total cost" to differentiate these costs from opportunity costs, which would include the lost wages from not entering the job market and instead entering postsecondary education. When we use the term "cost" throughout the remainder of the chapter, we are referring to outlays and not opportunity costs.

3. In its annual survey of state-funded expenditures for postsecondary student financial aid, the National Association of State Student Grant and Aid Programs (NASSGAP; 2012) found that for the 2010–2011 award year, total state aid from all sources increased 1.3% in constant dollars from the previous award year; need-based grants for undergraduates increased 1.7%, and total grants—both need-based and non-need-based—increased 4%. These increases in state need-based grant funding have not kept pace with public tuition increases as in-state tuition and fees at public four-year institutions increased by 7.9% between the 2009–2010 and 2010–2011 award years (College Board, 2010). In constant dollars, using the 2010–2011 award year as a base, state need-based grant assistance increased by 5.8% in 2007–2008, and the amount of increases in subsequent years has fluctuated to the current level of an increase of only 0.5% between 2009–2010 and 2010–2011. Total spending on grants—need- or non-need-based—hasn't fared much better. Conversely, increases in tuition and fees at public four-year institutions have outpaced state increases in need-based aid during this period (College Board, 2012).

4. The HOPE program began as a need-based program but eventually had the income caps eliminated. Also, during the program's inception, HOPE grants were created, and continue to exist, for certificate and diploma programs. The authors thank Nancy Ferguson at the University of Georgia's Office of Student Financial Aid for sharing her expertise on the particulars of the program and its history.

5. A recent study (Fitzpatrick & Jones, 2012) questions the strength of the claim that merit aid stanches brain drain, however.

6. Both plan types are often called "529 Plans" in recognition of the section of the Internal Revenue Code in which they are authorized. For purposes of clarity in this chapter, we reference each plan by its type name.

7. Although K–16, P–16, and P–20 efforts all have a similar goal of creating a comprehensive system of education that begins with early childhood and ends after college, each effort has its own focus. Specifically, K–16 systems generally span kindergarten through a four-year college degree, P–16 initiatives range from preschool through a four-year degree, and P–20 systems go beyond P–16 to include graduate school degrees and certificates (Krueger, 2006). For purposes of this chapter, we consistently use P–16 to generally refer to all such efforts.

8. For additional insight into the Common Core State Standards, see the Conley and Perna and Kurban chapters in this volume.

References

Advisory Committee on Student Financial Assistance (ACSFA). (2010). *The rising price of inequality: How inadequate grant aid limits college access and persistence.* Washington, DC: Author.

Advisory Committee on Student Financial Assistance (ACSFA). (2011a). *The bottom line: Ensuring that students and parents understand the net price of college.* Washington, DC: Author.

Advisory Committee on Student Financial Assistance (ACSFA). (2011b). *Higher education regulations study: Final report.* Washington, DC: Author.

Albright, B.N. (n.d.). *Reinventing higher education funding policies: Performance funding 2.0— Funding degrees*. Unpublished manuscript supported by the Making Opportunity Affordable Initiative of the Lumina Foundation for Education.

Baird, K. (2006a). Do prepaid tuition plans affect state support for higher education? *Journal of Education Finance, 31*(3), 255–275.

Baird, K. (2006b). The political economy of college prepaid tuition plans. *Review of Higher Education, 29*(2), 141–166.

Bettinger, E.P., Long, B.T., Oreopoulos, P., & Sanbonmatsu, L. (2012). The role of application assistance and information in college decisions: Results from the H&R Block FAFSA experiment. *Quarterly Journal of Economics, 127*(3), 1205–1242.

Binder, M., & Ganderton, P. (2002). Incentive effects of New Mexico's merit-based state scholarship program: Who responds and how? In D.E. Heller & P. Marin (Eds.), *Who should we help? The negative social consequences of merit scholarships* (pp. 41–56). Cambridge, MA: The Civil Rights Project at Harvard University.

Binder, M., & Ganderton, P. (2004). The New Mexico lottery scholarship: Does it help minority and low-income students? In D.E. Heller, & P. Marin (Eds.), *Who should we help? The negative social consequences of merit scholarships* (pp. 101–122). Cambridge, MA: The Civil Rights Project at Harvard University.

Blankinship, D.G. (2012, November 1). Prepaid tuition begins new year under scrutiny about funding. *The Spokesman-Review*. Retrieved from http://www.spokesman.com

Burke, J.C., & Minassians, H. (2003). *Performance reporting: "Real" accountability or accountability "lite."* Albany, NY: The Rockefeller Institute.

Burke, J. C., Rosen, J., Minassians, H., & Lessard, T. (2000). *Performance funding and budgeting: An emerging merger? The fourth annual survey*. Albany, NY: The Rockefeller Institute.

Cabrera, A.F., & LaNasa, S.M. (2000). Understanding the college-choice process. *New Directions for Institutional Research, 2000*(107), 5–22.

Carey, K. (2009, May 8). College savings plans: A bad gamble. *The Chronicle of Higher Education*. Retrieved from http://chronicle.com

Carey, K., & Aldeman, C. (2008). *Ready to assemble: A model state higher education accountability system*. Washington, DC: Education Sector.

Carey, K., & Kelly, A.P. (2011). *The truth behind higher education disclosure laws*. Washington, DC: Education Sector.

Clawson, D., & Leiblum, M. (2008). Class struggle in higher education. *Equity & Excellence in Education, 41*(1), 12–30.

Clotfelter, C.T. (2012). *Synopsis paper: Context for success: Measuring colleges' impact*. Washington, DC: HCM Strategists.

Clotfelter, C.T., & Cook. P.J. (1991). *Selling hope: State lotteries in America*. Cambridge, MA: Harvard University Press.

College Board. (2010). *Trends in college pricing, 2010*. New York, NY: Author.

College Board. (2012). *Trends in college pricing, 2012*. New York, NY: Author.

Community College League of California (1999). *Accountability measures: A comparison by type and state*. Sacramento, CA: Author. Retrieved from http://www.ccleague.org/i4a/pages/Index.cfm?pageID=3429#recom

Cornwell, C.M., Misztal, M., & Mustard, D.B. (2009). *The effect of large-scale merit scholarships on state sponsored need-based aid*. Unpublished manuscript. Retrieved from http://www.terry.uga.edu/~mustard/Need-Aid-2009.pdf

Cornwell, C., & Mustard, D.B. (2002). Race and the effects of Georgia's HOPE scholarship. In D.E. Heller, & P. Marin (Eds.), *Who should we help? The negative social consequences of merit scholarships* (pp. 57–72). Cambridge, MA: The Civil Rights Project at Harvard University.

Cornwell, C., & Mustard, D.B. (2004). Georgia's HOPE scholarship and minority and low-income students: Program effects and proposed reforms. In D.E. Heller & P. Marin (Eds.), *State merit scholarship programs and racial inequality* (pp. 77–100). Cambridge, MA: The Civil Rights Project at Harvard University.

Data Quality Campaign. (2009). *The next step: Using longitudinal data systems to improve student success.* Washington, DC: Author.

Dougherty, K.J., & Natow, R.S. (2009). *The demise of higher education performance funding systems in three states.* New York, NY: Community College Research Center, Teachers College, Columbia University.

Doyle, W.R. (2006). Adoption of merit-based student grant programs: An event history analysis. *Educational Evaluation and Policy Analysis, 28*(3), 259–285.

Doyle, W.R. (2010). Does merit-based aid "crowd out" need-based aid? *Research in Higher Education, 51*(5), 397–415.

Doyle, W.R., McLendon, M.K., & Hearn, J.C. (2010). The adoption of prepaid tuition and savings plans in the American states: An event history analysis. *Research in Higher Education, 51*(7), 659–686.

Dynarski, S. (2000). Hope for whom? Financial aid for the middle class and its impact on college attendance. *National Tax Journal, 53*(3), 629–663.

Dynarski, S. (2002). Race, income, and the impact of merit aid. In D.E. Heller & P. Marin (Eds.). *Who should we help? The negative social consequences of merit scholarships* (pp. 73–92). Cambridge, MA: The Civil Rights Project at Harvard University.

Dynarski, S. (2004). The new merit aid. In C.M. Hoxby (Ed.), *College choices: The economics of where to go, when to go, and how to pay for it* (pp. 63–100). Chicago, IL: University of Chicago Press.

Fitzpatrick, M.D., & Jones, D. (2012). *Higher education, merit-based scholarships and post-baccalaureate migration.* NBER Working Paper No. 18530. Cambridge, MA: National Bureau of Economic Research. Retrieved from http://www.nber.org/papers/w18530

Flint, T.A. (1992). Parental and planning influences on the formation of student college choice sets. *Research in Higher Education, 33*(6), 689–708.

Gladieux, L.E., & Wolanin, T.R. (1976). *Congress and the colleges: The national politics of higher education.* Lexington, MA: Lexington Books.

Hall, C., & Thomas, S.L. (2012). *"Advocacy philanthropy" and the public policy agenda: The role of modern foundations in American higher education.* Paper presented at the 93rd annual meeting of the American Educational Research Association, Vancouver, British Columbia.

Harnisch, T.L. (2011). *Performance-based funding: A re-emerging strategy in public higher education financing.* Washington, DC: American Association of State Colleges and Universities.

Hearn, J.C. (1993). The paradox of growth in federal aid for college students: 1965–1990. In J.C. Smart (Ed.), *Higher education: Handbook of theory and research* (Vol. 9, pp. 94–153). New York, NY: Agathon Press.

Hearn, J.C. (2001). Access to postsecondary education: Financing equity in an evolving context. In M.B. Paulsen & J.C. Smart (Eds.), *The finance of higher education: Theory, research, policy, and practice* (pp. 439–460). New York, NY: Agathon Press.

Hearn, J.C., & Holdsworth, J.M. (2002). Influences of state-level policies and practices on college students' learning. *Peabody Journal of Education, 73*(3), 6–39.

Hearn, J. C., & Longanecker, D. (1985). Enrollment effects of alternative postsecondary pricing policies. *Journal of Higher Education, 56,* 485–508.

Heller, D.E. (2002a). State merit scholarship programs: An overview. In D.E. Heller & P. Marin (Eds.), *State merit scholarship programs and racial inequality* (pp. 13–22). Cambridge, MA: The Civil Rights Project at Harvard University.

Heller, D.E. (2002b). The policy shift in state financial aid programs. In J.C. Smart (Ed.), *Higher education: Handbook of theory and research* (Vol. 17, pp. 221–261). New York, NY: Agathon Press.

Heller, D.E. (2006, March). *Merit aid and college access*. Paper presented at the Symposium on the Consequences of Merit-Based Student Aid, Madison, WI. Retrieved from http://php.scripts.psu.edu/deh29/papers/WISCAPE_2006_paper.pdf

Heller, D.E., & Rasmussen, C.J. (2002). Merit scholarships and college access: Evidence from Florida and Michigan. In D.E. Heller & P. Marin (Eds.), *Who should we help? The negative social consequences of merit scholarships* (pp. 25–40). Cambridge, MA: The Civil Rights Project at Harvard University.

Higher Education Opportunity Act, Pub. L. No. 110–135, §132(a), 122 Stat. 3098. (2008).

Kantrowitz, M. (2012a). *The college completion agenda may sacrifice college access for low-income, minority and other at-risk students*. FinAid Page, LLC. Retrieved from http://www.finaid.org/educators/20120910completionagenda.pdf

Kantrowitz, M. (2012b). *State section 529 plans*. FinAid Page, LLC. Retrieved from http://www.finaid.org/savings/state529plans.phtml

Kirst, M.W., & Bracco, K.R. (2004). Bridging the great divide: How the K–12 and postsecondary split hurts students, and what can be done about it. In M.W. Kirst & A. Venezia (Eds.), *From high school to college: Improving opportunities for success in postsecondary education* (pp. 1–30). San Francisco, CA: Jossey-Bass.

Kirst, M.W., & Venezia, A. (Eds.). (2004). *From high school to college: Improving opportunities for success in postsecondary education* San Francisco, CA: Jossey-Bass.

Krueger, C. (2002). *The case for P–16: Designing an integrated learning system, preschool through postsecondary education*. Denver, CO: Education Commission of the States.

Krueger, C. (2006). *P–16 collaboration in the states*. Denver, CO: Education Commission of the States.

Long, B. T., & Bettinger, E. P. (2011). *The early college planning initiative: A randomized experiment to increase college savings in Massachusetts*. Project description. Retrieved from http://isites.harvard.edu/fs/docs/icb.topic1232999.files//Long_Early_College_Planning_Initiative_Summary_2011.pdf

Longanecker, D.A. (2002). Is merit-based student aid really trumping need-based aid? *Change, 34*(2), 30–37.

Lumina Foundation. (2011). *Lumina foundation's strategic plan: Goal 2025*. Indianapolis, IN: Author. Retrieved from http://www.luminafoundation.org/wp-content/uploads/2011/02/Lumina_Strategic_Plan.pdf

McLendon, M.K., Hearn, J.C., & Deaton, R. (2006). Called to account: Analyzing the origins and spread of state performance-accountability policies for higher education. *Educational Evaluation and Policy Analysis, 28*(1), 1–24.

McLendon, M.K., Heller, D.E., & Lee, S. (2009). High school to college transition policy in the American states: Conceptual and analytic perspectives on conducting across-state study. *Educational Policy, 23*(2), 385–418.

McLendon, M.K., Mokher, C., & Flores, S.M. (2011). Legislative agenda-setting for in-state resident tuition policies: Immigration, representation, and educational access. *American Journal of Education, 117*(4), 563–602.

Miao, K. (2012). *Performance-based funding of higher education: A detailed look at best practices in 6 states*. Washington, DC: Center for American Progress.

National Association of State Student Grant and Aid Programs (NASSGAP). (2011). *41st annual survey report on state-sponsored student financial aid: 2009–2010 academic year*. Washington, DC: Author.

National Association of State Student Grant and Aid Programs (NASSGAP). (2012). *42nd annual survey report on state-sponsored student financial aid: 2010–2011 academic year.* Washington, DC: Author.

National Center for Higher Education Management Systems (NCHEMS). (n.d.). *Increasing college attainment in the United States: Variations in returns to states and their residents.* Retrieved from http://www.nchems.org/clasp.php

National Governors Association (NGA). (2012). *NGA key committee issues: Higher education.* Retrieved from http://www.nga.org/cms/home/federal-relations/nga-key-committee-issues/page-ecw-issues/col2-content/main-content-list/title_higher-education.html

National Governors Association (NGA) & Council of Chief State School Officers (CCSSO). (n.d.). *About the standards.* Retrieved from http://www.corestandards.org/about-the-standards

National Postsecondary Education Cooperative. (2009). *Information required to be disclosed under the Higher Education Act of 1965: Suggestions for dissemination* (NPEC 2010-831). Prepared by Carol Fuller and Carlo Salerno. Washington, DC: Coffey Consulting.

Ness, E.C. (2008). *Merit aid and the politics of education.* New York, NY: Routledge.

Ness, E.C., & Noland, B.E. (2007). Targeted merit aid: Implications of the Tennessee education lottery scholarship program. *Journal of Student Financial Aid, 37*(1), 7–17.

Ness, E.C., & Tucker, R. (2008). Eligibility effects on college access: Under-represented students' perceptions of Tennessee's merit aid program. *Research in Higher Education, 49*(7), 569–588.

O'Donnell, M.L., & Hattan, S.K. (2009). *Key HEOA compliance obligations.* Washington, DC: Higher Education Compliance Alliance, National Association of College and University Attorneys. Retrieved from http://www.higheredcompliance.org/wp-content/uploads/2012/02/xv-09–11–6b.pdf

Olivas, M.A. (2003). State college savings and prepaid tuition plans: A reappraisal and review. *Journal of Law & Education, 32*(4), 475–515.

Perna, L.W., Finney, J., & Callan, P. (2012). *Much accomplished, much at stake: Performance and policy in Maryland higher education.* Philadelphia: University of Pennsylvania Graduate School of Education, Institute for Research on Higher Education.

Perna, L.W., & Titus, M.A. (2005). The relationship between parental involvement as social capital and college enrollment: An examination of racial/ethnic group differences. *Journal of Higher Education, 76*(5), 485–518.

Pipho, C. (2001). *State policy options to support a P–16 system of public education: Preschool through postsecondary.* Denver, CO: Education Commission of the States.

Quinterno, J. (2012). *The great cost shift: How higher education cuts undermine the future middle class.* New York, NY: Demos. Retrieved from http://www.demos.org/sites/default/files/publications/thegreatcostshift_0.pdf

Roth, A.P. (2001). *Saving for college & the tax code: A new spin on the "who pays for higher education?" debate.* New York, NY: Garland Publishing.

Rowan-Kenyon, H.T., Bell, A.D., & Perna, L.W. (2008). Contextual influences on parental involvement in college going: Variations by socioeconomic class. *Journal of Higher Education, 79*(5), 564–586.

Sanford, T., & Hunter, J.M. (2011). Impact of performance-funding on retention and graduation rates. *Education Policy Analysis Archives, 19*(33), 1–30.

State Higher Education Executive Officers (SHEEO). (2008). Second to none in attainment, discovery, and innovation: The national agenda for higher education. *Change,* September/October, 42–49.

The Institute for College Access and Success (TICAS). (2011). *Adding it all up: An early look at net price calculators*. Oakland, CA: Author. Retrieved from http://ticas.org/files/pub/adding_it_all_up.pdf

University System of Georgia. (2011, April 12). *How HOPE changes will affect USG students*. Retrieved from http://www.usg.edu/student_affairs/students/how_hope_changes_will_affect_usg_students/

Venezia, A., Callan, P.M., Finney, J.E., Kirst, M.W., & Usdan, M.D. (2005). *The governance divide: A report on a four-state study on improving college readiness*. San Jose, CA: National Center for Public Policy and Higher Education.

Vernez, G., Krop, C., Vuollo, M., & Hansen, J.S. (2008). *Toward a K–20 student unit record data system for California*. Santa Monica, CA: RAND Corporation.

Zhang, L. (2009). Does state funding affect graduation rates at public four-year colleges and universities? *Educational Policy, 23*(5), 714–731.

Zhang, L., & Ness, E.C. (2010). Does state merit-based aid stem brain drain? *Educational Evaluation and Policy Analysis, 32*(2), 143–165.

10

NONEXPERIMENTAL DESIGNS AND CAUSAL ANALYSES OF COLLEGE ACCESS, PERSISTENCE, AND COMPLETION

Stephen L. DesJardins and Allyson Flaster

Access to college is limited for some students, especially those from disadvantaged or underrepresented groups. For example, the college enrollment rate of high-income high school graduates is about 80%, whereas only about 55% of their low-income counterparts enroll in college. This 25 percentage point difference remains substantial even though the gap has narrowed over the last two decades (Baum, Ma, & Payea, 2010).

As described in the preceding chapters in this volume, policymakers have implemented a variety of interventions such as precollege outreach programs, college-level remedial education, and the provision of financial aid in an effort to reduce disparities in college access and success for diverse groups of students. To determine if interventions perform as expected—and therefore are an efficient use of public resources—education researchers have produced a wide body of literature that examines the effectiveness of programs and practices in reducing postsecondary inequality.

In recent years, however, there has been increasing concern about the rigor of education research in general and of studies examining the effects of financial aid on student educational outcomes in particular. In an influential book published in 2007, a group of distinguished academics note:

> Among educational leaders and policymakers there has been increasing concern regarding the need for scientifically based evidence on which to base funding decisions for specific educational programs and practices. This concern is fundamentally about having better evidence for making decisions about what programs and practices do or do not work. The need for such evidence leads to causal questions, such as whether particular programs and practices improve student academic achievement, social development,

and educational attainment. (Schneider, Carnoy, Kilpatrick, Schmidt, & Shavelson, 2007, p. 1)

Issues about making causal inferences are not new (Cook, 2002; Morgan & Harding, 2006; Morgan & Winship, 2007; Shadish, Cook, & Campbell, 2002; Whitehurst, 2003; Winship & Morgan, 1999). Nonetheless, these issues are now dominating discussions in education research. Many stakeholders are now skeptical that the research designs and methodologies traditionally employed in education research have produced a body of work that provides sound findings (Kaestle, 1993; Levin & O'Donnell, 1999; Schneider et al., 2007; Sroufe, 1997), implying that a new approach to education research is needed.

Furthermore, the director of the U.S. Department of Education's Institute of Education Sciences (IES), Grover J. "Russ" Whitehurst, argued that "randomized trials are one tool in the toolbox" (Whitehurst, 2003, p. 8) often used to conduct education research. But IES has also made it clear that randomized controlled trials (RCTs) are not practicable in all research contexts. Other approaches, especially nonexperimental methods that account for nonrandom assignment into treatment/control groups, are also appropriate when using observational data to assess the causal effect of educational programs and interventions.

Experiments are characterized by the random assignment of subjects into treatment and control groups. "Nonexperimental" or "quasi-experimental" methods lack this randomization component, but take into account the nonrandom assignment of subjects into treatment and control groups using statistical techniques (in this chapter, we use these terms non- and quasi-experimental interchangeably). As Hossler, Dundar, and Shapiro note in their chapter in this volume, "Researchers should make the best use of quasi-experimental research methods . . . to avoid biases introduced by the absence of control groups and random assignment, and to isolate the effects of these programs with more confidence" (p. 159).

From an education research and policymaking perspective, the basic question is this: are there differences in educational outcomes between groups of students who are in an educational program or intervention and those students who are not? For example, are there differences in college access and completion rates depending on whether a student receives financial aid such as the Pell grant (the "treatment") or not (the "control" group)? The criteria used to allocate Pell grants (e.g., family income, number of children in college, net value of assets, etc.) make it infeasible to randomize students into the "treatment" and "control" groups in order to evaluate the impact of the grant on educational outcomes.

Ethical and logistical constraints to randomization are also often present when evaluating education programs and practices. The inability to randomly assign students can pose problems for making causal inferences because students who receive a Pell grant may be materially different (based on observed and unobserved factors) than their counterparts who do not receive the grant. For example, low-income students are more likely to receive Pell grants and also have lower probabilities of enrolling in and finishing college than students who do not receive a Pell grant. The nonrandom nature of Pell grant distribution makes it difficult to parse the *causal* effects of receiving the grant from the observed and unobserved differences (the *selection* effects) among students who do and do not receive this financial support.

Using the study of financial aid as an example, this chapter describes statistical techniques that education researchers might employ to produce rigorous statements about the effects of educational interventions, programs, and practices. We identify how student financial aid affects access to and success in postsecondary education, briefly describing prior research examining the impact of financial aid on access and completion, then discuss the limitations of earlier studies. We then present some of the newest methods in use by educational researchers that, when properly employed, permit rigorous statements about the effects of financial aid on students' educational outcomes. Our intention is to introduce researchers and policymakers to these methods and discuss their application to education policymaking.

The Effect of Financial Aid on Student Behavior

Researchers have studied the impact of financial resources on student postsecondary outcomes for decades. Surveys of this literature generally conclude that a reduction in college expenses—whether engendered through lower tuition, higher family income, or increased financial aid—can increase educational access and attainment (Dynarski, 2002; Heller, 1997; Leslie & Brinkman, 1987; Long, 2008). However, the estimated impact of financial aid is less consistent across studies than that of family income or tuition. Further, some studies of financial aid produce results that are contrary to expectations, such as the finding that offers of aid have a negative impact on college matriculation (e.g., Somers & St. John, 1997). Others use the same data and come to very different conclusions. For example, St. John and Starkey (1995) find no significant effect of grant aid on persistence, but their colleagues Cofer and Somers (2000) find grant and loans to be positively related to persistence. Thus, the literature reveals mixed results of the effect of financial aid on student access, persistence, and completion.[1]

Education stakeholders are concerned about the mixed conclusions drawn from existing literature on educational interventions, and methodological limitations have been identified as a probable source of these inconsistencies. Below, we describe financial aid studies that do not account for the nonrandom assignment of students into aid receipt (dubbed the "naïve" statistical approach), and discuss the implications of this omission for the study findings. For expository purposes, we focus our review on studies that employ a naive approach when the outcome is college enrollment. Nonexperimental studies of financial aid's effect on persistence and degree attainment may also exhibit conflicting results but are not discussed.[2]

Prior Research on Financial Aid and Enrollment

Among studies that do not account for nonrandom assignment or "selection" effects, some previous research on college access suggests that any offer of financial aid positively influences a student's decision to attend college (St. John & Noell, 1989) whereas other studies challenge this conclusion (Akerhielm, Berger, Hooker, & Wise, 1998; Braunstein, McGrath, & Pescatrice, 1999; McPherson & Schapiro, 1991; Somers & St. John, 1997). For example, Akerhielm et al. (1998) examine the college matriculation decisions of 1992 high school graduates in relation to a financial aid offer from a four-year college. Due to data limitations, they were not able to observe the *amount* of aid students were offered or why (i.e., due to merit or need)—they only observed whether a student was offered financial aid of any kind. When results are disaggregated by college sector and student family income, the authors find the probability of enrollment at a private college is significantly influenced by offers of aid for low- and middle-income students, but not for high-income students. This finding makes sense, as high-income students likely have access to other financial resources and have the social capital required to navigate the college decision-making process. Among students who apply to public colleges, Akerhielm and colleagues find that only middle-income student enrollment is sensitive to offers of financial aid; in fact, the odds of middle-income student enrollment are higher in response to aid offers at public colleges than private colleges. This is surprising because, on average, public institutions charge lower tuition and offer smaller aid packages than private institutions (Hearn, Griswold, & Marine, 1996).

Studies that examine the *size* rather than just the presence of aid awards should provide more detailed information about aid effects (Chen & DesJardins, 2010). Using national data on White students from 1974 to 1984, McPherson and Schapiro (1991) examine whether the net cost of college attendance (tuition minus financial aid) affects college enrollment. They find that increases in college net cost has a negative impact on the enrollment of low-income students at private colleges, no impact on their enrollment at public colleges, and a positive impact on middle- and high-income student enrollment at public and private colleges. The authors attribute the unexpected finding of a positive relationship between college costs and enrollment for wealthier students to the laws of supply and demand: due to limits in their short-term capacity (or desire) to expand, colleges may increase tuition in response to increased demand for a college education by affluent students. However, the authors do not control for institutional selectivity or student ability; thus, the positive relationship could arise because affluent students tend to meet admissions criteria at selective and expensive colleges.

Research studies that examine the effects of *total* financial aid or *total* net cost only do not account for the fact that different *types* of aid may have differing effects on student behavior (Chen & DesJardins, 2010). For example, "self-help" aid such as student loans and work-study, which must be repaid or earned, may be less desirable to students than "gift aid" such as grants and scholarships. Thus, self-help aid may be less likely to induce students to enroll than gift aid. However, when Somers and St. John (1997) examine the impact of aid types on enrollment at several four-year institutions, they find inconsistent and surprising results. Increased scholarship aid offers result in *decreases* in enrollment in three out of four schools. An increase in offered work-study aid has a negative effect on enrollment at two schools, a positive effect at one school, and no effect at another school. The authors attribute the negative relationship to high levels of unobserved unmet need among students who are offered financial aid.

In contrast, using nationally representative data that includes the *types* (but not amounts) of financial aid college applicants were offered in 1972, 1980, and 1982, St. John and Noell (1989) determine that all types of aid offers (e.g., grants/scholarships only, loans only, work-study only, aid packages that combine several types of aid) significantly increase the probability that a student attends college. However, the magnitude of these positive effects varies. Across all three cohorts, "work-study only" offers are associated with the greatest increase in enrollment, whereas in two out of the three cohorts, "grants/scholarships only" offers are associated with the lowest increase in enrollment. Based on these results, we are faced with a counterintuitive finding: college access appears to be more strongly supported by offering students self-help aid than gift aid.

Limitations

Drawing strong conclusions about the efficacy of financial aid from contradictory findings or those that run counter to basic economic precepts about price (tuition) and quantity demanded (enrollment) can be difficult. Conflicting and unexpected findings may result from the use of different samples, methods of measuring aid, and distributions of missing data. Studies may also exhibit a statistical bias referred to as "omitted variable bias," which occurs when a researcher employs regression methods and omits a factor from the statistical model that is correlated with both an independent variable (or variables) and the outcome. This omission causes an over- or underestimation of an independent variable, depending on whether the omitted variable has a positive or negative relationship with the outcome (Cellini, 2008).

Omitted variable bias is likely present in many studies of financial aid because students are not randomly provided with financial aid (Alon, 2005; Cellini, 2008). Rather, student receipt of financial aid is predicated on a selection process. First, students decide whether to apply for financial aid (i.e., they self-select into a group of aid applicants). Second, using criteria related to merit and/or need, aid-awarding organizations determine if applicants will be provided with financial aid. Students then must decide whether to accept any aid offered to them. Failing to account for this selection process in the analyses may introduce bias, because factors related to a student's decision to apply for financial aid or an organization's decision to award aid are also likely related to the student's probability of enrolling, persisting, or graduating from college (Alon, 2005; Cellini, 2008; van der Klaauw, 2002).

For example, researchers who study the effect of Pell grants, which are need-based, should account for factors related both to a student's Pell eligibility and the outcome of interest (e.g., college enrollment, persistence, graduation) to avoid omitted variable bias. Correlates of Pell eligibility, such as being unfamiliar with the college application process or needing to work to support family members, tend to be negatively related to college outcomes. Therefore, omissions of these correlates from analyses of Pell grant effects may suggest that grants are less effective than they really are.

Brief Introduction to the Counterfactual Framework

In an effort to make more appropriate assessments of the efficacy of education policies and practices, researchers have been employing a "counterfactual" framework to guide their analyses. Under the counterfactual framework, hypothetically each individual has two potential outcomes: one that is observed and another that is unobserved (Holland, 1986; Murnane & Willett, 2011; Rubin, 1974). Also, each individual can potentially either receive or not receive a treatment, but we only observe the individual as "treated" or "not treated" (Angrist & Pischke, 2009). Continuing the financial aid offer/college enrollment example, each high school graduate has two possible outcomes: (1) enroll in college or (2) not enroll in college. The student can either receive the treatment (an offer of financial aid) or not (no offer of financial aid)—otherwise known as the "control" condition.

Ideally, to determine whether differences in the probability of enrollment are *caused* by financial aid offers, we would prefer to compare each student's enrollment outcome in a world where he received an offer of aid, to his enrollment outcome in a counterfactual world, where he did not receive an offer of aid. If we could do this, we could compare the student to himself, thereby keeping constant all the observed factors (e.g., demographic, ability, experiences) and unobserved/unmeasured factors (e.g., motivation, grit) that may affect his enrollment status. Any difference in educational outcomes under the treatment and control conditions would represent the *causal* effect of financial aid on the outcome of interest because the treatment condition would be the only factor that was different across these two states of the world. Repeating this exercise over many students and averaging the outcomes would provide the researcher with the *average treatment effect*—an estimate purged of any potential bias and thus of great interest to policymakers seeking to increase college access and completion.

The empirical problem is that we observe students only under the factual condition (the world we can observe), whereas outcomes under the counterfactual condition remain unknown (see Murnane & Willett, 2011, for information about the counterfactual framework). Researchers attempt to approximate the counterfactual condition by employing randomized trials, which, when implemented correctly, result in treatment and control groups that have identical observable and unobservable characteristics (Murnane & Willet, 2011; Schneider et al., 2007). The groups differ only with regard to their treatment status; therefore, the average treatment effect can be obtained by simply comparing the average outcomes across the two groups.

However, implementing a randomized trial is not always feasible or ethically appropriate. There may be resistance to randomly providing only some low-income students with Pell grants, because of a perception that students who do not receive a Pell grant are being denied a benefit to which they are entitled.

Nonexperimental Methods: A Solution to the Application of the Naïve Statistical Model

Given that randomized trials are not always feasible, and the results of the naïve statistical approach often suspect, what are policymakers who want rigorous evidence of the effects of financial aid programs, interventions, and policies to do? Fortunately a number of nonexperimental methods may offer a remedy to this inferential problem. These techniques employ natural experiments or statistical methods that can be used to make causal inferences about an educational policy or practice using observational datasets (Schneider et al., 2007). Examples include regression discontinuity design (see Lesik, 2008; McCall & Bielby, 2012; Shadish et al., 2002; Thistlethwaite & Campbell, 1960, for additional details), difference-in-difference methods (see Ashenfelter & Krueger, 1994; Card, 1995; Zhang, 2010), instrumental variable techniques (see Angrist, Imbens, & Rubin, 1996; Bielby, House, Flaster, & DesJardins, 2013; Bound, Jaeger, & Baker, 1995; Imbens & Angrist, 1994), and propensity score matching methods (see Caliendo & Kopeinig, 2008; Dehejia & Wahba, 1999, 2002; Heckman, Ichimura, & Todd, 1997; Morgan & Harding, 2006; Reynolds & DesJardins, 2009; Rosenbaum & Rubin, 1983; Smith & Todd, 2005). We briefly discuss these techniques below and describe a few studies that have employed them to analyze the effects of financial aid on education outcomes such as enrollment and persistence.

Regression Discontinuity Design

One nonexperimental method that has become increasingly popular is regression discontinuity (RD) analysis. RD is employed when subjects are assigned to treatment and control groups based on a score on a prespecified criterion or criteria. When appropriately applied, RD mimics the desirable properties of randomized experiments, thereby allowing strong ("causal") claims about the effects of the policy, program, or intervention being studied.

Thistlethwaite and Campbell (1960) initially applied RD in the field of education to study the effects of the National Merit Scholarship program. More recently the RD method was used by DesJardins, McCall, and colleagues (Des-Jardins & McCall, 2006a, 2006b, 2008; DesJardins, McCall, Ott, & Kim, 2010) to study the Gates Millennium Scholars (GMS) program. GMS administrators assign students to receive the scholarship based on their Pell eligibility, grades in high school, and score on application essays. Students are then awarded the scholarship based on whether their index score is greater than a threshold defined by the program administrators. One might expect that students very near to this "cut score" are distributed randomly above and below the threshold. For example, a student who scored one point above the threshold may have simply had a good day when writing the application essays and, if given another chance, would likely be in the other group. If students are randomly distributed around this threshold, then the observed and unobserved characteristics of the students are very similar, mimicking the desirable properties of a randomized experiment. DesJardins, McCall, and associates (DesJardins & McCall, 2006a, 2006b, 2008; DesJardins et al., 2010) found that, compared to non-GMS students, GMS scholars (i.e., the treatment group) had higher persistence rates, lower loan debt, higher graduation rates, worked fewer hours while enrolled in college, and had higher aspirations for graduate school.

Van der Klaauw (2002) used the RD approach and found that the enrollment of students who applied for federal aid was more sensitive to the offer of college grants than their counterparts who did not apply for federal aid, most likely because, their family income or residency status may have made them ineligible to receive it. Van der Klaauw also demonstrated that estimates based on the naïve approach of including the actual aid offer (which is the result of a nonrandom selection process) in an enrollment equation were unstable and biased, "providing a partial explanation for the wide range of reported aid effects in the literature" (van der Klaauw, 2002, p. 1280).

Although a useful technique for providing rigorous estimates of program and policy effects, RD has not been widely adopted by higher education researchers (McCall & Bielby, 2012). Given the criteria often used to distribute financial aid, thresholds on test scores or grades, or student/parent income levels, RD could be applied more often to study the effects of financial aid on college access and completion. Its use may be hampered by a lack of awareness of its merits and by overreliance on traditional methodologies (e.g., linear and nonlinear regression).

Difference-in-Differences

Difference-in-differences (DD) is another nonexperimental method often used to study the effects of education policies and practices on student outcomes. A simple hypothetical example may be instructive: Assume for two groups of students we observe an educational outcome (e.g., persistence) over two time periods. One group of students (the treated; denoted below as t) receives a treatment (e.g., a scholarship) in the second year (denoted by 2) but not in the first year (denoted by *1*). A second group of students (the controls; denoted by *c*) is not exposed to the treatment. A statistically naïve way to ascertain the effect of the scholarship on persistence (denoted by *Persist*) would be to do a before (pre) and after (post) comparison. That is, one could subtract the average persistence rate of the treated in year 1 ($Persist_{t1}$) from the pretreatment persistence rate for the treated in year 2 ($Persist_{t2}$) (the first difference shown in equation 1 below). However, this simple estimate may be biased because there may have already been an underlying trend in persistence rates that was unrelated to the provision of the scholarship, or the treated group may have characteristics that are related to higher persistence rates (e.g., higher ability, more support from family, etc.) regardless of receipt of the scholarship. Employing this simple pre/post method will not permit us to establish whether any observed change in persistence is due to the scholarship, preexisting trends in these rates, or the characteristics of students receiving the scholarship.

A more rigorous estimate of the effect of the scholarship can be ascertained by subtracting the average difference in persistence in the counterfactual (i.e., control group) ($Persist_{c2}$—$Persist_{c1}$) from the average difference in persistence in the treated group ($Persist_{t2}$—$Persist_{t1}$) across the two time periods (represented in algebraic form in equation 1). Using regression methods to estimate this difference removes any bias that may result from nonrandom differences in the students and any pre-existing trends in persistence rates, thereby isolating the effect of the scholarship on differences in persistence between the treated and control groups over time.

$$Impact\ of\ Scholarship = (Persist_{t2} - Persist_{t1}) - (Persist_{c2} - Persist_{c1}) \tag{10.1}$$

The DD method has been used extensively to study the effect of education policies and practices, and, in particular, to examine the effect of implementing new statewide financial aid policies on educational outcomes. For example, Dynarski (2000) finds that Georgia's HOPE (Helping Outstanding Pupils Educationally) Scholarship increases college attendance among 18- and 19-year-old students by 7 to 8 percentage points, although 80% of HOPE funds flow to students who would have attended college in the absence of the program. Cornwell, Mustard, and Sridhar (2006) estimate that HOPE increases first-time freshmen enrollment in Georgia colleges by nearly 6%. The scholarship also induces some students to remain in the state instead of attending college out of state. There is no evidence that HOPE increases enrollment at two-year colleges, although the authors did find evidence that Black enrollments increase at technical colleges in response to HOPE availability.

Kane (2007) used DD to analyze students' enrollment responses to the introduction of the DC Tuition Assistance Grant (DCTAG) program. DCTAG allows recent Washington, D.C., high school graduates to pay the in-state tuition rate at public colleges in any of the 50 states. Kane's (2007) estimates indicate that after the program's implementation, D.C. resident enrollments at out-of-state four-year colleges increased. There was no corresponding increase at out-of-state two-year colleges, most likely because a local inexpensive two-year option already existed.

In addition, individuals from middle- and high-income neighborhoods used the DCTAG grant more extensively than their counterparts from low-income neighborhoods. This finding suggests that grants such as DCTAG that are not means-tested benefit students who are likely to attend college in the absence of the subsidy.

When properly applied, the DD approach allows the researcher to create an appropriate counterfactual and to account for any preexisting trends, thereby allowing legitimate comparisons of the treated and control groups. Compared to the naïve statistical approaches often applied by education researchers, the results obtained from DD studies may be more reliable and therefore more useful for informing educational policy. Collectively, recent DD studies of the effectiveness of financial aid policies support the contention that reducing the cost of college attendance has a causal effect on student enrollment behavior, either by inducing marginal students to enroll or by modifying the institutional choice of college-bound students.

Instrumental Variables Techniques

Another method of statistically controlling for nonrandom assignment into treatment is an instrumental variables (IV) approach. This technique allows the researcher to estimate the causal effect of a variable (e.g., receipt of financial aid) on an outcome (e.g., graduation from college) using a third variable (i.e., an "instrument"). To determine causality, an instrument must be related to the variable of interest (the "treatment"—e.g., Pell grant receipt), but not directly affect the educational outcome (e.g., degree attainment; see Bielby et al., 2013; or Newhouse & McClellan, 1998, for more details on what constitutes an effective IV). Various factors may determine whether a student receives a treatment, many of which are either under the control of the student or another actor with knowledge of the student's characteristics, such as a financial aid officer. The instrument is used to "carve out" the portion of an individual's treatment status (e.g., grant receipt) that is determined by factors outside the control of the student or other educational actors. This "exogenous" source of variation—that which is outside the control of the student or other actors—is then used to estimate the causal effect of the treatment on the outcome.

IV approaches have promising applications to higher educational issues related to student access, persistence, and completion. Nonetheless, finding effective IVs is not an easy task. As Angrist and Pischke (2009) conclude, "Good instruments come from a combination of institutional knowledge and ideas about the processes determining the variable of interest" (p. 117). A sound understanding of the mechanisms and processes related to any educational outcomes studied is necessary, but not sufficient, to apply this technique successfully.

An instrument used in the study of financial aid is the number of siblings a student has that are concurrently enrolled in college (Alon, 2011). This instrument is derived from the federal formula that determines the expected family contribution (EFC): parents who have multiple children enrolled in college at the same time are expected to provide less funding to each child than parents who have only one child enrolled in college (Baum, 1999; Brown, Scholz, & Seshadri, 2009). Assuming students do not strategically synchronize their college enrollment with a sibling, the number of siblings concurrently enrolled in college predicts aid receipt using a factor outside the control of the student or other educational actors. Controlling for family size (to account for resource dilution) and other student and college-level variables, sibling enrollment serves as a good instrument for studying the effects of federal financial aid because it is strongly related to a student's aid eligibility but does not directly determine his or her postsecondary outcomes (Alon, 2011).

When applying the sibling college enrollment IV to national data, Alon (2011) finds that each additional $1,000 in need-based aid increases first-year persistence by 5% across all income groups. However, restricting the analysis to lower middle-income students, that is, students who are on the cusp of Pell eligibility and for whom sibling enrollment has a substantial effect on the amount of need-based aid received, suggests that each $1,000 increase in aid results in a 5% increase in first-year persistence. This result leads Alon to conclude: "Clearly, for students in this income bracket, means-tested grants are critical to their ability to persist in college" (p. 819).

Researchers have also used other policy-related variables as instruments. In the 2006–2007 academic year, Ohio implemented the Ohio College Opportunity Grant (OCOG), which changed the amount of need-based aid for which students in the state were eligible (Bettinger, 2010). This resulted in policy "winners" (students who received more aid in 2006–2007 than in 2005–2006) and policy "losers" (students who received less aid in 2006–2007 than in 2005–2006). Using an interaction between a student's year in college (i.e., their "cohort") and policy winner/loser status as an IV, Bettinger (2010) finds that each $1,000 increase in need-based aid decreases dropout or transfer in the first year by 1.6 to 2.4 percentage points. These results are largely driven by changes in aid amounts for students in the bottom of the income distribution, that is, those students who were exposed to the greatest change in their aid packages after the implementation of the OCOG.

The preceding instrumental variable approaches demonstrate the potential of their application to higher education research. However, additional scholarship using this technique is needed. To find effective instrumental variables, education researchers should seek out data sources not conventionally used in the study of higher education. For example, data on students' labor market contexts from government agencies may provide information about factors that predict program participation, but do not affect educational outcomes (Bielby et al., 2013).

Propensity Score Matching

Propensity score matching (PSM) is another method that uses observational data to mimic the desirable properties of randomized experiments (see Reynolds &

DesJardins [2009] for a detailed description of the conceptual and statistical underpinnings of matching methods). The intuition behind PSM is to find individuals who do not receive the "treatment" who have observable pretreatment characteristics that are similar to individuals actually receiving the treatment. PSM controls for pretreatment differences by balancing each group's set of observable characteristics on a single "propensity score," an estimate of the probability of treatment for all subjects after accounting for observable factors thought to be related to treatment. This score is obtained by using regression techniques to estimate the probability of treatment for each student and using this probability to match treated students to students who were not treated but had similar propensity scores.

When properly conducted, matching on the propensity score balances the distribution of observable characteristics across the treated and untreated groups; thus, the probability that any treated individual has a specific trait will be the same as the probability that any untreated individual has that same characteristic. The observed outcome for untreated cases serves as the correct counterfactual, allowing for more rigorous claims of the effect of the treatment.

Few studies have employed PSM to examine the effects of financial aid and undergraduate outcomes, but researchers have applied the technique to studying other facets of college access and success. For instance, Melguizo (2010) examined whether college selectivity has an effect on college completion for low-income, high-achieving students of color using data on applicants to the Gates Millennium Scholars (GMS) program. She matched students with similar observable characteristics, including noncognitive factors such as leadership potential, by their propensity to attend institutions of varying selectivity and found that students who attend a highly selective college (the treated) instead of a less selective college experience an 8% increase in their probability of degree completion.

Using PSM, Reynolds and DesJardins (2009) indicate that students who initially attend a two-year college but move on to a four-year institution have lower probabilities of being retained in the four-year institution, have lower probabilities of completing a bachelor's degree, and earn fewer college credits over their college careers. Their results also indicate that the naïve statistical methods often employed to estimate education "treatments" may produce results that are materially different than when one employs PSM and that the estimates of the treatment effects vary depending on the matching method used and educational outcome being examined.

PSM methods are promising tools for studying the effects of financial aid on student access and completion. However, the extent to which PSM actually results in equivalent treatment and comparison groups is an issue. PSM may not provide accurate estimates of causal effects if factors involved in receiving treatment are excluded from the model that estimates the propensity scores. Therefore, to ensure that treatment and control groups are equivalent, researchers must have a solid understanding of the mechanisms that determine whether students receive a treatment. If the propensity scores are not correctly estimated, then the two groups may not be equivalent. PSM methods might then lead to spurious results, making no improvement over results obtained from naïve statistical methods (Agodini & Dynarski, 2004).

Conclusions

The issue of causal inference is garnering considerable attention in education research and policymaking circles. Additionally, disparities in college enrollment across racial/ethnic groups and between individuals from low- and high-income backgrounds remain prevalent. In order to successfully improve college access and success for underserved groups, policymakers and practitioners need access to rigorous analysis of the programs and policies that are intended to reduce educational inequality.

Higher education researchers have been very successful in informing educational decision makers about factors *related* to educational outcomes, but less successful in determining whether there are *causal* linkages. One reason may be researchers' failure to apply designs and methods that can help unravel the causal effects of educational treatments on outcomes, thereby providing more accurate information. This chapter describes analytical methods that can remedy some of these difficulties and be applied to study the effects of financial aid, remedial education, community college transfer, and other topics discussed in this volume.

Recommendations

Practitioners and policymakers play an important role in promoting the rigorous evaluation of educational interventions. In particular, college staff, such as institutional researchers or program managers, may advance our collective understanding about the educational practices that support the success of students. They also have a wealth of data at their disposal, understand the backgrounds of the students they serve, and have detailed knowledge about institutional practices and systems that can be used to identify policy shifts for DD studies, criteria thresholds for RD analysis, and instruments that affect whether students receive an intervention but do not affect their educational outcomes. Institutional leaders should provide college staff responsible for program evaluation, but unfamiliar with the techniques discussed in this chapter, with training in quasi-experimental methodologies. In many institutions such courses are taught in graduate programs in statistics, political science/public policy, sociology, economics, and in some education schools.

The American Educational Research Association has promoted the use of rigorous analytic methods by supporting the book cited at the opening of the chapter (Schneider et al., 2007). The Association for Institutional Research (AIR) and/or the Association for the Study of Higher Education could play a role by providing professional development for institutional and educational researchers.

In addition to AIR instruction on the application of statistical methods, adding modules on the nonexperimental methods discussed above may be fruitful. Additionally, graduate schools, especially education schools, need to provide training in quasi-experimental studies. Providing statistical training that stops at basic linear and nonlinear regression is a major barrier to the widespread adoption of research methodologies that better support claims of cause and effect in the field of higher education.

Widespread adoption of quasi-experimental methods in education research is more likely to occur when state and federal policymakers leverage their influence to promote these analytical techniques. Through the Institute for Education Sciences (IES), the U.S. Department of Education has promoted the application of experimental and quasi-experimental methods through multiple channels. In partnership with the Institute for Policy Research at Northwestern University, IES has sponsored summer workshops on quasi-experimental methods for postsecondary and K–12 employees. However, the number of individuals who can participate is limited. Expanding the availability of these summer workshops across the country could help provide access to important training opportunities for education staff and researchers.

IES also compiles the results of rigorous studies of educational interventions—the majority of which employ experimental or quasi-experimental methods—in their What Works Clearinghouse (WWC) website (http://ies.ed.gov/ncee/wwc/). The inclusion of quasi-experimental studies on the WWC site is, in effect, an endorsement of the use of these methodologies. However, the vast majority of research reviewed on the website is specific to primary and secondary education. The inclusion of more topics and research related to higher education appears warranted. At the state level, IES has put hundreds of millions of dollars into the construction of student unit-record databases, the main objective of which is to help inform policymaking and improve educational outcomes. IES has also allocated funds to promote access to these data, and additional funding could encourage the application of methods that may help state and federal stakeholders make strong inferences about "what works" in education.

Additionally, policymakers can serve as powerful supporters of quasi-experimental methods in education research by leveraging their "power of the purse." Currently, the use of methods like those discussed above is practically a prerequisite for receiving funding through the IES research grant program. If all federal agencies that provide funding to organizations to support general education and dissertation research followed the lead of IES, applicants may be incentivized to learn and apply new methods, thereby changing the research base available for education decision makers. Finally, by linking the use of state-level data with federal support for the adoption of rigorous research methods, policymakers could provide a strong foundation for a new research agenda that focuses on the programs and practices that *causally improve* college access and success for underserved students across the nation.

Notes

1. Over the past four decades, numerous studies of the effects of college price on college access, persistence, and completion have been conducted. For meta-analyses of these studies, see Leslie and Brinkman (1987), Heller (1997), Gallett (2007), and Kim (2010).
2. We do not attempt to provide a comprehensive survey of the financial aid literature in this chapter because many such surveys already exist. See Dynarski (2003) and Long (2008) for thoughtful discussions of the role of financial aid and college expenses in postsecondary access and success. Other chapters in this edited volume also provide more detail about the results of existing financial aid research.

References

Agodini, R., & Dynarski, M. (2004). Are experiments the only option? A look at dropout prevention programs. *Review of Economics and Statistics, 86,* 180–194.

Akerhielm, K., Berger, J., Hooker, M., & Wise, D. (1998). *Factors related to college enrollment: Final report.* Washington, DC: U.S. Department of Education, Office of the Undersecretary.

Alon, S. (2005). Model mis-specification in assessing the impact of financial aid on academic outcomes. *Research in Higher Education, 46*(1), 109–125.

Alon, S. (2011). Who benefits most from financial aid? The heterogeneous effect of need-based grants on students' college persistence. *Social Science Quarterly, 92*(3), 807–829.

Angrist, J.D., Imbens, G.W., & Rubin, D.B. (1996). Identification of causal effects using instrumental variables. *Journal of the American Statistical Association, 91*(434), 444–455.

Angrist, J.D., & Pischke, J.S. (2009). *Mostly harmless econometrics: An empiricist's companion.* Princeton, NJ: Princeton University Press.

Ashenfelter, O., & Krueger, A. (1994). Estimates of the economic return to schooling from a new sample of twins. *American Economic Review, 84*(5), 1157–1173.

Baum, S. (1999). Need analysis: How we decide who gets what. In Jacqueline E. King (Ed.), *Financing a college education: How it works, how it is changing* (pp. 48–63). Phoenix, AZ: The American Council on Education and the Oryx Press Series on Higher Education.

Baum, S., Ma, J., & Payea, K. (2010). *Education pays 2010: The benefits of higher education for individuals and society.* New York, NY: College Board.

Bettinger, E.P. (2010). *Need-based aid and student outcomes: The effects of the Ohio College Opportunity Grant.* Unpublished manuscript, Stanford University School of Education, Stanford, CA. Retrieved from https://www.sesp.northwestern.edu/docs/need-based-aid-why.pdf

Bielby, R.M., House, E., Flaster, A., & DesJardins, S.L. (2013). Instrumental variables: Conceptual issues and an application considering high school coursetaking. In M.B. Paulsen (Ed.), *Higher education: Handbook of theory and research* (Vol. 28). New York, NY: Springer.

Bound, J., Jaeger, D.A., & Baker, R.M. (1995). Problems with instrumental variables estimation when the correlation between the instruments and the endogenous explanatory variable is weak. *Journal of the American Statistical Association, 90*(430), 443–450.

Braunstein, A., McGrath, M., & Pescatrice, D. (1999). Measuring the impact of income and financial aid offers on college enrollment decisions. *Research in Higher Education, 40*(3), 247–259.

Brown, M., Scholz, J.K., & Seshadri, A. (2009). *A new test of borrowing constraints for Education* (NBER Working Paper No. 14879). Cambridge, MA: National Bureau of Economic Research. Retrieved from http://www.nber.org

Caliendo, M., & Kopeinig, S. (2008). Some practical guidance for the implementation of propensity score matching. *Journal of Economic Surveys, 22*(1), 31–72.

Card, D. (1995). Using geographic variation in college proximity to estimate the return to schooling. In L.N. Christofides, E.K. Grant, and R. Swidinsky (Eds.), *Aspects of labour market behaviour: Essays in honour of John Vanderkamp* (pp. 201–222). Toronto, Canada: University of Toronto Press.

Cellini, S.R. (2008). Causal inference and omitted variable bias in financial aid research: Assessing solutions. *Review of Higher Education, 31*(3), 329–354.

Chen, R., & DesJardins, S.L. (2010). Investigating the impact of financial aid on student dropout risks: Racial and ethnic differences. *Journal of Higher Education, 81*(2), 179–208.

Cofer, J., & Somers, P. (2000). A comparison of the influence of debtload on the persistence of students at public and private colleges. *Journal of Student Financial Aid, 30*(2), 39–58.

Cook, T.D. (2002). Randomized experiments in educational policy research: A critical examination of the reasons the educational evaluation community has offered for not doing them. *Educational Evaluation and Policy Analysis, 24*(3), 175–199.

Cornwell, C., Mustard, D.B., & Sridhar, D.J. (2006). The enrollment effects of merit-based financial aid: Evidence from Georgia's HOPE Program. *Journal of Labor Economics, 24*(4), 761–786.

Dehejia, R.H., & Wahba, S. (1999). Causal effects in nonexperimental studies: Reevaluating the evaluation of training programs. *Journal of the American Statistical Association, 94*(448), 1053–1062.

Dehejia, R.H., & Wahba, S. (2002). Propensity score-matching methods for nonexperimental causal studies. *Review of Economics and Statistics, 84*(1), 151–161.

DesJardins, S.L., & McCall, B.P. (2006a). *The impact of the Gates Millennium Scholars Program on selected academic and non-cognitive outcomes: A regression discontinuity analysis.* A Report to the Bill and Melinda Gates Foundation.

DesJardins, S.L., & McCall, B.P. (2006b). *The impact of the Gates Millennium Scholars Program on the college enrollment, borrowing and work behavior of low-income minority students.* A Report to the Bill and Melinda Gates Foundation.

DesJardins, S.L., & McCall, B.P. (2008). *Investigating the causal impact of the Gates Millennium Scholars Program on the correlates of college completion, graduation from college, and future educational aspirations of low-income minority students.* A Report to the Bill and Melinda Gates Foundation.

DesJardins, S.L., McCall, B.P., Ott, M., & Kim, J. (2010). A quasi-experimental investigation of how the Gates Millennium Scholars program is related to college students' time use and activities. *Educational Evaluation and Policy Analysis, 32*(4), 456–475.

Dynarski, S. (2000). *Hope for whom? Financial aid for the middle class and its impact on college attendance* (NBER Working Paper No. 7756). Cambridge, MA: National Bureau of Economic Research. Retrieved from http://www.nber.org

Dynarski, S. (2002). The consequences of lowering the cost of college: The behavioral and distributional implications of aid for college. *AEA Papers and Proceedings, 92*(2), 279–285.

Dynarski, S. (2003). Does aid matter? Measuring the effect of student aid on college attendance and completion. *American Economic Review, 93*(1), 279–288.

Gallet, C. (2007). A comparative analysis of the demand for higher education: Results from a meta-analysis of elasticities. *Economics Bulletin, 9*(7), 1–14.

Hearn, J.C., Griswold, C.P., & Marine, G.M. (1996). Region, resources, and reason: A contextual analysis of state tuition and student aid policies. *Research in Higher Education, 37*(3), 241–278.

Heckman, J.J., Ichimura, H., & Todd, P.E. (1997). Matching as an econometric evaluation estimator: Evidence from evaluating a job training programme. *Review of Economic Studies, 64*(4), 605–654.

Heller, D.E. (1997). Student price response in higher education: An update to Leslie and Brinkman. *Journal of Higher Education, 68*(6), 624–657.

Holland, P.W. (1986). Statistics and causal inference. *Journal of the American Statistical Association, 81*, 945–970.

Imbens, G.W. & Angrist, J.D. (1994). Identification and estimation of local average treatment effects. *Econometrica, 62*(2), 467–475.

Kaestle, C.F. (1993). The awful reputation of educational research. *Educational Researcher, 22*, 23–31.

Kane, T.J. (2007). Evaluating the impact of the DC Tuition Assistance Grant Program. *Journal of Human Resources, 42*(3), 555–582.

Kim, J. (2010). The effect of prices on postsecondary access: An update to Heller. *Higher Education in Review, 7*, 23–46.

Lesik, S.A. (2008). Studying the effectiveness of programs and initiatives in higher education using the regression-discontinuity design. In J.C. Smart (Ed.), *Higher education: Handbook of theory and research*. (Vol. 23). New York, NY: Springer.

Leslie, L.L., & Brinkman, P.T. (1987). Student price response in higher education. *Journal of Higher Education, 58*(2), 181–204.

Levin, J.R., & O'Donnell, A.M. (1999). What to do about educational research's credibility gaps? *Issues in Education, 5*(2), 177–229.

Long, B.T. (2008). *What is known about the impact of financial aid? Implications for policy* (An NCPR Working Paper). New York, NY: National Center for Postsecondary Research.

McCall, B.P., & Bielby, R.M. (2012). Regression discontinuity design: Recent developments and a guide to practice for researchers in higher education. In J.C. Smart and M.B. Paulsen (Eds.), *Higher education: Handbook of theory and research* (Vol. 27). New York, NY: Springer.

McPherson, M.S., & Schapiro, M.O. (1991). Does student aid affect college enrollment? New evidence on a persistent controversy. *The American Economic Review, 81*(1), 309–318.

Melguizo, T. (2010). Are students of color more likely to graduate from college if they attend more selective institutions? Evidence from a cohort of recipients and nonrecipients of the Gates Millennium Scholarship program. *Educational Evaluation and Policy Analysis, 32*(2), 230–248.

Morgan, S.L., & Harding, D.J. (2006). Matching estimators of causal effects: Prospects and pitfalls in theory and practice. *Sociological Methods and Research, 35*(1), 3–60.

Morgan, S.L., & Winship, C. (2007). *Counterfactuals and causal inference: Methods and principles for social research.* Cambridge, UK: Cambridge University Press.

Murnane, R.J., & Willett, J.B. (2011). *Methods matter: Improving causal inference in educational and social science research.* New York, NY: Oxford University Press.

Newhouse, J., & McClellan, M. (1998). Econometrics in outcomes research: The use of instrumental variables. *Annual Review of Public Health, 19*, 17–34.

Reynolds, C.L., & DesJardins, S.L. (2009). The use of matching methods in higher education research: Answering whether attendance at a two-year institution results in differences in educational attainment. In J.C. Smart (Ed.), *Higher education: Handbook of theory and research* (Vol. 24). New York, NY: Springer.

Rosenbaum, P., & Rubin, D.B. (1983). The central role of the propensity score in observational studies for causal effects. *Biometrika, 70*, 41–55.

Rubin, D. (1974). Estimating causal effects of treatments in randomized and non-random-ized studies. *Journal of Educational Psychology, 66,* 688–701.

Schneider, B., Carnoy, M., Kilpatrick, J., Schmidt, W.H., & Shavelson, R.J. (2007). *Estimat-ing causal effects using experimental and observational designs.* Washington, DC: American Educational Research Association.

Shadish, W.R., Cook, T.D., & Campbell, D.T. (2002). *Experimental and quasi-experimental designs for generalized causal inference.* Boston, MA: Houghton-Mifflin.

Smith, J.A., & Todd, P.E. (2005). Does matching overcome LaLonde's critique of nonex-perimental estimators? *Journal of Econometrics, 125*(1–2), 305–353.

Somers, P.A., & St. John, E.P. (1997). Analyzing the role of financial aid in student per-sistence. In J.S. Davis. (Ed.), *Student aid research: A manual for financial aid administrators.* Washington, DC: National Association of Student Financial Aid Administrators.

Sroufe, G.E. (1997). Improving the "awful reputation" of education research. *Educational Researcher, 26*(7), 26–28.

St. John, E.P., & Noell, J. (1989). The effects of student financial aid on access to higher education: An analysis of progress with special consideration of minority enrollment. *Research in Higher Education, 30*(6), 563–581.

St. John, E.P., & Starkey, J.B. (1995). An alternative to net price: Assessing the influences of prices and subsidies on within-year persistence. *Journal of Higher Education, 66,* 156–186.

Thistlethwaite, D.L., & Campbell, D.T. (1960). Regression-discontinuity analysis: An alter-native to the ex-post facto experiment. *Journal of Educational Psychology, 51,* 309–317.

van der Klaauw, W. (2002). Estimating the effect of financial aid offers on college en-rollment: A regression–discontinuity approach. *International Economic Review, 43*(4), 1249–1287.

Whitehurst, G.J. (2003, April). *The Institute of Education Sciences: New wine, new bottles.* Speech to the American Educational Research Association's Annual Conference, New Orleans, LA. Retrieved from http://ies.ed.gov/director/pdf/2003_04_22.pdf

Winship, C., & Morgan, S.L. (1999). The estimation of causal effects from observational data. *Annual Review of Sociology, 25,* 659–707.

Zhang, L. (2010). The use of panel data models in higher education policy studies. In J.C. Smart (Ed.), *Higher education: Handbook of theory and research* (Vol. 25). New York, NY: Springer.

11

CONCLUSIONS

Improving College Access, Persistence, and Completion: Lessons Learned

Laura W. Perna

As illustrated by the preceding chapters in this volume, the United States has made substantial progress in improving some outcomes on the path from college access to degree completion. Growth in college enrollment has been particularly impressive. As Elizabeth Kurban and I observe in our chapter in this volume, the number of students enrolled in college increased 74% over the past three decades (National Center for Education Statistics [NCES], 2012).

Despite this progress, however, substantial concerns remain. One problem, as Don Hossler and his coauthors note in their chapter, is that college completion rates have not increased over time. Only 58% of students seeking bachelor's degrees who entered a four-year college or university for the first time on a full-time basis in 2004 completed a bachelor's degree within six years. This completion rate is only marginally higher than the completion rate for students who first enrolled a decade earlier, as 55% of those who first enrolled in 1996 completed a bachelor's degree within six years (NCES, 2012). There has also been little improvement over time in completion rates at two-year colleges. Only 30% of students who first enrolled on a full-time basis at a two-year college in 2007 completed a certificate or degree within three years, the same completion rate as for students who first entered in 2000 (NCES, 2012).

At least in part because of this stagnation in completion rates, educational attainment is now lower for the U.S. population than the population of several other nations. As other chapters in this volume observe, the United States leads the world in the share of older adults (e.g., adults age 45 to 54) who hold at least a baccalaureate-level degree, but lags other nations in the educational attainment of younger adults (e.g., adults age 25 to 34). In 2007, the percentage of adults age 25 to 34 with at least a bachelor's type of degree was lower in the United States than in Norway, The Netherlands, Korea, New Zealand, and Denmark (Baum,

Ma, & Payea, 2010). Essentially, educational attainment has stalled in the United States, with about 30% of adults in each age cohort holding at least a bachelor's degree. Over this same period, however, educational attainment has been rising dramatically in some other nations (Baum et al., 2010). Of particular note, in Korea, 34% of adults age 25 to 34 now hold at least a bachelor's type of post-secondary degree, up from only 17% of adults age 45 to 54. Following the same pattern, 30% of younger adults (age 25 to 34) in Poland hold at least a bachelor's degree, compared with only 13% of older (age 45 to 54) adults (Baum et al., 2010).

Why Is It Critical to Improve Educational Attainment in the United States?

As noted elsewhere in this volume, President Obama and other U.S. presidents, members of Congress, U.S. Department of Education officials, state governors, foundation leaders, and others have all called for the United States to raise the educational attainment of the population for international competitiveness reasons. Based on trends in degree production and population growth, the National Center for Higher Education Management Systems estimates that the number of associate's and bachelor's degrees must increase by 7.9% each year from 2009 through 2020 in order for 55% of the U.S. population age 25 to 64 to hold at least an associate's degree—the level of educational attainment in the best-performing nation (Kelly, 2010).

As Anthony Jones articulates in the introductory chapter to this volume, improvements in educational attainment will come only with improvements in the multiple junctures on the pathway from college access through degree completion. Clearly—as demonstrated by data presented throughout this volume—too many students are lost at too many critical junctures in the pipeline. Too few students successfully transition from high school into college, as described in my chapter with Elizabeth Kurban. Too many lack the academic preparation required to enroll in college-credit courses without the need for remedial or development courses, as discussed in chapters by David Conley and by Bridget Terry Long and Angela Boatman. Too many lack the financial resources required to pay the costs of enrolling and persisting in college, as Don Heller describes in his chapter. Too few successfully transfer from community colleges to complete bachelor's degrees at four-year colleges and universities, as illustrated in the chapter by Tatiana Melguizo, Gregory Kienzl, and Holly Kosiewicz. Too few students are retained at the institution at which they first enroll or persist through multiple institutions to degree completion, as demonstrated by the chapter by Don Hossler, Afet Dundar, and Doug Shapiro.

Students from low-income families, Black and Hispanic students, and potential first-generation college students are substantially less likely than their peers from higher-income families, who are White and Asian, and whose parents have entered and completed college, to have the academic preparation and financial resources required to enroll and persist in college and complete degrees. As Debra Bragg argues in her chapter, these groups are not only underrepresented among college enrollees and degree completers, but are also underserved by our nation's educational system. As just one indicator of the very large differences in educational outcomes across groups, only 9.8% of Hispanic men and 17.6% of Black men between the ages of 25 and 29 in 2009 had completed at least a bachelor's degree, compared with 32.3% of their White male counterparts. The pattern of racial/ethnic group differences is the same for women: only 14.9% of Hispanic and 21.4% of Black women age 25 to 29 in 2009 had completed at least a bachelor's degree, compared with 41% of White women (Baum et al., 2010).

Underscoring the need to improve the educational outcomes for young adults is the reality that our nation's educational system does not have a strong record of promoting educational outcomes for adult students—that is, individuals who did not successfully progress through these transition points at earlier stages in their lives. Although entering college as an adult (i.e., beyond the traditional 18- to 24-year-old range) is not without challenges, adults now represent a sizable share of the nation's college students. In fall 2009, about a third (33%) of all undergraduates were age 25 and older. Adults represent a higher share of undergraduates who are enrolled part time (53%) rather than full time (12%) (NCES, 2012). As Debra Bragg demonstrates in her chapter in this volume, adult students often face a unique set of hurdles to college access, success, and completion, and would benefit from clear pathways into and through college to employment.

Improving the many critical transition points, closing gaps in outcomes across demographic groups, and promoting attainment of not only traditional-age students but also adults are all essential to raising the nation's overall educational attainment. Improvement in educational attainment is required not only to meet international competitiveness goals but also to ensure that the educational qualifications of the nation's workers match the educational requirements necessary for current and future jobs. Based on their analyses of data from the Bureau of Labor Statistics, Carnevale, Smith, and Strohl (2010) project that, by 2018, 63% of all new and replacement jobs will require at least some college education. In contrast, in 1973, 72% of available jobs required no more than a high school education. Carnevale and colleagues estimate that, at the current rate of degree production, the demand for workers with at least an associate's degree will exceed the supply by 3 million by 2018.

Raising educational attainment to meet international competitiveness goals and workforce demands will produce countless other benefits both to society and individuals, as noted by Anthony Jones in the introductory chapter as well as other chapter authors. Among the many other societal benefits, higher levels of attainment generate greater economic productivity as well as an expanded tax base (because of the higher earnings of better-educated workers), higher labor force participation and employment rates, lower unemployment rates and less reliance on social support programs, and higher rates of volunteerism and voting (Baum et al., 2010).

Individuals also realize countless economic and noneconomic benefits when they complete higher levels of education. At the individual level, increased educational attainment is associated with higher annual earnings, greater job satisfaction, lower likelihood of unemployment and poverty, greater likelihood of employer-provided health insurance, better health, and improved educational outcomes for one's children (Baum et al., 2010). Moreover, since the early 1990s, the wage premium associated with holding a bachelor's degree rather than an associate's degree, some college, or a high school diploma has grown, as illustrated by Don Heller in his chapter in this volume and observed by others (e.g., Baum et al., 2010; Carnevale et al., 2010). Median earnings of full-time, year-round workers were 79% higher in 2008 for women age 25 to 34 who held at least a bachelor's degree rather than a high school diploma; the earnings premium was 60% in 1998. For men, the earnings premium associated with having at least a bachelor's degree rather than a high school diploma increased from 54% in 1998 to 74% in 2008 (Baum et al., 2010).

Consideration of these individual benefits also further underscores the need to close gaps in attainment across groups. The failure to close gaps in college access, persistence, and completion means that individuals from lower-achieving groups are less likely to realize the many economic and social benefits that are associated with higher education. Moreover, the failure to eliminate gaps across groups in educational outcomes has contributed to the increased economic and social stratification of our society over time. Over the past 40 years, individuals without a college education have become increasingly concentrated in the lower-income class. In 2007, 35% of high school graduates were in the lowest three income quartiles, up from only 22% in 1970. Over the same period, those with a bachelor's degree or graduate degree represented a growing share of those in the upper-income class. In 2007, 48% of individuals with a bachelor's degree and 61% of individuals with a graduate degree were in the upper three income deciles, up from 37% and 41% respectively in 1970 (Carnevale et al., 2010).

The importance of closing racial/ethnic group gaps in attainment is more important now than ever before, given the changing demographic characteristics of the U.S. population. Hispanics, the group with among the lowest current educational attainment, are among the nation's fastest growing racial/ethnic groups (Western Interstate Commission on Higher Education, 2008). By 2021, the majority of high school graduates will be students of color; a number of states (e.g., Maryland, Texas) are already "majority-minority."

Why Is Educational Attainment in the United States Not Higher?

Many forces restrict college access, persistence, and completion and contribute to the perpetuation of gaps in these outcomes across groups. As described in several chapters in this volume (e.g., Perna & Kurban; Conley; Long & Boatman), too many students are inadequately academically prepared to enroll and succeed in college without the need for remedial or developmental coursework. Too many students are unable to pay the costs of higher education, even with the availability of financial aid, as discussed in chapters by Perna and Kurban, as well as Heller. Too many students continue to lack access to necessary information about their academic readiness for college, or about college and financial aid, early enough in the educational pipeline, as described in chapters by Long and Boatman, as well as Perna and Kurban. Too many nontraditional and adult students lack the information required to navigate their way into and through college and into careers, as described in the chapter by Bragg.

Addressing the barriers to college access, persistence, and completion that are associated with inadequate academic preparation; insufficient financial resources to pay the financial costs; and inadequate information about academic readiness, college requirements and application procedures, and financial aid availability and processes is complicated by numerous forces. Of particular importance are the continued disconnects between the nation's K–12 and higher education systems; the number, diversity, and autonomy of the nation's higher education institutions; and the deficiencies of existing research.

Misalignment of K–12 and Higher Education "Systems"

One force that challenges efforts to improve academic readiness for college is the fact that K–12 education and higher education in the United States are operated as separate, largely uncoordinated systems. A particularly problematic consequence of this separation is the lack of alignment of curricula and assessment, as well as data and accountability mechanisms, between secondary and higher education (Kirst & Venezia, 2004). As described by other chapters in this volume (e.g., Conley; Hearn et al.; Long & Boatman; Perna & Kurban), this situation creates substantial problems for ensuring that high school students are academically ready to enter and succeed in college. Over the past decade, states have made little tangible progress improving the alignment between K–12 and higher education. For example, although a number of states ($n = 25$) require students to take and pass an "exit exam" in order to receive a regular high school diploma, only 8 states (Florida, Massachusetts, Mississippi, New York, Oklahoma, Oregon, Rhode Island, and Virginia) have aligned the exam content to college- and career-readiness standards (Center on Education Policy, 2012). As a result, many high schools in most states are preparing students to receive a high school diploma, rather than to academically succeed in college (Kirst & Usdan, 2009; Venezia, Callan, Finney, Kirst, & Usdan, 2005).

With financial support from the U.S. Department of Education, the PARCC (Partnership for Assessment of Readiness for College and Careers) Consortium and the Smarter Balanced Assessment Consortium are developing assessments in English language arts/literacy and mathematics that are aligned with the Common Core State Standards (CCSS). PARCC has 24 member states (including the District of Columbia), whereas Smarter Balanced has 27 member states; 5 states are members of both (Alabama, Colorado, North Dakota, Pennsylvania, and South Carolina). Released in 2010 by the National Governors Association and Council of Chief State School Officers, the Common Core State Standards have been adopted by 45 states (Center for K–12 Assessment & Performance Management, 2012). States that are members of the PARCC and/or Smarter Balanced Consortia have agreed to implement the new assessments starting with the 2014–2015 academic year. Although states may also adopt state-specific standards, CCSS must represent at least 85% of a state's total standards (Center for K–12 Assessment & Performance Management, 2012). As Hearn and colleagues argue in their chapter, these efforts hold promise for improving the alignment of curricula and assessments between K–12 and higher education, and raising the likelihood that a student who meets the requirements for graduating from high school is academically qualified to enter college without requiring remedial or developmental education. Nonetheless, as David Conley observes in his chapter, the effectiveness of these and other efforts will not be demonstrated for several more years.

What we do know now is that the prevailing mechanism for improving college readiness for those who enter college without being adequately prepared during high school—that is, remedial or developmental education—has substantial weaknesses. As Long and Boatman describe in their chapter, college persistence rates are lower for those placed in remedial courses than for other students. Too few students who are placed in remedial and developmental education courses successfully move through these courses and into credit-bearing courses (Bailey, Jeong, & Cho, 2010). And, providing and receiving remedial education comes at a substantial cost to states and students (Long & Boatman, this volume). As Long and Boatman discuss in their chapter, greater attention is required to redesigning and reconfiguring the approaches used to provide remedial education, meeting the nonacademic barriers that limit academic success of underprepared students, and reducing the need for students to participate in remedial education (by, for example, informing high school students of their insufficient readiness and offering opportunities for them to raise their readiness before entering college). Clearly, more work is required to more clearly define what is meant by "college readiness" and how to best measure college readiness and communicate to students, parents, and schools whether students are "college ready." Ideally, "remedial education" (however it is redesigned or reconfigured) should not be a barrier that prevents students from gaining access to credit-bearing college coursework, but a gateway on the road to college-degree completion.

Characteristics of the Nation's Higher Education System

Efforts to improve college access, persistence, and completion are also complicated by the number, diversity, and autonomy of our nation's colleges and universities.

In 2010–2011 there were 4,599 degree-granting colleges and universities in the United States (including branch campuses) (NCES, 2012). These institutions vary in countless dimensions, including control (i.e., public, private not-for-profit, for-profit), level (i.e., two-year or four-year), Carnegie classification (e.g., research university, master's, baccalaureate, special focus), location, selectivity, tuition and fees, major field offerings, size, minority-serving status, religious affiliation, and more. This diversity has numerous advantages, particularly in terms of student choice: hypothetically, this diversity should ensure that every student has the opportunity to attend an institution that best meets his or her needs and interests. As Kurban and I demonstrate in our chapter earlier in this volume, however, this ideal is not the reality: the distribution of students across our nation's colleges and universities continues to be stratified based on students' race/ethnicity and family income, as well as other student demographic characteristics.

With the benefits of diversity also come other challenges. One complexity is that educational outcomes vary tremendously across different types of colleges and universities. As Don Hossler, Afet Dundar, and Doug Shapiro describe in their chapter, college persistence rates are generally higher at four-year than two-year colleges, more rather than less selective colleges and universities, private rather than public colleges and universities, and institutions with higher rather than lower tuition and expenditures on instruction and other functions. As an example of this variation, Table 11.1 shows that the percentage of first-time full-time students who entered four-year colleges and universities in 2004 and completed bachelor's degrees within six years ranged from 29% at institutions with open admission, to 45% at institutions where more than 90% of applicants are admitted, to

TABLE 11.1 Six-Year Graduation Rates of First-Time Postsecondary Students Who Started as Full-Time Degree/Certificate-Seeking Students at Four-Year Institutions in 2004 by Institutional Selectivity

	Total	Public	Private Not-for-profit	For-profit
Total	58.3	56.0	65.4	28.4
Open admissions	29.2	28.8	36.4	
90% or more accepted	45.4	44.2	50.0	
75.0% to 89.9% accepted	56.3	54.9	60.3	
50.0% to 74.9% accepted	60.7	59.9	63.8	
25.0% to 49.9% accepted	70.3	62.2	79.3	
Less than 25.0% accepted	87.2	82.2	90.5	

Source: National Center for Education Statistics (2012).

87% at institutions where fewer than 25% of applicants are admitted. In addition, at each level of selectivity, completion rates are higher at private not-for-profit institutions than at public institutions (NCES, 2012).

Of particular concern is the reality that degree completion rates tend to be lower at the colleges and universities that enroll the highest shares of students from low-income families, racial/ethnic minority groups, and first-generation college students. For instance, as Kurban and I describe in our chapter earlier in this volume, students from lower-income families are disproportionately represented at for-profit colleges and universities. But, as Table 11.1 shows, six-year bachelor's degree completion rates are substantially lower at for-profit institutions (28%) than at private not-for-profit four-year colleges and universities (65%) and public colleges and universities (56%). The institutions that enroll the highest shares of low-income students, racial/ethnic minorities, and first-generation college students also tend to have fewer financial resources (from endowments and resources) to allocate to institutional financial aid and other types of student support.

The size and diversity of the U.S. higher education system also creates difficulties for students who seek to move between colleges and universities. As Melguizo, Kienzl, and Kosiewicz describe in their chapter, students often have difficulty transferring from a community college to a four-year college or university, thus limiting their likelihood of earning a bachelor's degree. The extent to which statewide articulation agreements, one strategy designed to improve the transfer from two-year to four-year colleges without loss of credit, actually improve transfer is unclear (Roksa & Keith, 2008). Nonetheless, identifying mechanisms to promote the transfer of students across institutions is critical, given the mobility of today's college students. Data from the National Student Clearinghouse (2012) show that 8% of all students (both undergraduate and graduate) attended more than one institution in 2010–2011. Most (56%) of these students attended a two-year and four-year institution; about one-fourth (25%) attended two different four-year institutions (National Student Clearinghouse Research Center, 2012).

Another fundamental characteristic of the U.S. higher education system—the high level of institutional autonomy (Schmidtlein & Berdahl, 2005)—also has both benefits and challenges especially for efforts to improve college access and success. With high levels of autonomy, colleges and universities in the United States are able to determine their own mission and goals, determine the nature and characteristics of their curricular programs, and identify their own criteria for hiring faculty and admitting students (Schmidtlein & Berdahl, 2005). But, institutional autonomy is often viewed as at odds with accountability. As Jim Hearn, Anthony Jones, and Elizabeth Kurban describe in their chapter, policymakers are increasingly calling for greater accountability from our nation's colleges and universities. The quest for greater accountability is not surprising, as policymakers seek to ensure that the public dollars that are invested in higher education result in a more-educated workforce. Public resources at the federal and state levels will likely continue to be constrained into the near future, in the wake of the Great Recession, accelerating demand for Pell grants (at the federal level), and structural budget deficits (at the state level). These constraints, coupled with the growing awareness of the need for improved educational attainment, will likely result in even greater demands for institutional accountability into the future.

Inadequacy of Existing Research

A third force that restricts improvements in college access, success, and completion pertains to gaps in our knowledge of the most effective policies and practices. Although numerous studies have been conducted to understand the predictors of many college-related outcomes, substantial limitations in knowledge remain. For instance, based on our review and synthesis of prior research, Kurban and I conclude our chapter by noting the absence of research about the college enrollment and choice decisions of nontraditional students, "nontraditional" college enrollment choices including the decision to enroll part time and in a for-profit college or university, and whether and how particular federal and institutional policies and programs improve college enrollment and choice for students of different groups. Similarly, Debra Bragg notes the absence of theoretically grounded research on adult pathways into and through college, and into careers. Long and Boatman observe the need for more research that identifies the most promising and cost-effective remedial education programs, determines how and why the effects of remedial education programs vary based on students' background characteristics and level of academic preparation, identifies the most appropriate process for determining placement into remedial coursework, and demonstrates the most effective instructional approaches for delivering remedial courses. Hossler and colleagues also call for more research, noting the absence of knowledge about such critical topics as the ways that colleges and universities organize themselves so as to promote student retention as well as the effectiveness of particular institutional policies and practices for improving retention. They also argue that little is known about the forces that contribute to the persistence of students who attend multiple institutions or the role of state public policies in raising persistence and degree completion.

Some of the gaps in knowledge are attributable to limitations in the data available to examine these topics. As described by Hossler and colleagues and other chapters in this volume, little data are now available to examine the effects of institutional or state policies and practices on the persistence and degree completion of students who attend more than one college or university. Many states are now investing substantial resources to develop and enhance state longitudinal data systems, but few are building interoperability of data systems across states (Hossler et al., this volume). The National Student Clearinghouse holds data that could address this challenge but has insufficient resources to publish regular benchmarking reports from its data system or to make its data available to other researchers without charging a fee (Hossler et al., this volume).

Knowledge of the most effective policies and practices for improving college access, persistence, and completion for traditional, nontraditional, and various other subgroups of students is also limited by methodological limitations of existing research. As described in the chapter by Stephen DesJardins and Allyson Flaster as well as the chapters by Long and Boatman and by Hossler and colleagues, these methodological limitations restrict the conclusions that may be drawn even from many of the studies that have been conducted. A primary limitation is the inability of many research designs to take into account the effects on the outcomes of students' selection into the programs. In other words, many existing studies are unable to identify whether the outcomes would have improved even if the program were not provided. Some research, including research described by Long and Boatman in their chapter, has effectively used randomized controlled trials (RCTs) to eliminate the selection problem, and thereby determine the extent to which participating in a particular intervention (such as a remedial education program) actually improves students' outcomes.

Nonetheless, for practical, ethical, and other reasons, this type of experimental design is often difficult to implement. The types of quasi- or non-experimental designs that DesJardins and Flaster describe in their chapter offer a methodological alternative to identifying causal relationships. DesJardins and Flaster, as well as Hossler, Dundar, and Shapiro, argue that regression discontinuity, difference-in-differences, instrumental variables techniques, and propensity score matching are among the approaches that future research should use in order to provide more rigorous assessments of the extent to which particular policies and programs cause improvements in college access, persistence, and completion. Other research approaches have value in understanding how or why a program may or may not "work" overall and for different groups of students, as well as for more fully understanding the experiences of different groups of students on the path from college entrance to college completion and the forces that limit and promote these outcomes. Nonetheless, the paucity of research using experimental and quasi-experimental designs to assess program effects must be addressed.

What Can Be Done to Improve College Access, Persistence, and Completion?

Although identifying gaps in existing knowledge about how to improve college access, persistence, and completion, together the chapters in this volume do point to a number of ways that federal and state public policymakers, as well as institutional leaders, can improve college access, persistence, and completion, as well as close gaps across groups in these critical outcomes.

Clearly there is no simple or easy solution: A one-size-fits-all approach is not appropriate given the many variations in the characteristics of students, the characteristics of the higher education institutions they attend, and the characteristics of the states in which they are located. As Kurban and I argue in our chapter, the contexts in which students are embedded have a profound impact on their educational experiences and outcomes. Also recognizing the role of context, Long and Boatman conclude that approaches to remedial education must recognize variations in the effects of remediation based on state and institution characteristics as well as students' initial level of academic preparation. Hearn and colleagues also recognize the role of context, cautioning state public policymakers about the dangers of adopting a reform initiative from another state without considering the historical, cultural, and other relevant characteristics of the state. In short, to create meaningful improvements in college access, persistence, and completion, public and institutional policies and programs must be tailored to reflect the characteristics of the federal and state context, the characteristics of targeted colleges and universities, and the characteristics and needs of current and prospective targeted students.

Recognizing the role of and variations in context, the chapters in this volume also suggest that improvements in college access, persistence, and completion will occur only if the following six steps are taken:

1. Improve academic readiness for college;
2. Improve the alignment across and within educational sectors and levels;
3. Improve college affordability;
4. Ensure early awareness of and knowledge of college and financial aid;
5. Adapt approaches to reflect the diverse needs of current and prospective students, the characteristics of the institutions they attend, and the state and other contexts in which they are embedded; and
6. Collect and use data to monitor college access and completion and identify refinements in existing policies and practices.

Public policymakers should consider ways to coordinate policies at the federal and state levels to promote these six goals. As Hearn and colleagues argue, collaboration and partnership between the federal and state governments holds great promise for maximizing available resources and achieving the shared goal of improving educational attainment. Reflecting this view, Bragg proposes that the federal government consider mechanisms that encourage states to use need-based aid to promote the college enrollment of nontraditional students. One example of a federal government initiative that successfully created incentives for states to engage in behaviors that promoted college opportunity is the Leveraging Educational Assistance Partnership (LEAP) Program, formerly known as the State Student Incentive Grant (SSIG) program. Originally authorized by the federal government in 1972, this program provided matching funding to states that award grants to students based on financial need and successfully incentivized the establishment of state-sponsored need-based financial aid programs in many states (Heller, 2004). Nonetheless, funding for the LEAP Program was discontinued as of July 1, 2011.

Public policymakers should also consider ways to use public policies to incentivize colleges and universities to promote college access, persistence, and completion, particularly for students from underserved and underrepresented groups. Identifying the most appropriate and effective mechanisms for incentivizing institutions is not easy, however, as Hearn, Jones, and Kurban discuss in their chapter. The desired goals must be defined and particular attention must be paid to determining the optimal definition of "postsecondary success" (Hearn et al.). Moreover, although performance funding may appear to be a fruitful approach to creating improvements in college access, persistence, and completion, many states have experienced difficulties developing and implementing an effective performance funding system (Hearn et al.).

Improve Academic Readiness for College

Clearly federal and state policymakers and institutional leaders need to do more to ensure that students graduate from high school, academically ready to enter college without the need for remediation and to persist to degree completion. As Kurban and I recommend earlier in this volume, federal and state policymakers should encourage efforts that expand the availability of rigorous coursework, particularly in schools with high shares of low-income students and racial/ethnic minorities, and continue to support efforts that improve the alignment of academic curricula, assessments, and expectations between K–12 and higher education.

The proficiency-based model that Conley recommends offers promise for identifying the cognitive strategies, content knowledge, learning skills, and transition skills that students need to academically succeed in college. This approach may also effectively provide students with early and regular feedback about the extent to which they meet college expectations. Emerging research suggests that a proficiency-based approach provides better and more useful information about high school students' academic readiness for college (Conley, this volume).

Public policies should also encourage mechanisms that provide feedback to high schools about the extent to which students meet proficiency standards, as Conley recommends, and are academically ready to enter college-level courses without the need for remediation, as Long and Boatman recommend. High schools should then be encouraged to use this feedback to offer supplemental instruction to students who are not meeting minimum expectations and adopt reforms that raise all students' academic readiness.

Colleges and universities should also assess the strategies that they use to improve academic readiness of students who enter unprepared for college-level work. Long and Boatman encourage more attention to determining which institutions should deliver remedial education and urge colleges and universities to redefine remediation as academic support designed to promote students' future academic success rather than as only a mechanism for ensuring that students meet standards that were not fulfilled in the past and that may not predict success in college. Melguizo and colleagues point to the importance of academic and social readiness to transfer and bachelor's degree attainment, especially for low-income students and racial/ethnic minorities. Nonetheless, available research shows mixed results about the effects of such commonly adopted approaches as student success courses, supplemental instruction, summer bridge programs, accelerated courses, and learning communities. Therefore, colleges and universities should build in strategies for assessing the extent to which these and other practices cause improvements in academic and social readiness.

Improve Alignment across Educational Sectors and Levels

Federal and state policymakers should also encourage efforts that promote alignment and coordination across educational sectors and levels. In addition to improving the alignment of college readiness expectations between K–12 and higher education (as described in the prior section), policymakers should also consider ways that governance, finance, data, and accountability structures can encourage greater coordination between K–12 and higher education, as recommended by Perna and Kurban; Conley; and Hearn et al. in this volume, as well as other scholars (e.g., Kirst & Venezia, 2004; Venezia et al., 2005).

Policymakers should also support efforts that facilitate the movement of students across colleges and universities without loss of academic credit. As Hossler and his colleagues observe, substantial numbers of students are attending multiple colleges and universities on the path to degree completion. But as Melguizo and her coauthors argue, better alignment of educational and organizational policies between community colleges and four-year colleges and universities is required to ensure seamless transfer. Public and institutional policies should be designed to address current limitations on the availability of counseling about transfer at community colleges and improve availability of transfer-related information. Reforms should also encourage systemic reform through statewide articulation and transfer policies, rather than rely on agreements negotiated between individual institutions.

Improve College Affordability

Another critical step toward improving college access, persistence, and degree completion is ensuring that college is affordable and that students have the resources required to pay the costs. The chapters in this volume demonstrate that financial resources are a critical determinant of college enrollment and choice (Perna & Kurban), transfer between community colleges and four-year colleges and universities (Melguizo et al.), and student retention and persistence (Hossler et al.), and are particularly important for students from low-income families (Heller) and nontraditional students (Bragg). But, in recent years, tuition and fees have increased dramatically (Heller; Hearn et al.). States have not only permitted tuition to rise substantially at public colleges and universities but also advanced efforts that tend to promote the ability to pay among students from middle- and upper-income families rather than lower-income families (Hearn et al.). These policy initiatives include state-sponsored merit-based financial aid programs as well as college savings and prepaid tuition programs (Hearn et al.).

Colleges and universities, state governments, and the federal government must share the responsibility for ensuring the affordability of higher education. To improve college affordability, greater effort is needed by all three groups to control tuition increases, ensure the availability of state appropriations to higher education institutions, and ensure the availability of need-based financial aid. Federal and state governments as well as colleges and universities should strive to target available grant aid to the lowest-income students, as argued in several chapters (e.g., Hearn et al; Heller; Hossler et al.; Perna & Kurban). As Heller also recommends, colleges and universities should strive to allocate financial aid so as to hold low-income students harmless when tuition increases.

Ensure Early Awareness and Knowledge of College and Financial Aid

Related to the need to improve college affordability is the need to improve students' early awareness and knowledge of student financial aid. As discussed in several chapters (e.g., Heller; Melguizo et al.; Perna & Kurban), insufficient knowledge or understanding of financial aid is one force that continues to limit college access, transfer, and completion for too many students. The lack of knowledge is attributable at least in part to insufficient numbers of counselors at the high school and community college levels (Melguizo et al.; Perna & Kurban).

As recommended in earlier chapters in this volume, more work is required to reduce the complexity of the process for applying for financial aid, provide information about the availability of and eligibility for financial aid early enough in the educational pipeline so as to encourage students to engage in the behaviors that will improve their likelihood of college access and success; and support early commitment programs like Indiana's 21st Century Scholars Program and precollege outreach programs that provide college and financial aid-related information. The federal government should also build on such efforts as the recent net price calculator requirement to encourage greater transparency and uniformity in the information that colleges and universities provide to students about their financial aid awards.

Adapt Approaches to Reflect Students' Needs and the Context

So many of the policies and practices that have been adopted to improve college access and completion have focused on addressing the needs of traditional-age students who are enrolling in a public or nonprofit college or university on a full-time basis immediately after graduating from high school. Nonetheless, as several chapters discuss (e.g., Bragg; Perna & Kurban), this focus fails to recognize the different but still important needs of numerous other students. In her chapter, Debra Bragg stresses the need for adult career pathways that integrate academic and social supports that promote program completion and lead to employment. Adult learners may face particular challenges with regard to learning how to navigate the higher education system and managing family and work responsibilities that may compete with student responsibilities (Bragg, this volume). Thus, policies and programs must be adapted to recognize not only the state and institutional context (as described above), but also the characteristics of the targeted students.

Collect and Use Data to Monitor College Access and Completion

In addition, public policymakers and institutional leaders must also provide financial support and incentives for efforts that build even greater understanding of the forces that limit and promote college access, persistence, and completion, and the strategies that most effectively promote these outcomes for students of different groups. As DesJardins and Flaster argue, research organizations and schools of education should do more to ensure that researchers possess the skills required to conduct rigorous evaluations of policies and programs. Policymakers and other grant-making organizations should encourage the use of rigorous research methods for understanding program effectiveness through their award criteria.

Additionally, federal and state policymakers and institutional leaders should ensure the availability of data for researchers to examine by continuing efforts to build state longitudinal data systems. As Hearn and his colleagues discuss, student-level data that track students' educational experiences, progress, and outcomes over time are essential for understanding, monitoring, and improving college access, persistence, and completion. For maximum utility, these data systems should permit the tracking of students across K–12 and higher education systems, between public and private colleges and universities, across state lines, and into the labor market. Better data are also required to understand the educational experiences and outcomes of nontraditional students, as Bragg argues.

Although essential, simply collecting more and better data alone is insufficient. Such data must also be used to inform policy and practice. As other chapters describe (e.g., Hearn et al.; Hossler et al.), data are essential for assessing progress toward reaching college access, persistence, and completion goals, identifying problems with prevailing policies and approaches, and identifying solutions that effectively achieve the goals.

Concluding Note

Clearly, the United States must do more to improve college access, persistence, and completion—especially for students from low-income families, racial/ethnic minority groups, and other underserved and underrepresented groups. Although further research is needed to more fully understand the most effective policies and programs, the chapters in this volume offer much guidance about the actions that the federal government, state governments, and colleges and universities all can—and must—take now. Efforts that focus on raising academic readiness for college, improving the alignment across and within educational sectors, ensuring college affordability, promoting early awareness and knowledge of financial aid, adapting approaches to meet the needs and characteristics of targeted students, and using data to monitor progress will go a long way toward realizing the nation's educational attainment goals, ensuring that our nation's workers are qualified for available jobs, and improving equity in attainment across groups.

References

Bailey, T., Jeong, D.W., & Cho, S.-W. (2010). Referral, enrollment, and completion in developmental education sequences in community colleges. *Economics of Education Review, 29*(2), 255–270.

Baum, S., Ma, J., & Payea, K. (2010). *Education pays 2010.* Washington, DC: College Board. Retrieved from http://trends.collegeboard.org/downloads/Education_Pays_2010.pdf

Carnevale, A., Smith, N., & Stohl, J. (2010). *Help wanted: Projections of jobs and education requirements through 2018.* Washington, DC: Georgetown Center on Education and the Workforce. Retrieved from http://www9.georgetown.edu/grad/gppi/hpi/cew/pdfs/FullReport.pdf

Center for K–12 Assessment & Performance Management. (2012). *Coming together to raise achievement: New assessments for the Common Core State standards.* Princeton, NJ: Education Testing Service. Retrieved from http://www.k12center.org/rsc/pdf/Coming_Together_April_2012_Final.PDF

Center on Education Policy (2012). *State high school exit exams: A policy in transition.* Washington, DC: Author. Retrieved from http://www.cep-dc.org/displayDocument.cfm?DocumentID=408

Heller, D.E. (2004). The changing nature of financial aid. *Academe.* Retrieved from http://www.aaup.org/AAUP/pubsres/academe/2004/JA/Feat/hell.htm

Kelly, P. (2010). *Projected degree gap: Percent of 25 to 64 year olds with associate degrees or higher.* Unpublished table, Boulder, CO, National Center for Higher Education Management Systems (NCHEMS).

Kirst, M.W., & Usdan, M.D. (2009). The historical context of the divide between K–12 and higher education. *In States, schools, and colleges: Policies to improve student readiness for college and strengthen coordination between schools and colleges* (pp. 5–22). San Jose, CA: National Center for Public Policy and Higher Education.

Kirst, M.W., & Venezia, A. (2004). *From high school to college: Improving opportunities for success in postsecondary education.* San Francisco, CA: Jossey-Bass.

National Center for Education Statistics (NCES). (2012). *Digest of education statistics 2011.* Washington, DC: Author.

National Student Clearinghouse Research Center (2012). *Snapshot report: Mobility.* Retrieved November 30, 2012 from http://www.studentclearinghouse.info/snapshot/

Roksa, J., & Keith, B. (2008). Credits, time, and attainment. Articulation policies and success after transfer. *Educational Evaluation and Policy Analysis, 30*(2), 236–254.

Schmidtlein, F., & Berdahl, R.O. (2005). Autonomy and accountability: Who controls academe? In P.G. Altbach, R.O. Berdahl, & P.J. Gumport (Eds.), *American higher education in the twenty-first century* (2nd ed.). Baltimore, MD: Johns Hopkins University.

Venezia, A., Callan, P.M., Finney, J.E., Kirst, M.W., & Usdan, M.D. (2005). *The governance divide: A report on a four-state study on improving college readiness*. San Jose, CA: National Center for Public Policy and Higher Education.

Western Interstate Commission on Higher Education (2008). *Knocking at the college door*. Boulder, CO: Author. Retrieved from http://www.wiche.edu/knocking

CONTRIBUTOR BIOGRAPHIES

Angela Boatman's research focuses on the evaluation of college access policies, particularly in the areas of postsecondary remediation and financial aid. Current projects include an evaluation of the impact of innovations in the delivery of remedial courses, including the use of instructional technology, on collegiate student outcomes. In other recent work, she has examined the effects of more traditional remedial and developmental courses in Tennessee and conducted a multi-cohort evaluation of the Gates Millennium Scholars Program, both co-authored with Dr. Bridget Terry Long. Dr. Boatman previously worked as an intern at the State Higher Education Executive Officers (SHEEO) researching state tuition, fees, and financial aid policies, and as a postdoctoral scholar at the Center for Education Policy Analysis at Stanford University. Boatman received her doctoral degree from the Harvard Graduate School of Education and holds a M.P.P in Public Policy and a M.A. in Higher Education, both from the University of Michigan. In the fall of 2013 she will begin a faculty position in the Department of Leadership, Policy, and Organizations in Peabody College at Vanderbilt University.

Debra D. Bragg is Professor in the Department of Educational Policy, Organization, and Leadership at the University of Illinois at Urbana-Champaign. In addition to being Director of the Office of Community College Research and Leadership, Dr. Bragg is Director of the Illinois Collaborative for Education Policy Research, a strategic initiative of the state of Illinois to increase access to state longitudinal data systems by faculty and policy researchers. Her research focuses on transition to college by youth and adults, especially student populations that have not, historically, attended college. She is particularly interested in how underserved youth and adult students use the community college to transition to postsecondary education and employment. The expanding mission of community colleges, including the increasing importance of linkages to high schools, adult education, and the workforce is of particular interest. Recent publications include *Examining Pathways to and Through the Community College for Youth and Adults* (2011) and *The Two Year College Curriculum in Mathematics* (2012). Dr. Bragg holds a PhD in Comprehensive Vocational Education from The Ohio State University.

David T. Conley is Professor of Educational Policy and Leadership in the College of Education at the University of Oregon. He is the Founder and Director of the Center for Educational Policy Research (CEPR) at the University of Oregon, and Founder and Chief Executive Officer of the Educational Policy Improvement Center, a 501(c)3 not-for-profit educational research organization. Before joining the faculty of the University of Oregon in 1989, he spent a total of 20 years in Colorado and California as a school-level and central office administrator in several districts; an executive in a state education department; and as a teacher in two public, multicultural, alternative schools. His areas of teaching and research include the high school-to-college transition, standards-based education, systemic school reform, educational governance, and adequacy funding models. His recent publications include *College and Career Readiness: Same or Different?* (2012), *College and Career Ready: Helping All Students Succeed Beyond High School* (2010), and *Rethinking College Readiness* (2008). Dr. Conley received a BA with honors in Social Sciences from the University of California, Berkeley. He earned his master's degree in Social, Multicultural, and Bilingual Foundations of Education and his doctoral degree in Curriculum, Administration, and Supervision at the University of Colorado, Boulder.

Stephen L. DesJardins is Professor and former Director of the Center for the Study of Higher and Postsecondary Education in the School of Education at the University of Michigan. He also has an academic appointment in the Ford School of Public Policy at Michigan. Prior to joining academia, he worked in market research in the private sector and was a policy analyst and institutional researcher for 13 years at the University of Minnesota. His research interests include student transitions from high school to college, what happens to students once they enroll in college, the economics of postsecondary education, and applying new statistical techniques to the study of these issues. Recent publications include *A Quasi-Experimental Investigation of How the Gates Millennium Scholars Program is Related to College Students' Time Use and Activities* (2010), *Investigating the Impact of Financial Aid on Student Dropout Risks: Racial and Ethnic Differences* (2010), *Simulating the Effects of Financial Aid Packages on College Student Stopout and Reenrollment Spells and Graduation Chances* (2010), and *Exploring the Effects of Student Expectations about Financial Aid on Postsecondary Choice* (2009). Dr. DesJardins received a BS in economics from Northern Michigan University, an MA in policy analysis and labor economics from the Hubert H. Humphrey Institute of Public Affairs at the University of Minnesota, and a PhD in higher education with a concentration in research and evaluation methods, also from the University of Minnesota.

Afet Dundar is Associate Director of the Research Center at the National Student Clearinghouse. The Clearinghouse Research Center conducts research on issues of importance to the Clearinghouse participating institutions and to the broader education and public policy community. Prior to joining the Clearinghouse Research Center, Dr. Dundar was Assistant Director for Research at the Project on Academic Success (PAS) at Indiana University Bloomington, where she was responsible for maintaining the state student unit-record database. During her time at PAS, she was also closely involved in the design and implementation of a national survey to identify and document policies and practices associated with student persistence at institutions across the United States as part of the College Board Study on Student Retention, and in the Mobile Working Student Collaborative project, funded by the Lumina Foundation. She has published and presented at professional conferences on student transfer, and other postsecondary student access and success outcomes. Dr. Dundar earned her PhD in Education Policy Studies from Indiana University Bloomington.

Allyson Flaster is a PhD student in the Center for the Study of Higher and Postsecondary Education at the University of Michigan. She has an EdM in Higher Education Administration from Harvard University and is a former TRIO program staff member. Her research interests are the causes and consequences of postsecondary inequality and the effects of financial aid on student outcomes.

James C. Hearn is Professor of Higher Education and Interim Director at the University of Georgia Institute of Higher Education. Prior to joining the faculty at the University of Georgia, Dr. Hearn served as a faculty member at the University of Minnesota and Vanderbilt University. Dr. Hearn's research and teaching focus on organization, policy, and finance in postsecondary education. He has particular interest in the origins, planning, management, effects, and evaluation of governmental policies and programs; the financing of postsecondary education at the state and federal levels; and policies relating to access, choice, and persistence in postsecondary education. He currently serves as a consulting editor for *Research in Higher Education*. In the past, he has served as an associate editor of the *Educational Researcher and Research in Higher Education* and on the editorial boards of the *Journal of Higher Education*, the *Review of Higher Education*, *Teachers College Record*, and *Sociology of Education*. Dr. Hearn earned a PhD in the sociology of education and an MA in sociology from Stanford University. He also holds an MBA in finance from the University of Pennsylvania (Wharton) and an AB from Duke University.

Donald E. Heller is Dean of the College of Education and Professor of Education at Michigan State University. Prior to his appointment in January 2012, he was Director of the Center for the Study of Higher Education and Professor of Education and Senior Scientist at The Pennsylvania State University. He also held a faculty appointment at the University of Michigan. His teaching and research is in the areas of educational economics, public policy, and finance, with a primary focus on issues of college access and choice for low-income and minority students. His recent publications include *The States and Public Higher Education Policy: Affordability, Access, and Accountability* (2nd edition, 2011); "The Financial Aid Picture: Realism, Surrealism, or Cubism?" (*Higher Education: Handbook of Theory and Research*, 2011); and the forthcoming edited volume (with Claire Callender), *Student Financing of Higher Education: A Comparative Perspective*. Dr. Heller completed his EdD in Higher Education at the Harvard Graduate School of Education (HGSE). He also has an EdM degree from HGSE, and a bachelor's degree in economics and political science from Tufts University.

Donald Hossler is a Consultant to the National Student Clearinghouse Research Center and also serves as Professor of Educational Leadership & Policy Studies at Indiana University Bloomington. Dr. Hossler has served as the Vice Chancellor for Enrollment Services for Indiana University Bloomington, and the Associate Vice President for Enrollment Services for the seven campuses of the Indiana University system, the Executive Associate Dean of the School of Education, and as Chair of the Department of Educational Leadership & Policy Studies. His areas of specialization include college choice, student persistence, student financial aid policy, and enrollment management. Dr. Hossler has consulted with more than 50 colleges, universities, and related educational organizations including The College Board, Educational Testing Services, the University of Cincinnati, Inter-American University of Puerto Rico, the Pew Charitable Trust, the University of Missouri, Colorado State University, the University of Alabama, and the General Accounting Office of the United States government. He has presented more than 130 scholarly papers and invited lectures and is the author, or coauthor, of 12 books and monographs and more than 70 articles and book chapters. Dr. Hossler is currently directing funded projects of The College Board, the Lumina Foundation for Education, and the Spencer Foundation, focusing on student success and persistence. He has received career achievement awards for his research, scholarship, and service from the American College Personnel Association, the Association for Institutional Research, the College Board, and the National Association of Student Personnel Administrators.

Anthony P. Jones serves as the Deputy Director and Director of Policy Research for the Advisory Committee on Student Financial Assistance in Washington, DC. Prior to joining the Advisory Committee staff in February 2010, he worked for the U.S. Department of Education for more than eight years, including serving as the Grants and Campus-Based Programs Section Chief in the Office of Federal Student Aid, and as a policy analyst/program specialist in the Office of

Postsecondary Education's Policy and Budget Development Service. Mr. Jones has been a financial aid administrator at three institutions, including serving as director of the financial aid office at Tusculum College. He also previously worked for the National Association of Student Financial Aid Administrators providing training and regulatory assistance to financial aid administrators at member institutions. Mr. Jones holds a BA in speech communication studies from the University of North Carolina at Greensboro and an MA in adult education from Tusculum College. He has advanced to doctoral candidacy at the University of Georgia's Institute of Higher Education. Mr. Jones currently serves on the editorial board of the *Journal of Student Financial Aid*.

Gregory Kienzl is an independent education consultant, who specializes in the fields of higher education and financial aid policy. He has authored or coauthored 25 peer-reviewed journal articles and reports for the National Center for Education Statistics and prominent national foundations. He has been invited to discuss the implications of his research at recent meetings of the Federal Reserve Bank of Dallas, the New Mexico Workforce and Education Strategy Academy, the College Board Forum, and the Jack Kent Cooke Foundation. Dr. Kienzl received a PhD in Economics of Education from Teachers College, Columbia University, and an MA in Public Policy and Management from the H. John Heinz III School of Public Policy and Management, Carnegie Mellon University.

Holly Kosiewicz is a PhD student in Urban Education Policy at the University of Southern California's Rossier School of Education. Her research interests center on evaluating policies that impact success of low-income and underrepresented college students living in the United States and abroad. She earned a bachelor's degree in Government and Spanish from the University of Texas at Austin and a master's degree in Sustainable International Development from Brandeis University.

Elizabeth R. Kurban serves as the Assistant Director of Policy Research for the Advisory Committee on Student Financial Assistance in Washington, DC. Prior to joining the Advisory Committee staff in July 2012, Elizabeth attended the University of Pennsylvania Graduate School of Education, where she earned an MSEd in higher education. She also holds an MA in cognitive science and linguistics, and a BA in psychology from the University of Delaware. Elizabeth plans to return to graduate school in the future for a doctoral degree.

Bridget Terry Long is the Xander Professor of Education and Economics at the Harvard Graduate School of Education. An economist specializing in education, Dr. Long studies the transition from high school to higher education and beyond. Her work focuses on college access and choice, factors that influence student outcomes, and the behavior of postsecondary institutions. Current and past projects examine the role of information and simplification in college decisions, the effects of financial aid programs, and the impact of postsecondary remediation on student outcomes. Her recent publications include "The Role of Application Assistance and Information in College Decisions: Results from the H&R Block FAFSA Experiment" (2012) and "Remediation: The Challenge of Helping Underprepared Students" (2012). Dr. Long is a Faculty Research Associate of the National Bureau of Economic Research (NBER) and, since 2011, has served as Chair of the National Board of Education Sciences, the advisory panel of the Institute of Education Sciences in the U.S. Department of Education. Dr. Long received her PhD and MA from the Harvard University Department of Economics and her AB from Princeton University.

Tatiana Melguizo is Associate Professor in the Rossier School of Education at the University of Southern California. She works in the field of economics of higher education. She uses quantitative methods of analysis and large-scale longitudinal survey data to study the association of different factors such as student trajectories and specific institutional characteristics on the persistence and educational outcomes of minority (African American and Hispanic) and low-income students. Her work has been published in *Education Evaluation and Policy Analysis*, *Teachers College Record*, *The Journal of Higher Education*, *The Review of Higher Education*, *Research in Higher Education*, and *Higher Education*. She is a recipient of the American Education Research Association (AERA) dissertation grant. Dr. Melguizo has also received grants from AERA, Association for Institutional Research/National Postsecondary Education Cooperative (AIR/NPEC), Bill and Melinda Gates Foundation, Institute of Education Sciences (IES), Jack Kent Cooke Foundation, Lumina Foundation, Nellie Mae Education Foundation, and Spencer Foundation. Dr. Melguizo received a PhD in Economics of Education from Stanford University and an MA in Social Policy from the London School of Economics.

Brian E. Noland currently serves as the ninth President of East Tennessee State University (ETSU) in Johnson City, Tennessee. Prior to joining ETSU in 2012, he served as Chancellor of the West Virginia Higher Education Policy Commission and worked at the Tennessee Higher Education Commission. He has also served as a faculty member at Vanderbilt University, Tennessee State University, and Nashville State Community College. He has authored or coauthored several scholarly publications on higher education topics, including *Targeted Merit Aid: Implications of the Tennessee Education Lottery Scholarship Program* (2007) and *Changing Perceptions and Outcomes: The Accountability Paradox in Tennessee* (2006). Dr. Noland received his BA in political science and MA in public policy studies from West Virginia University and his PhD in political science from the University of Tennessee Knoxville.

Laura W. Perna is Professor in the Graduate School of Education and Faculty Fellow at the Institute for Urban Research at the University of Pennsylvania. Her current scholarship draws on multiple theoretical perspectives and a variety of analytical techniques to understand the ways that social structures, institutional practices, and public policies separately and together enable and restrict the ability of women, racial/ethnic minorities, and individuals of lower socioeconomic status to enroll and succeed in college. Recent publications include *Understanding the Working College Student: New Research and Its Implications for Policy and Practice* (2010, Stylus) and *Preparing Today's Students for Tomorrow's Jobs in Metropolitan America: The Policy, Practice, and Research Issues* (2012, University of Pennsylvania Press). She is currently serving as Vice President of the Postsecondary Education Division of the American Education Research Association and Associate Editor of the *Journal of Higher Education* and is a member of the editorial boards of a number of other leading journals (e.g., *Educational Researcher, Educational Evaluation and Policy Analysis, Research in Higher Education*). Dr. Perna holds a BA in psychology and BS in economics from the University of Pennsylvania, and a master's of public policy and PhD in education from the University of Michigan.

Douglas T. Shapiro is Executive Research Director of the Research Center at the National Student Clearinghouse, where he is responsible for research projects utilizing a student-level database that covers 93 percent of all postsecondary enrollments in the United States. The Research Center is currently completing a Gates-funded project to build school, district, and state feedback reports analyzing the postsecondary enrollment and progress of high school graduates. The Center recently published a report that analyzes patterns of postsecondary student transfer and mobility. A report on completion rates will follow later in 2012. Dr. Shapiro was previously the Director of Institutional Research at The New School in New York City. Prior to that, he served as Vice President for Research and Policy Development at the Minnesota Private College Council, where he conducted research on postsecondary student access and success, college affordability and financial aid, labor markets for college-educated workers, and academic performance of recruited student-athletes. He also built and managed the Council's 17-institution student unit-record database covering enrollment, academics, and financial aid. Dr. Shapiro has been an Associate at the National Center for Public Policy in Higher Education and holds a master's degree in Mathematics from the University of Michigan and a PhD from Michigan's Center for the Study of Higher and Postsecondary Education.

INDEX

ability to benefit (ATB) program 47, 51
academic content standards 59, 61–2, 133
academic preparedness: achievement and
18–20; college enrollment and 16; of
community college students 118–19;
early assessment 85; enhancement of
128–30; financial aid and 24; human
capital theory 12; of minority students
27, 37, 57, 209–10; overview 27–8;
prior levels of 86, 90; programs for 115,
125; remedial education for 80, 81–3;
role of 5–6, 15; of transfer students 115
Access and Completion Incentive Fund 140
ACCUPLACER exam 91–5
Achieve's American Diploma Project 19
Achieving the Dream (AtD) 50
ACT scores 103
Adelman, C. 10, 120, 141, 149, 158
Adult Basic Education (ABE) 36, 40, 42
Adult Basic Skills (ABS) 41
adult career pathways 40–3, 115
adult education: enrollment in 36;
importance of 226; by nontraditional
students 49–50; overview 48; as pathway
program 42, 115; postsecondary
education and 39, 40
Adult Education and Family Literacy Act 48
Adult Secondary Education (ASE) 36
Advanced Placement (AP) 19, 60–1, 71
Advisory Committee on Student Financial
Assistance (ACFSA) 11, 22, 29, 35,
179–80

affordability initiatives 167–9, 172
African American students: academic
coursework 18; academic preparation
209–10; characteristics of 42; as college
applicants 37; college enrollment 10–11,
123; college retention 144, 150; in
community college 118; remedial
classes 79
Akerhielm, K. 193
Alfeld, C. 38
Alliance for Excellent Education 79
Alternative Exit pathway 44, 45
American College Testing (ACT) 62–3, 87
American Diploma Project 63
American Educational Research
Association 202
Angrist, J. D. 199
articulation agreements for transfer
students 124–5
Asian American students: academic
preparation 209–10; college retention
144, 150; in community college 118
Assessment of Skills for Successful Entry
and Transfer (ASSET) 91n5
Associate Completion Degree 44, 82
associate degrees 34, 44–5, 82, 132
Associate of Applied Science (AAS) 44
Associate of Arts (AA) 44
Associate of Arts in Teaching (AAT) 132
Associate of Science (AS) 44
Association for Institutional Research
(AIR) 202–3